THE ROSWELL FILE

6 —

THE ROSWELL FILE

TIM SHAWCROSS

BLOOMSBURY

First published in Great Britain 1997
This paperback edition published 1998
Bloomsbury Publishing Plc, 38 Soho Square, London W1V 5DF

Copyright © 1997 by Tim Shawcross

The moral right of the author has been asserted

PICTURE SOURCES

Associated Press: page 3 *top right*
Author's collection: pages 2 *top*, 3 *top left, bottom*, 4 *top left, bottom*, 5, 6, 7
Fort Worth Star Telegram (Special Collections Division,
The University of Texas at Arlington Libraries): page 4 *top right*
The Historical Society for Southeast New Mexico: page 1
US Department of Energy (Johnson Controls World Services): page 2 *bottom*

A CIP catalogue record for this book
is available from the British Library

ISBN 0 7475 3507 8

10 9 8 7 6 5 4 3 2 1

Typeset by Hewer Text Composition Services, Edinburgh
Printed by Clays Ltd, St Ives plc

INTRODUCTION

'The Roswell Incident' has become the world's most celebrated UFO mystery. It has instigated two official US government inquiries, engaged the office of a respected Republican congressman for New Mexico, been the subject of a 1995 General Audit Office investigation on behalf of Congress, led to the creation of two museums in the town and has produced what is by all accounts one of the most intriguing and controversial pieces of black and white film ever seen.

Despite all of the above, the Roswell Incident remains a mystery. As such it demands further investigation, elucidation and clarification. It inspires an insatiable appetite from the curious and the committed, the sceptics and the believers, the fans of *The X Files* and *Star Trek* as well as those who keep an open mind on the whole subject.

On newsagents' shelves throughout Europe and America there is currently a plethora of magazines dealing with the area where the paranormal intersects with the extraterrestrial. Titles like *Focus*, *Encounters*, *Alien*, *UFO* and *Fortean Times* (the last has been in existence somewhat longer than the brasher new arrivals) point to a huge and apparently growing appetite for subjects and stories which are quite literally out of this world. But it's not just magazines. On television recently there has been what seems like an endless succession of rather badly produced programmes attempting both to tap into and to cash in on the phenomenal interest in extraterrestrial phenomena – from aliens and UFOs to poltergeists and telekinesis. The quality of most of these programmes puts the reputation of British television rather dangerously on the line. But then, as television executives are quick to counter, you can't argue with the ratings. Almost irrespective of their quality, such programmes are attracting viewers by the million.

Significantly, people are apparently watching them not because the programmes are good but simply because of the subject matter.

Why should there be such a massive and seemingly expanding market for these phenomena? Particularly popular with viewers are UFOs and the myth of life on other planets. But we mustn't forget the ever-expanding number of people, mainly in the United States, who claim to have been abducted by aliens in flying saucers and then undergone terrifying and often painful and humiliating probes by sinister extraterrestrials with a mission to discover physiological data about the human race.

The other medium which has been swamped by the UFO community is the Internet. Cyberspace has been virtually colonized by people obsessed with outer space. What the magazine world and the Internet community have in common is a belief in conspiracy theory. Beneath the hype lies an apparent need to believe in the reality of something for which there is no tangible evidence. With the approach of the millennium it is perhaps no coincidence that such faith suggests an alternative 'religion'. There is a correlation between the decline of Christianity and the rise of New Age philosophies and the widespread acceptance of the existence of both flying saucers and their other worldly inhabitants. For the second is a belief system which requires exactly the same leap of faith as that made by those who subscribe to the more accepted religions. As a quasi-religion the UFO world has coined its own phraseology and language: the aliens are known by the pseudo-scientific term 'Extra-Terrestrial Biological Entities', or EBEs; they are also known as 'Greys'.

While eyewitnesses to abductions are understandably vague as to the exact whereabouts of the planet whence the aliens have come, there is a surprising unanimity in the descriptions of their physical characteristics: they are a race with large heads and huge, black, almond-shaped eyes, a minuscule slit for a mouth and two tiny apertures for a nose.

Their limbs are disproportionately long for their short bodies and they tend to have six digits on their hands and feet. Details concerning the language they speak and the controls and the furniture inside the alien craft are always slightly more open to debate but the image of the aliens is accepted as being fairly exhaustively documented by adherents of the UFO world.

While some of the accounts of the abductees border on the wilder fringes of the imagination in free flight, there are a puzzlingly large number of detailed reports from people with a respectable background which are utterly convincing in their sincerity. A large number of people who do not have anything to gain by fabricating such outlandish tall stories have told researchers and psychiatrists that they have been 'kidnapped' by aliens. Alien abduction may lie at the extreme edge of the UFO world, but once again the magazines and the Internet have a number of recurring stories with mythical status that form the foundation of the whole 'extraterrestrial experience'. Abduction is one, UFO sightings from the mundane to the spectacular is another, and the third is the shadowy photographs of the surface of the planet Mars. The fourth is 'Area 51' or 'Dreamland': the site of the US government's most highly classified defence experiments, including the testing of actual craft recovered from alien incursions into our atmosphere.

The final 'myth' – which in many ways is the most outlandish and yet for which there is the most evidence – has become known as 'The Roswell Incident'. To the sceptical outsider, the bare bones of the story appear even more ridiculous than all the other legends of the UFO world which are feverishly disseminated among the illuminati known as ufologists and their followers. For what is one to make of the claim that a 'flying saucer' crashed into the desert wasteland of a desolate ranch in New Mexico in the summer of 1947 and was tracked by radar operators from the US Air Force? Not only that: the craft was located and a USAF recovery team was dispatched to the stricken extraterrestrial vehicle. There they discovered an object never before seen on this planet and containing the bodies of five small, humanoid creatures wearing tight-fitting silver foil-like uniforms. Descriptions of their being childlike, large-headed and having enormous eyes and hands with six fingers pre-date all the later accounts of Greys with uncanny accuracy.

Then, the story goes, the craft and its (dead) inhabitants were loaded on to a military flatbed truck and taken back to the nearest Army Air Field (at that time the Air Force and the Army came under the same administration), which was at Roswell. After being temporarily stored in a hangar and closely guarded by armed military sentries, the wreckage was carefully crated into boxes and sent to Wright Air Field, the headquarters of Air Technical Intelligence Command, and from there to Washington. All of which sounds most unlikely, until it is remembered that the military authorities issued a press release at the time confirming the origins of the story.

The Roswell mystery has attracted the attention of eminent scientists, politicians and the Pentagon. They may differ in their views as to what actually happened but there is a surprising unanimity about a conspiracy and a cover-up.

I have always been fascinated by the UFO phenomenon and in collaboration with my producer John Purdie recently wrote and directed the documentary which comprises the most exhaustive study of the Roswell Incident to date. It has been acquired by television networks across the world and achieved one of the highest-ever ratings for any factual programme to be shown on the UK's Channel Four.

This book is an attempt to provide an objective account of the Roswell Incident and an assessment of the sensational and controversial 'alien autopsy'. This black and white newsreel film may depict a post-mortem conducted in a secret US government facility on the bodies of the creatures recovered from the craft that crashed in the New Mexico desert in the summer of 1947. Alternatively, it is an elaborate hoax which is so clever that no one has yet succeeded in unmasking its perpetrators.

Yet this sensational film, full details of which have never been revealed, is only a minor part of the story of the extraordinary events that took place that year in the small town of Roswell. In the course of making our film, we discovered a catalogue of events that were even more remarkable than the sensational footage: testimony that was at times so unbelievable that one began to question the sanity of the person telling the story. By virtue of our access to witnesses and official government sources, both those who believe and those who disparage the Roswell Incident, *The Roswell File* details the events that surround the story of what some believe to be the first evidence of an actual extraterrestrial visitation to this planet. Naturally, others remain convinced that the whole episode was a collective act of self-delusion which makes accounts of visitations by the bleeding or weeping Virgin and other religious miracles look almost credible and respectable by comparison.

The book draws on first-hand testimony from those who witnessed the strange events in Roswell in 1947. Among these are former US military officers who served with the 509th Bomber Squadron at their home base, Roswell Army Air Field. This was the top-secret headquarters for the elite atomic bomb wing of the USAF – at the time the only air force in the world with nuclear capability. It was the 509th

Bomb Group that had dropped the bombs on Hiroshima and Nagasaki – and it was Colonel Jesse Marcel, their intelligence officer, who first discovered evidence of the crashed UFO on a ranch north-west of Roswell.

Crucial evidence as to the nature of the Roswell Incident revolves around the sequence of events that took place in July 1947 and the reactions of the local Air Force command, which issued a press release stating that a 'flying disc' had been recovered – a story which was reported all over the world. The author has access to those who were at the base at the time and newspaper editors and radio reporters who were on the spot.

The book details the extraordinary retraction by the United States Air Force in a staged press conference and photo-call where it was announced that the original news release had been a mistake and that what had been recovered was nothing more than a weather balloon!

We include testimony from the participants in what is now admitted, even by the Air Force, to be nothing more than a clumsy cover-up. The book also reveals some of the top-secret experiments that were taking place in the area at the time. Roswell Army Air Field was just one of a number of highly classified defence areas in New Mexico, which included Alamogordo Air Field, Los Alamos and White Sands Rocket Range, where experiments with V-2 rockets, captured from the Nazis, were being conducted under the command of Wernher von Braun, the Nazi scientist who led the team that pioneered America's early efforts in space and missile research.

Other secret experiments, many of which were esoteric in the extreme, were being conducted in remote areas of New Mexico. The area's history of covert experimentation has led many to believe that it was some strange military operation that was responsible for the Roswell Incident. The book undertakes an exhaustive investigation into this possibility, to determine whether it could account for the Roswell Incident.

The abiding mystery of Roswell is the sheer number of eyewitness accounts of a strange craft and the presence of bodies whose appearance precluded any terrestrial origin. It is the credibility of these witnesses which has given the mystery such a powerful resonance: either they are all deluded or lying, or they are telling the truth. If the latter is the case it follows that either they did indeed witness a genuine extraterrestrial phenomenon or they genuinely mistook a secret experiment for an alien visitation.

The background of these witnesses, ordinary townsfolk, the sheriff, firemen, policemen and soldiers, is far removed from the 'cranks' who one now expects to subscribe to the notion of alien visitors and abductions. It is the credibility of their testimony which has elevated the Roswell Incident into a subject worthy of serious study.

This book is the story of what those witnesses saw, what they believed it to represent and the official cover-up that followed. It is a story which offers tantalizing 'evidence' of alien beings in a small town in America. But unlike most accounts of UFOs, it is a serious examination of a sequence of events which, whatever the final explanation, amount to a fascinating and mysterious episode in recent American history. For the Roswell Incident deserves an authoritative investigation aimed at providing a definitive account of a dramatic mystery which – if only half true – could be one of the greatest stories yet to be told!

1

If someone told you that they had seen a flying saucer, you could be forgiven for being sceptical. If that same person then told you that they had not only seen one but that they had also captured it, your scepticism might turn to incredulity. Yet that is precisely what the US Air Force told the world in the summer of 1947.

'Flying Disc Captured' was the sensational banner headline blazoned across America's local and national newspapers on July 8, 1947. The radio networks, the major source of news before the saturation coverage of the television age, issued hourly bulletins about the 'disc' and its curious properties. At first little emerged and then more details began to trickle out. It was of a flimsy construction and made of strange material. And that was about as far as it went. By now the world's media was getting in on the act. Newsrooms and wire services across the globe were literally humming with excitement. Art McQuiddy, the editor of the *Roswell Morning Despatch* at the time, remembers getting calls from all over the world, including Tokyo and London. Just as this international clamour began to build up, journalists and correspondents found themselves confronted by a deafening silence. Twelve hours after the initial announcement the Air Force appeared to have imposed a news blackout on the whole affair.

The event was all the more extraordinary because it took place at a time when flying saucers were a relatively new phenomenon. The term is believed to have first been coined in June 1947 when Kenneth Arnold, an American pilot, reported his observation of nine disc-shaped objects over the Cascade Mountains, Washington State. There had been many sightings before then loosely described under the umbrella title of Unidentified Flying Objects, or UFOs, but no reports of anything crashing to earth apart from the odd meteorite. Hence the worldwide sensation that greeted the Air Force's announcement.

The following day the curiosity of the massed journalists and an excited public had reached fever pitch. Word leaked out that the 'flying disc' had been flown to 'Higher Headquarters'. At Fort Worth, Texas, Brigadier General Roger Ramey, Commander of the Eighth Air Force and Major Jesse Marcel, the Intelligence Officer from Roswell Army Air Field, gave a press conference and exhibited some of the debris from the 'flying disc'.

Photos were flashed around the United States, accompanied by the text of the new official announcement. In an embarrassing volte-face for the Air Force, the remains of the mysterious disc had metamorphosed into tin foil, burnt rubber and scraps of material used in the construction of weather balloons.

The following day's headline read: 'GENERAL RAMEY EMP-TIES SAUCER! "FLYING DISC" A WEATHER BALLOON.' For a disappointed press and public that was the end of the matter. But the story didn't die – it just lay dormant for a number of years. Those who had been in Roswell at the time remembered not only the incident but also a whole series of strange events that surrounded the mystery.

There were the Military Police units that cordoned off the highway for several miles after the Independence Day weekend, three days before the press release was issued. There were the witnesses to strange lights in the sky, many days before, and accounts of radar observations picking up traces of unknown aircraft. There had been a host of unexplained sightings at the top-secret White Sands Proving Ground, a missile range less than 200 miles from Roswell.

There was the story of the rancher who found mysterious debris on the land he worked and how he had boxed some of it up and brought it into the local sheriff's office, only to be held incommunicado for over a week.

There were the radio announcers who found themselves warned by mysterious voices in Washington against broadcasting anything about 'the incident'. The warnings were not to be taken lightly: the owner of one station was told they would simply close him down.

There were dark tales of townsfolk receiving unannounced visits and unwarranted threats. One young girl who claimed she had handled some material with unearthly properties, which 'spread like water, right across the table', said a military policeman told her that if she didn't keep quiet she ought to remember that there was a big desert out there and that no one would find her bones.

A young boy remembered his excited father coming home in the small hours of the summer morning carrying a variety of debris covered in strange symbols and hieroglyphics. They were indecipherable.

A local Air Force sergeant, who still lives in Roswell, spoke of a midnight encounter with a craft that emitted a strange light and presence.

The local undertaker from Ballard's Funeral Home remembers the agitated voice of the mortuary officer from Roswell Army Air Field calling him up to enquire about methods for embalming a body. There was another call, this time to ask about the availability of small coffins: suitable for children.

There was a meeting with a beautiful young nurse who worked at Roswell Army Air Field who described how she had been hurriedly forced into assisting two doctors in the operating theatre doing a post-mortem on a body unlike anything she had ever seen before. Traumatized by the experience, she had described a strange odour coming from the corpse – so bad that eventually they all had to leave the room.

These accounts from a variety of people read like a script from *The X Files* except that this all happened before television had even begun to invade the living room. This was a sheltered part of small-town America, a rural community in the heartland of a country where the values of truth, justice and loyalty to the flag were unquestioned. Its law-abiding citizens shared ideals and beliefs typical of countless communities across the nation and fundamental to its cohesion.

The summer of 1947 was typical for Roswell: long and hot, with spectacular blue skies and sweeping sunsets. By day the unrelenting sun baked the rocks; at night the cool desert air sent the temperature plunging.

It was classic small-town America with an annual circus parade, pretty dancing girls in the long, swirling dresses of the Wild West and cowboys wearing hats and holding lasso contests. There were bands and competitions, a fly-past by the four-engined B-29s from the local Air Force base, stunt riding by the ranch hands on beautifully groomed horses wearing ornate hand-tooled leather saddles. In the evenings there would be barbecues and drinking and those few who had cars would make the occasional expedition into the nearest large town, Albuquerque, about four hours' drive away.

At that time Roswell was a small, tight-knit rural community of the sort which barely exists today. It was also one of the most secret places on earth. The natural beauty of the sprawling desert landscape, the sheer stature of the mountains and the spectacular sunsets formed a stark contrast to the terror that lay behind some of the highly classified experiments then being conducted on the land and in the skies of New Mexico. The tranquil scenery offered few clues to the fact that the desolate landscape was nurturing experiments with the power to destroy the world.

It was partly the wide open spaces and seemingly infinite blue skies which made the landscape of New Mexico so attractive to those whose lives were dedicated to masterminding the means of mass destruction. The lonely and isolated nature of the terrain made it ideally suited for the establishment of large defence establishments safe from the prying eyes of potential spies. And there were hundreds of thousands of acres of space for rocket, missile and bomb tests which could be carried out in the secure knowledge of minimal risk to the surrounding population.

The first atomic bomb was exploded at the Trinity test site not far from Roswell. Robert Oppenheimer and his team for the Manhattan Project, America's secret programme to make the first atomic bomb, had been based at a sprawling complex of laboratories and workshops in Los Alamos, New Mexico. Such was the state of nuclear physics and their venture into the unknown that it was seriously considered at the time that the Trinity test might spark a chain reaction which could lead to the end of the world. Oppenheimer and his team of scientists watched aghast as their fearsome device exploded high above the New Mexico desert, bestowing on the world a sense of its own mortality. They breathed a collective sigh of relief when the feared chain reaction failed to occur.

At Alamogordo, in the same state, highly classified tests were being undertaken at another airbase. The relatively straightforward technology of hot-air balloons was being used to send acoustic probes high into the earth's upper atmosphere to see whether they could detect any signals from the fallout of the atomic bomb tests that the Americans were convinced the Soviet Union was conducting. Less than one hundred miles away, adjacent to the geological phenomenon known as White Sands – a small patch of desert distinguished by a series of sand dunes so snow-white that they dazzle the eye – was the centre for the United States' nascent space programme at the White Sands Proving Ground. 'Space programme' was something of a euphemism: at that time the research was being directed towards missile technology. Rockets were being designed to wreak mass destruction at the greatest distance and with the highest accuracy.

The entire operation was being conducted with captured German V-2 rockets and a team of Nazi scientists who had been smuggled out of Germany by American intelligence agents at the end of the war. Enjoying the good fortune to escape the War Crimes Tribunal at Nuremberg, they were free to pursue the ambitions in space which had cost so many lives in the slave factories of Peenemünde, where the V-2 was developed. The head of the programme was the legendary scientist Wernher von Braun, aided and abetted by a team of American technicians and engineers.

Roswell itself was the home and headquarters to the 509th Bomb Group, America's elite Air Force squadron and the only unit in the world which had the capability of flying and dropping the atomic bomb. It was the 509th that, at the end of the Second World War, had dropped the bombs on Hiroshima and Nagasaki from their base in the Pacific. The commander of the base at Roswell Army Air Field was a swashbuckling Air Force pilot, Colonel William 'Butch' Blanchard.

Admired and respected by his men, Blanchard had engaged in exploits that were legendary, including one infamous occasion when he flew a trainer jet down to Mexico with a colleague and came back laden with so much whiskey that the plane buckled on landing and crashed to a smoking halt. Remarkably, he succeeded in not only jumping out of the stricken craft but also quickly returning to the scene to demand that the Military Police track down the pilot and court-martial him. Whether the plane crashed because of the weight of the bootleg booze on board or its in-flight consumption by the inhabitants of the cockpit never emerged at the court-martial proceedings because the pilot mysteriously disappeared!

The base for the 509th dominated Roswell, fuelling its economy and employing its citizens, while the town's social life brought many of the local community's most attractive girls into close proximity with the eligible bachelors of the Air Force. Local romance flourished between military personnel at the base and the young daughters of farmers and agricultural workers. The base even had its own newspaper, *Atom Blast*.

The base, with its perimeter fences patrolled night and day by armed sentries, the constant taxiing, take-offs and landings of a variety of aircraft, the numerous personnel – some pilots, some navigators, others working in security and intelligence – and at the same time being at the centre of the town's life was the first place that Sheriff George Wilcox thought of when Mac Brazel rode into town with a garbled story and a box of strange debris that he said had fallen from the skies, littering the ground of the ranch where he worked. Brazel didn't even have to go to the trouble of making his own way to the base: two military sentries drove over to Sheriff Wilcox's office and picked him up in an open-topped jeep. In the first week of July 1947, Roswell Army Air Field was about to get its hands on its first 'flying saucer'.

The man who started the whole welter of myth or reality – depending upon which view one takes of the Roswell Incident – is unfortunately now dead. But Mac Brazel is still remembered by many who knew him at the time.

One key witness is Loretta Proctor, a diminutive eighty-year-old who to this day lives on an isolated ranch some thirty-five miles outside the town of Roswell, the same spot where she was accosted one day by her neighbour and friend, Mac Brazel. Despite her advancing years and fading memory, Loretta can still recall with seeming accuracy the day that he turned up in an excited state to regale her and her husband with the story of what he had come across, after a storm, on his horseback round of the ranch. Brazel was a frequent visitor who helped the Proctors on their farm, while they in turn lent him a hand whenever he needed it. One day in the summer of 1947 Brazel showed up unannounced. 'He brought a small piece of material up and he said that he couldn't get any of the other loose, so I don't know whether it was scattered as much as they've said later that it was or not because he described to me this piece that looked like plastic. There was some metallic-looking stuff that when you crushed it, it straightened back out. It wouldn't stay crushed and there was some beams or something that kind of had pinkish-purple printing on it and some tape – I don't know whether he meant like freezer tape or some other type, I don't know what other kind of tape but he said it was some kind of tape that he couldn't get loose or cut. He and my husband tried to burn this piece of material that he brought me, take their knives and try to whittle it and it would make no dent on it or anything. It was very, at that time, strange-looking material, different to anything we'd ever seen. You'd say it was like plastic but that was before we had plastic.'

I asked Loretta whether she and Brazel could have been mistaken and merely stumbled across a balloon as the Air Force was later to claim. 'I don't think so,' she replied, 'because he had found weather balloons and other people had and this was strange to him. No, I don't think it was.'

Loretta actually saw and handled a piece of the material and remembers its properties to this day. 'What he brought up was about a little larger round than a lead pencil, just a regular pencil, and it was a light tan in colour. Looked like a lightweight wood. I just don't know how you would describe it. I'd say now some kind of plastic, but it's been a long time.' When she felt the material it felt very light: 'a real light weight, it was lighter than a lead pencil would have been because we remarked on how lightweight it was. But it was different to anything we had ever seen. The material and the way you couldn't burn it and you couldn't cut it. He said that he had tried to cut off some of the foil stuff with his knife and he couldn't touch it, you know, but he described it kinda like aluminum foil – only he said when you crushed it, it straightened back out, it wouldn't hold a crease or anything.'

This description of the physical properties of Brazel's find is remarkably similar to other eyewitness accounts of the debris – in particular the notion that it was a material that regained its shape when it was crushed, bounding back to its original form. So long after the event there is the inevitable suspicion that the descriptions tally because interviewees read others' accounts and perhaps superimposed those recollections on their own. Yet Loretta Proctor was potentially one of the very first to have handled some of the 'debris' that Brazel had discovered. Mrs Proctor is a down-to-earth countrywoman, of a type that you would scarcely credit with the inclination to embellish a story or embroider her experience to make it fit with a prevailing fashion or a conventional wisdom whether it favoured the mystery or the more mundane explanation of the balloon theory. She is emphatic that the material was different from 'anything that we had ever seen' and that it seemed resistant to being burnt or cut. Loretta and her husband ended up telling Brazel that it was probably a UFO and that he should report it.

'We had heard there was a reward and I don't remember how much of a reward but there was a lot of sightings at that time and people were talking about them and we decided that's what it was and he should report it. And then when he did report it they kept him at Roswell for about nearly a week. When he came back out we heard that they'd brought him back out there in an airplane and he showed them where the debris field was and they took him back to Roswell and they kept him down there while they sent somebody out to clean it up. So I don't know, but I know they didn't let him come back home and stay. He was down there about a week.'

If we accept that the Air Force's cover story of the 'weather balloon' is correct, it is all the more puzzling why they should have held Brazel incommunicado for seven days. And even if we accept the official Air Force explanation that their initial story was a cover-up for a more secret balloon, 'Project Mogul', it still does not square with the imposition of a restraining order on a rancher and the necessity of flying him out over the area. If the balloon project was that secret, then it would hardly have made sense to draw that much attention to it. Yet, as even those involved admit, the balloon and the materials used in it were perfectly ordinary – it was merely the mission that was secret: an attempt to record Soviet atomic tests via acoustic echoes in the upper atmosphere. While none of this proves the case of the UFO supporters, it does add to the mystery in the sense that it suggests that something was happening that the authorities were extremely sensitive about and that something had crashed or gone missing that they were extremely anxious to recover. A weather balloon in any shape or form – even if it was a top-secret project to eavesdrop on the innermost counsels of the Kremlin with a super-secret advanced microphone capable of detecting conversations inside the Politburo – would hardly have warranted such extreme measures: if for no other reason than that the more secret the purpose of the balloon was the less likelihood there could have been of anyone compromising its mission.

When Loretta Proctor and her husband saw their neighbour again he had some telling words to communicate to them. 'Well, the next time we saw him,' recalls Loretta, 'he said, "They told me it was a weather balloon, but if I ever find another nobody will know anything about it."' She adds: 'He didn't think it was a weather balloon but he said they told him it was so he wouldn't talk about it.'

Confirmation that Brazel was leant upon by the military comes from Frank Joyce, who was working as a radio reporter for KGFL in Roswell at the time. He had been tipped off early on by Sheriff Wilcox's office that there might be a news story. 'I'm not completely clear about whether I called the sheriff's office or they called me, but I found myself on the phone with a man named W.W. Brazel and he wanted to tell me about some sort of crash that had happened on his ranch.' Joyce listened to what Brazel had to say and although he is reluctant to give a full account of everything Brazel said (because of a later encounter in which he gave an undertaking to Brazel), he does admit that some of it was unbelievable and he remembers suggesting that Brazel should contact the local Air Force base.

The next that Joyce heard was when Walter Haut, the public information officer at the airbase, contacted him. 'I had a friend named Walter Haut who was the PIO at the Roswell Army Air Corps base at that time. By coincidence I had told Walter several times before that he hadn't been giving me any stories out of Roswell base, so he says you get the next one. He calls me before he came and says, "Joyce, I've got a release for you. I'll be down in thirty minutes and give you this and you will have a little time to get it out before anybody else does." So Walter comes down to the station and hands me the information which basically says a flying saucer has been recovered on a ranch north of Roswell. It seemed to be written in a way by someone who had been told there was a crash of a flying saucer out there but no one gave him any details so he just wrote it out as best he could.'

Frank Joyce was amazed to discover that the story that he had heard by telephone from Brazel was now appearing in print as a press release. 'And I'm looking at this release which was on onionskin paper rather than mimeograph and I said, "Walter, wait a minute! I know about this story, I sent this guy to you!" And he's going out of the door not really paying attention to what I say and I'm going out the door hollering, "Hey, wait a minute, I know about this story. I want to talk to you . . . I don't think you should release this story. And he hopped in his car . . . he's on the run and goes back to the base. So I sit there and read this story about the US Army Air Force says it has a flying saucer and I think, well, I really shouldn't do this because it hasn't been proved and having been in the military I know how the military works, and at the very least I could see some of the top brass saying this is not right. So I called Walter at the base – he had apparently just got out of his car there – and I said, Walter, I don't think you should use this story . . . this man came to me and it seemed like a pretty unbelievable story, and he said, "Frank, it's OK, the old man, Blanchard" – I believe it was Blanchard, or something to that effect . . . I can't give you his exact words – "has cleared this and it's all right for you to put that story on the air."'

Joyce practically ran out of the door to reach the Western Union offices, two blocks away, and instructed the operator to send the release word for word on the wire to Santa Fe. By the time he got back to the office, the wires were buzzing with local and national news organizations trying to get more details and confirmation of the story. Twenty minutes later all the wires went quiet and Joyce believes that they were deliberately shut down. The owner of the radio station then came to ask Joyce what all the commotion was about and as Joyce searched for the press release to show him the telephone rang. 'I got a number of phone calls,' he recalls. 'But the one that really got my attention was purportedly from the Pentagon. There was a young lady on the line saying Colonel So and So from the Pentagon was calling and this was within a few minutes of it going out on the wire and the voice on the line says, "Who's this?" I tell him and he says, "Did you put that story on the air about the flying saucers?" and I mean his voice was, you know, the type that really conveys menace and power. I said, "Yes, I did." And he says, "You're going to get in a lot of trouble for this . . ." And I say, "Look, I'm a civilian, you can't talk to me this way, you can't treat me this way, you can't tell me what to do and what stories I put on the air" and he says, "I'll show you what I can do" and hung up the phone.'

Later that afternoon Joyce was surprised to get a phone call from Brazel, who told him that they hadn't quite got the story right and asked if he could come over and talk to him about it. Joyce readily agreed. 'So along about dusk Brazel comes to the station. I go out and meet him at the door and we meet physically for the first time. So he comes in and I bring him into the control room and we're sitting there with small talk for a few minutes and then he says, "I wanted to come over and tell you that we didn't get this story quite right and some of the things I said the other day may have misled you. Actually what came down on my ranch was a weather balloon and there was a lot of wreckage strewn around." I said this is not at all like what you told me the other day. I said it is a completely different story, nothing like what they say about "little green men", and I said that and I looked away because I couldn't really look him in the eye when I said this – in effect calling him a liar – and he said the most profound words up to that point. There is a little pause and he said, "They weren't green."'

Joyce was convinced this meant that what Brazel had originally told him was the truth. 'He immediately said, "OK Frank, I'll tell you just between me and you. They told me to come here to the station and tell you this story about the weather balloon that's what they want you to think it is. He said they wanted me to tell you this story about the weather balloon and if I didn't do that it would go hard with me and then he looked at me and he said it would also go hard with you. So at this point I really blew my top. I said, "Look, we're American citizens, you know. Whoever they are, they can't tell us how to run our lives, they can't tell us what to do and they can't tell you" and I'm making this little speech to him and at the end of it he says, "I'm not so sure about that."'

As far as Joyce is concerned, he is convinced that Brazel was put under a lot of pressure by the military not to say anything and although Joyce did not broadcast anything on the radio, an article did appear the following day in the July 9 edition of the *Roswell Daily Record*, headlined 'Harassed Rancher Who Located "Saucer" Sorry He Told About It.' A full-scale press conference seems to have been organized by the authorities in the presence of R.D. Adair, the wire chief of the Albuquerque office of Associated Press, and Jason Kellahin, also of AP. Brazel was brought to the office of the newspaper, apparently still accompanied by a military escort. The new story quoted Brazel as saying that he had come across the wreckage on June 14 when out with his eight-year-old son, Vernon, and it was described as 'a large area of bright wreckage made up of rubber strips, tinfoil, a rather tough paper and sticks'.

In the new version Brazel did not return to collect the debris until July 4 and it was only the next day that he heard about the 'flying discs' and wondered if he had found one. It was not until Monday July 7 that Brazel went into Roswell and mentioned his find to the sheriff. The article continues: 'Wilcox got in touch with the Roswell Army Air Field and Maj Jesse A. Marcel and a man in plain clothes accompanied him home where they picked up the rest of the pieces of the "disk" and went to his home to try to reconstruct it.'

According to Brazel, they simply could not reconstruct it at all. They tried to make a kite out of it but could not do this; nor could they find any way to put it back together so that it would fit.

Then Major Marcel took the find to Roswell and that was the last Brazel heard of it until the story broke that he had found a flying disc. Brazel said that he neither saw it fall from the sky nor saw it before it was torn up, so he didn't know the size or shape it might have been, but he thought it might have been about as large as a table top. The balloon which held it up, if that was how it worked, must have been about twelve feet long, he felt, measuring the distance by the size of the room in which he sat. The rubber was smoky grey in colour and scattered over an area about 200 yards in diameter.

When the debris was gathered up, the tinfoil, paper, tape and sticks made a bundle about eighteen to twenty inches long and about eight inches thick. In all, he estimated, the entire lot would have weighed maybe five pounds.

There was no sign of any metal in the area which might have been used for an engine and no sign of any propellers of any kind, although at least one paper fin had been glued on to some of the tinfoil.

There were no words to be found anywhere on the instrument, although there were letters on some of the parts. A considerable amount of adhesive tape and some tape with flowers printed on it had been used in the construction. No strings or wire were to be found but there were some eyelets in the paper to indicate that some form of attachment may have been used.

Brazel said that he had previously found two weather balloons on the ranch, but that what he found this time did not in any way resemble either of these. 'I am sure what I found was not any weather observation balloon,' he said. 'But if I find anything else, besides a bomb, they are going to have a hard time getting me to say anything about it.'

There are some curious features to this story, even accepting that Joyce is right and that Brazel was pressured into making this statement. It is strange that they were able to offer such a detailed analysis of the debris when this had already been flown to Fort Worth. Also, if this was what had been found by Brazel it becomes almost inconceivable to believe that the Army Air Force could have mistaken it for a flying disc. Finally, Brazel's last comment seems to indicate his resentment at being held and questioned by the military and suggests that what he was saying was against his will.

Even to his friends and neighbours, Brazel remained tight-lipped about his experience in later years. The Proctors felt that he had been intimidated in some way and that because of the time just after the Second World War, when people had a natural deference to the military authorities – Brazel would have knuckled under and kept quiet. Again, a puzzling attitude, given that they were all excited originally about their find. And if it had turned out to be disappointingly a mere weather balloon then there would have been no reason not to talk and even joke about it later – but they didn't. Once again, none of this proves that there was anything extraterrestrial, but it does suggest something rather more serious than a weather instrument or a 'Project Mogul' balloon. It raises the possibility of either something that was highly secret and experimental or a UFO which the authorities were unable to explain.

Before he was questioned by the military, Brazel had reportedly handed in the debris that he had found on the Foster ranch to the local sheriff's office. A picture of Sheriff George Wilcox, of Chaves County, was featured in the *Roswell Daily Record*, bravely manning the telephone as calls came in from all over the world about the historic announcement of the crashed flying saucer in Roswell. Although George Wilcox died several years ago, members of his family are still alive and his daughter remembers clearly that the incident affected her father and had a serious impact on his later life. Phyllis McGuire still lives in the area. A sprightly seventy-year-old, she lives in a house in a pretty side road some miles out of Roswell in a rural and agricultural part of New Mexico where many of the old buildings and wooden shacks still survive. Her front porch reaches out towards a large lake in a picturesque setting while inside there is a swing door leading to a spotless interior and a homely kitchen.

Phyllis remembers both her parents and the incident of the 'flying saucer' with great clarity. 'I was in my early twenties and I was visiting my father, George Wilcox, and my mother, and Brazel came to town and brought the material and the article came out in the newspaper. I went of course, the office was not as busy then as it would be now so I did go and ask my father if he thought this was true, what was in the paper, and he said, "I don't know what Brazel would bother to bring all this stuff into town for if there wasn't something to this." And he sent deputies out, and I think he went himself, but very shortly after it went public and the Army refuted the claim that there was a flying saucer, plus they encircled the ranch with so many soldiers and jeeps and armed people that no one could get in. They closed it off. That was virtually the end of the information. There was some material in the sheriff's office in a little room – the office had two rooms: the larger office and a little one. The material was in there and the Army came in three or four days to pick it up; they really put a lid on the information that got out about it. I did not see the material, I knew it was there, I did have an opportunity to see the material but I just didn't do it at the time. I really was very interested and excited about this possibility and I asked so many questions that my mother

said, "Your father doesn't want you to ask any more questions." I
realize now that he had trouble saying he didn't know anything to
me at that time. He was forced to say over the phone that he did
not know anything and to direct them to the Air Force any time that
any questions came over the phone and lots and lots of questions did
come, calls from London and all over the United States.'

For what they claimed was a mere weather balloon (although,
arguably, they didn't know at the time), the military turned up in
surprisingly large numbers at the sheriff's office. Phyllis McGuire
was there at the time and remembers a number of military jeeps and
military cars with at least eight soldiers. 'They told him they didn't
want him to say anything about it all,' she recalls. 'My mother said
they were very hard on [my] father at that time and threatened him
and his family if he did mention or tell anyone about it.'

Even with his own family, Sheriff Wilcox was strangely reticent
about the incident. 'My mother and father were very close,' recalls
Phyllis. 'I could ask them any questions that I wanted to and we
talked about all kinds of things. I had always talked to my mother
a great deal so I felt a little strange when my father cut me off and
said he wasn't going to answer the phone about the UFOs and that
he was leaving it up to the Army entirely and my mother said to me,
"Don't ask your father any more questions, he doesn't want to talk
about that." It bothered me a little bit but someone told me that they
thought it was an experimental plane, that the Army did have a lot of
experiments going on and that perhaps that was it. And I just went
on with my life after that."

In later life George Wilcox was indeed curiously reluctant to say
anything about the incident, an odd attitude to take, particularly if
the whole affair was nothing more than a balloon. Many years later,
after he had died, his widow was slightly more forthcoming to their
daughter. 'My mother, years later, said that there was a crash, that
they were asked, told, not to say anything, so we didn't and she said
there was a saucer and that there were bodies: three bodies. She said
that one of them was alive when they went out there. So I assume
that my father told her that and that she didn't tell it until many
years later.'

Although she did not hear it directly from her father, Phyllis
McGuire is in no doubt that, bearing in mind what her mother
told her, 'He knew it was true. I think he believed it to be true. I
really believed it was true. I feel badly that we didn't have TV and

helicopters and things to go find out about things like that – then we could have known. But the distance that ranch where it landed was seventy-five miles from Roswell. The communication that we have nowadays and take for granted was not there then.'

Sheriff Wilcox's daughter also believes that the 'Incident' and the pressure and the threats that came from the Roswell airbase had an effect on her father's health. She remembers him as a very open, gregarious and easygoing sort of person who, for the times, was very progressive when it came to dealing with prisoners and juvenile delinquents. Wilcox introduced a new system of separating juveniles from adult prisoners in the Roswell jail – a fairly radical innovation at the time. Today Phyllis thinks the whole affair 'had a lot of an effect on my father. I didn't realize at the time but I think it did bother him a great deal. It sort of broke his health.' According to her mother, the military had threatened the lives of the sheriff and his family – threats that were taken very seriously and could account for the change that the daughter noticed in her father.

If it is difficult to believe that Phyllis McGuire would fabricate a story, then, even without knowing her, it is nigh impossible to conceive of her mother, the wife of Sheriff Wilcox, as capable of such a wild invention. When I gently challenged Phyllis and intimated that most people would find it very difficult to believe that any of these stories about flying saucers and aliens could possibly be true, she agreed. 'I know that's true and there are some fringes that are far-out and nutty but basically I think you will find that people who are telling you this story are very ordinary Americans.'

Phyllis's sister, Elizabeth Tulk, is a lively and animated lady who lives and works with her horses and cattle. I went to meet her one early morning at the Roswell Cattle Market, which was teeming with cows and steers and ranch hands expertly guiding frisky horses between narrow rails into pens where they would await appraisal before going to auction. Large trucks and small trailers turned up throughout the day to discharge their animal cargo, and the noise of barking dogs, braying horses, cattle mooing and grunting, shouting cow-hands and clanging gates all combined to produce a rural cacophony that almost drowned out conversation.

'I remember coming to Roswell to do shopping and going to the sheriff's office, where my mother and father lived and my mother prepared meals for the prisoners and she had a special dining room,' recalls Elizabeth. 'And when we drove up that day I remember seeing two or three, I think it was two, MP trucks, jeeps, outside, and I just remarked, I wonder what these jeeps are doing out there, and then we went on into the building and at lunchtime my mother said, "Well, George won't be able to come to lunch today because they thought a flying saucer had landed out north of Roswell and he's been on the telephone all night and all day talking about the flying saucer!" Now my husband went into the office and said, "What did you do, George?" and he said, "Well, we went out to the crash site and it was a lot of burnt area out there" but he didn't tell him any more.'

The presence of burnt grass is something of an anomaly, not mentioned in any of the other accounts, but Elizabeth is confident that her father mentioned it. 'My father, the Sheriff, told my husband that because we asked him over and over, "Well, what did you find?" and he said, "We found burnt grass out at the crash."'

I asked Elizabeth if either she or her father could have been mistaken about this particular detail and she replied, 'No, no. He was very sane and very fit. Just like you and I, he wouldn't dare tell something that he didn't know, my goodness, no! But then he didn't talk about it, you know. From then on I didn't . . . we didn't. But my mother wrote [in a letter to Elizabeth] one time that a rancher came into the sheriff's office and brought some debris and said there was a flying saucer had landed out there.'

Like her sister, Elizabeth Tulk recalls that her father never spoke of the incident afterwards, and although she was unable to confirm whether he was threatened or anything else untoward, his subsequent behaviour does not seem consistent with the explanation that it was merely a weather balloon that had been found. Besides, people like the sheriff, who were involved from the outset, would surely have dismissed the episode in later life or made fun of it? No one seems to have done this so either they are all tremendously lacking in a sense of humour or there was something rather serious about the sequence of events.

Other accounts of the 'Roswell Incident' have referred to a group of archaeologists who were digging in the area and came across a crashed flying saucer. The story has become somewhat apocryphal as no one has succeeded in identifying the group or their university. It may just be a rumour but one distinguished archaeologist has a story which lends some credence to the accounts. Dr George Agogino is one of America's foremost archaeologists and is famous for his work on sites containing the bones of mammoths killed by humans, particularly at the Black Water site in New Mexico, one of the most important and historic mammoth 'kill sites' in the Americas. Agogino is still active both on digs and as a lecturer at the University of New Mexico. When I met him he was amused to be still associated with such a celebrated case. 'Well, I was claimed to be one of the archaeologists who saw the site,' he told me. 'It's not true! But I was working at the University of New Mexico on a degree – I forget which one it was – and went out to the field very frequently with surveys, so when this incident occurred and four archaeologists were supposed to have been at the scene of the crash, the only institute in the whole state which taught archaeology was the University of New Mexico, so we were all interrogated, so that's the first time I heard about it.'

Clearly, the rumour had also reached the eyes and ears of the military because, according to Agogino, a deputation arrived to question the faculty, along with some journalists. 'We had military, we had some newspaper people from Albuquerque heard about it, the Roswell Incident, and they came up and more or less accused each of us of being there and I think some of our people were there but everyone had denied it, but I had my own suspicion but I don't want to mention it.'

According to Agogino, the military officials questioned several people at the University, including him. 'They asked me what we saw, if we saw the disabled rocket or spaceship with dead occupants. The nature of the question was: were we the people? They wanted to identify the individuals, the archaeologists who were at that site. Now the only group I knew of who was out there is a Canadian archaeologist and I don't want to mention his name. He had five people with him and one of the people was a woman who was supposed to be the one who died in Florida. Now this person from Canada tells me that he was not at the site and never saw it but some of the people on his crew talked about a flying saucer wreck after he had left the area. Now everybody has denied it and will continue to deny it and I don't know what the reason is. I know originally what the reason was. If they found those archaeologists in 1947 there was about seventy professional jobs in the whole country, archaeologists who graduated and made their living by doing salvage work, getting grants from government to clear up river surveys and things like that. Those people were contacted by the military – they gave them two choices: talk at all, ever, and you don't get any more grant, don't talk and we will be very liberal and you'll be given your grants. I'm sure that's what happened there.'

2

Frank Kaufmann is a grizzled and grey-haired American in his late seventies. A man of large build with a steady walk and a firm handshake, he is both open and approachable and seemingly untroubled for an individual who claims to be privy to one of the greatest secrets of mankind.

He and his wife live in a neat bungalow decorated with dark wooden furniture and oil paintings in fake-antique gilt frames. Many of the paintings have an amateurish quality about them although some display a good sense of the landscape and light of New Mexico. The pictures were painted by Kaufmann himself and he is proud of the achievement, although he makes no great claims for his artistic abilities.

Adjoining the sitting room, which has a brick fireplace surround that appears somewhat incongruous in the fiery summer heat of New Mexico, is a spotlessly kept kitchen where Juanita Kaufmann cooks and cleans and makes remarkable lemon pies. A photograph on the wall reveals that the Kaufmanns campaigned for Bill Clinton during the 1992 election. Smiling photographs of dark-suited young men, women and children adorn the walls and testify to a large family of children, grandchildren and in-laws.

For many years Kaufmann was the head of the Roswell Chamber of Commerce and he is fast approaching the celebrations for his fiftieth wedding anniversary. His ordinary demeanour and background merely serve to highlight the extraordinary nature of his story. He claims to have entered military service in 1941 and to have been assigned to Roswell the following year as an NCOIC: a Non-Commissioned Officer in Charge. His commanding officer was General Scanlon and his duties were concerned with security at the base. As the 509th was the only air squadron capable of carrying atomic bombs, not just in America but the whole world, it would inevitably have been surrounded by a fairly high level of security. On the other hand it was on the edge of the town of Roswell, so access to the base was fairly relaxed, but there were occasions when the military could be distinctly unfriendly towards their civilian neighbours. In addition to the atomic weapons that were stored at the base, the 509th was also in possession of the Norton bomb-sight, a precision instrument for pinpoint bombing which had given the Americans a distinct advantage over first, the Germans and later the Russians. Along with any atomic secrets, the device would have been a prized target for any foreign agent on an espionage mission.

Kaufmann left the military in October 1945 but says he was asked to rejoin almost immediately to take up his old duties in a civilian capacity, helping to maintain security at the base. It was towards the end of June 1947, he remembers, that he was sent to Alamogordo, to White Sands, which had more powerful radar antennae than Roswell, on a mission to monitor strange movements that were being detected on the radar screens. He recalls that 'the blips were just dancing from one end of the screen to the other and all of a sudden there was kind of a white flash and it just disappeared. Well, that indicated that possibly it may be a plane or a missile or something just went down.' A report about a possible crash was then radioed into Roswell and to the Commanding Officer, Colonel Blanchard, who would almost certainly have reported the event up the line to General Roger Ramey, Commander of the Eighth Air Force at Fort Worth, Texas.

Kaufmann was then ordered to make his way back to Roswell from White Sands – in those days a three- or four-hour drive. On the way they radioed back to Roswell Army Air Field to have a crew drive north on Highway 285 to see if they could locate anything that might have crashed in the vicinity. The patrol from Roswell radioed back that they had spotted something that appeared to be glowing at some distance from the main road. Kaufmann and his team drove for over two hours before they joined them. 'We just started to clip some of the wire fence and drove into the area because we saw this glow of light, this kind of halo of light just kind of beaming out, and we got to about two hundred yards, maybe three hundred yards, from where it was and we learned then and there that it wasn't a plane, it wasn't a missile it was kind of a strange-looking craft that was embedded in the arroyo.'

A searchlight on one of the trucks was used to illuminate the area and a radio dispatch was sent back to Roswell to request special suits as they were uncertain as to what they had come across. The glow from the object had alerted them to the danger of some form of radiation but later the glow appeared to subside and fade, so the patrol decided to move in to take a closer look.

'We saw this odd-shaped craft almost looked like a heel [of a shoe], something like that,' Kaufmann recalls, 'and it was open halfway and one body was thrown up against the wall of the arroyo; the other one was half in and half out of the craft and when we got in close we noticed that there were three others inside the craft . . .'

The craft itself, which was later roughly sketched by Kaufmann, was an estimated six feet high, twenty to twenty-five feet long and about fifteen feet wide. It was somewhere between a 'V' shape and a 'Delta' shape, with a wrap-around window at the front, and the whole contraption appeared to have split in half along its horizontal edge. Inside the craft, Kaufmann says, they saw panels of controls and some writing which they couldn't make out. Explaining why they did not make a more thorough examination at the crash site, he says that the operational priority was to clear the area and get the craft out and back to the Roswell base, where they were clearing an entire hangar to deposit the wreckage and study it further. There was also the problem of the severe thunderstorms which had been raging across the desert for the past few days and nights and which could delay the recovery procedure.

Kaufmann claims that he was told later about a possible reason for the crash of the strange aerial object. 'This is something that was maybe one in a trillion that it happened,' he recalls. 'There was no fuel on the craft but the underbelly had a series of cells – you know, quartz type cells, glass-looking cells, octagon-shaped. And lightning, as you know, starts from the ground up and it just so happens that at that time that lightning hit that craft and knocked it out of commission and it crashed. That's what we were told happened.'

A further radio call was made to headquarters and a request was made for a flatbed truck and a crane to come out to the site. Apparently no one was terribly sure about the exact nature of what they had come across or what they were witnessing. But they were unanimous that what they were seeing was something that none of them had ever experienced before. Kaufmann says it is hard to describe their reaction to what they saw. 'You see something out of this world, it was a little frightening . . . we kept staring at it and not saying a word and just looking at it until we finally snapped out of it. But it's hard to describe just how we felt about it at the time.'

Kaufmann, who has an eerie oil painting of an 'alien face' hanging in his sitting room, recalls: 'They didn't look anything like you see portrayed in your science fiction magazines – they didn't have any horns or spiny fingers. They were smooth-looking individuals, no hair, very fine skin and a silver type of uniform. I would say about five four or five six in height, but very fine features, small nose, small ears and they didn't have any of the big eyes, you know the slanted eyes of that type.' He remembers that there was a sense of urgency and haste communicated from base headquarters. 'We didn't spend too much time going over that craft at the site. What we wanted to do was clear everything out, get it out of the way because dawn was approaching. We felt that during the daytime we may be in deep trouble, maybe draw a crowd, and this is something we wanted to get out of the way, so our mission was to clear that area out *muy pronto* and put it on the flatbed and get it out to the base.'

The bodies were put into lead-lined body bags and taken back to the base hospital. Kaufmann says there was no medical examination of them at the site nor was he aware that there were any survivors. There was 'just a quick review . . . making sure that we wouldn't be contaminated or anything of that nature . . we noticed one thing and that was that deterioration was starting to set in on one of the bodies. We noticed the edge of the skin trying to shrivel up and that's the reason why we put them in the bags in a hurry and got them out to the base hospital. We radioed in to have another crew to come out to the site and they were given instructions to clear the area to search for any other debris that had to do with the craft or anything else and to restore it to its natural state just as quickly as possible – and that crew came out. Meantime Thomas [the officer in command of the operation] and I and several others in our group, we were heading back to the base. We stopped at the hospital and were told that a pathologist from Beaumont General Hospital was being flown in and I understand they called the mortuary here to find out if there was any way they could preserve the bodies, and they were kind of in a quandary about what to do. So we went to headquarters and to file our reports and Colonel Blanchard was there, and Jesse Marcel, who was the Intelligence Officer, Major Easley, who was the Provost Marshal, were all there in a room kind of comparing notes and making arrangements to have the craft and the bodies shipped out. I didn't have anything to do with that. We had another group who handled that portion of it.'

According to Kaufmann, the centre of operations was a large hangar in the middle of the airfield, Hangar 84. Although the airfield closed down many years ago, some of the original buildings are still standing and that hangar is still in use. I revisited the hangar with Kaufmann and inside it was an old DC10 being serviced by a group of aviation engineers. One of them was curious to know what we were doing and when I explained he led me to the side of the hangar, where there was a small room, and confided to me that this was where it was believed the 'extraterrestrial' bodies had been stored back in 1947! When they found out who we were they shook Kaufmann's hand as if welcoming a veteran war hero! Kaufmann looked around the vast and cavernous interior of the hangar, and confirmed that the area became the makeshift headquarters for the recovery operation. 'The craft and the bodies were actually brought into this hangar and later on it was flown out of this area here into Fort Worth and Wright Patterson Field. There was a lot of activity in this area and inside the hangar right on top there was a spotlight shining down on the craft and the bodies were laid out – there were five of them – and there was a cordon of military police around the area to keep people from getting too close.

'The bodies were brought in and they were laid out on the floor, side by side, and they were examined by several officers and the pathologist from Beaumont General Hospital and the craft was on the east side of the building and there were several pictures taken and then the planes came on the tarmac right here and the craft itself was taken on a kind of cargo ship and loaded and I didn't pay too much attention to the loading and then they took off. Actually there were three diversionary flights: one flight went east, one flight went north, and another flight went west, and that was primarily to divert attention from the activity here because we noticed that there were some people still along the fence and we noticed some of them had cameras and we figured that some of them were trying to squeeze in a picture but, using the diversionary tactics, they didn't know exactly what was going on. I think it was early in the morning – around 3 a.m. or maybe 4 a.m., I am not quite sure – that they actually left Roswell Army Air Field and one flight went to Fort Worth and one went to Wright Patterson but they all wound up at Wright Patterson Field.'

In fact, Kaufmann is mistaken here: in 1947 it was at Wright Field, Ohio, that the headquarters of the US Air Force's research and development operations was based; Patterson was an adjoining but separate base which was later amalgamated. At that time Wright Field was the headquarters for the Foreign Technology Division of what was then the Army Air Force and soon to become the Air Force – when the command of the Army and the Air Force was separate in September of the same year. There is no doubt that if a craft had landed from outer space it would have been taken to Wright Field. A number of former airmen from the 509th base at Roswell have confirmed that there was unusual activity at this time, and there is evidence of crates being loaded and flown to Wright Field amid high security and secrecy. One pilot is reported to have remarked that their flight had 'made history', while another, Pappy Henderson, a much-decorated Second World War veteran, later told his wife that he had flown a transport plane that had carried the alien bodies. Those involved on the ground were not sure of what was inside the boxes but there were rumours of debris from a flying saucer and of bodies recovered from a craft. Not evidence in itself but an indication that something unusual had occurred – the movements, the secrecy and the rumours could all relate to an alternative scenario: an experimental craft that had crashed and killed its occupants or even civilians. There is even the possibility of what is known by the military as a 'broken arrow': a crash involving a craft carrying nuclear weapons. But those who have been questioned about this point out the fact that where this has occurred in the past – and there have been several incidents of this nature – it has always been discovered or openly reported.

One officer who would certainly have known all about the incident would have been Colonel Blanchard. Kaufmann remembers Blanchard, who 'went and viewed the craft and saw the bodies', being as puzzled by the crash as everyone else. Mysteriously, Blanchard never discussed the episode in later life. At a reunion dinner in Roswell several years after the event he was guest of honour and, after the meal and several glasses of whiskey, some of the Roswell locals pressed him to tell them what had really happened. Blanchard remained tight-lipped but was heard by several people, including the former mayor of Roswell, to remark, 'What I saw was the damnedest thing I've ever seen!'

Art McQuiddy, editor of the *Roswell Morning Despatch* at the time, who remained friends with Blanchard, saw him on several occasions after the July 1947 incident and constantly badgered him about what had really happened, only to find his friend unusually reticent. 'We were very good friends,' he remembers, 'and I saw him quite often socially and having been a Navy pilot in World War Two and having some interest in flight and all that was going on at the base we shared a common interest in our love of aviation, so he was a good friend of mine. Almost every time I had a drink with him, which was not infrequent, he never would discuss what happened but one night, he said, "Well . . ." and he paused. He said, "I'll tell you this", and I'm paraphrasing him because I don't remember exactly how he said it but in essence he said, "What I saw I'd never seen before . . ."'

It was Blanchard who would have had to authorize the press release about the Army Air Force capturing the 'flying disc'. One possibility is that the news release was a mistake, that the debris brought in by Mac Brazel, combined with the sightings that had occurred in and around Roswell in the early days of July and the national news of 'flying discs' which had swept across America, all contributed to what was nothing more than an overexcited press release which was simply wrong. But, given that in those days the military was governed by an almost implacable bureaucracy, this seems unlikely.

It is certainly true that the description that was issued of the recovered material, 'flimsy, like a box kite', was used in one of the network news radio bulletins. This phrase has been seized on by sceptics as a clear indication that the original material recovered was indeed a balloon of some description that was innocently mistaken for a 'flying disc'. There was also a suggestion that a reward had been offered for the recovery of one of these 'flying discs', a factor which might have influenced both Brazel and an overeager public information officer at the Roswell airbase. Might not all this have persuaded people to suspend their critical faculties and become convinced that they had perhaps got hold of something from outer space when all along it was nothing more than parts of a balloon? It is a plausible explanation. After all, Brazel himself had been told by his neighbour Loretta Proctor that perhaps he had happened upon 'one of them flying discs' and that maybe there was a reward for handing it in. He could have then told the sheriff it was a 'flying disc' and the description could have been passed on, along with the material, to the Air Force. However, for the Air Force to have mistaken bits of balsa-wood and foil from a balloon for a 'flying disc' – an object which by its very nature could not resemble anything man-made from earthly materials – seems almost incredible. Yet for those who remain convinced that it was a craft of extraterrestrial origin there are a large number of descriptions from eyewitnesses which tally with the materials that we know were used on balloons. Tape, foil, balsa wood, I-beams and material that was incredibly lightweight are all typical components of balloons and they all figure in many of the eyewitness accounts.

It may just be that the 'saucer' hysteria in the summer of 1947 suspended judgement and replaced it with a readiness to believe that the 'flying discs' were real.

Frank Kaufmann has an intriguing spin on the confused accounts of the incompatible stories. He claims that from the moment the original 'flying disc' press release was put out a carefully designed disinformation programme was underway. 'It was a beautiful job of confusion,' he laughs. 'If you want to cover up something, confuse the hell out of it!' Thus the plan could have been to admit that a 'flying disc' had been recovered but to include few details of what it was like, except for the descriptions of the craft being 'flimsy, like a box kite'. This would have paved the way for the second press release and photo session at Fort Worth where the balloon material could be produced. If one accepts that a craft really had crashed and that a number of people inside and outside the military knew of its existence, then the strategy makes sense. The partial admission would initially satisfy those who were convinced of the reality while the later retraction would cast doubt on anyone who came forward to claim otherwise.

In Kaufmann's version, Major Jesse Marcel was made the fall guy, and ordered to display the balloon at the press conference. His son, Jesse Marcel junior, who has studied the photographs of the time with great care, is convinced that the material was switched. He states categorically that the material in the pictures is not what his father brought home that night in Roswell when they studied the material and the I-beams with the strange hieroglyphics. This theory is further supported by Marcel's admission on an American television programme thirty years later that what they had seen was 'not of this world'. If this scenario is to be believed then it follows that Marcel senior was under orders to go along with the deception, even though by implication it made him look a complete fool, since he was the one responsible for misidentifying an ordinary weather balloon as the remnants of a flying saucer. If the whole thing had been the result of a catastrophic error, involving the base commander, the public information officer and the base intelligence officer, Marcel, then it follows that the Air Force would have taken some action to reprimand those responsible. In fact, both Blanchard and Marcel were subsequently promoted: Marcel was posted to Washington and Blanchard progressed to the rank of general and then to the office of the Chiefs of Staff, also in the US capital. Arguably, the military establishment found the whole affair so acutely embarrassing that they ignored the errors of the junior officers and did nothing – this seems unlikely and in addition there are no reports of any of the personnel involved putting this forward as a plausible scenario.

Kaufmann is adamant that the whole news management policy was deliberately manipulated to confuse the press and the public – although by the time the story came under the control of the Eighth Air Force Headquarters at Carswell Airbase, in Fort Worth, Texas it nearly fell apart.

'Well they almost blew it on the first press release,' explains Kaufmann. 'General Ramey told his aide, "We're going to have a press conference and we want you to get some material and the press will be there taking some pictures." The aide apparently got hold of some of the actual debris and placed it in the room where the press conference was due to be held while General Ramey was standing out in the hall – when he opened the door and saw that the original [and presumably the real debris from the actual craft] was in place, Ramey quickly closed the door and said, "God Almighty, let's get that stuff out of here" and they quickly gathered some other material that was balloon material and some cellophane, aluminum, some sticks and what have you and that's the one Jesse Marcel was holding up, that's the way it was but they almost blew it!'

If disinformation was being bandied about with such skill it raises the question of whether Kaufmann himself might still be part of a campaign to conceal the truth or even that his whole story is a complete fabrication. I tackled him on this on a number of occasions and he was always disarmingly straightforward about the 'veracity' of his story.

'How long have you kept this secret, Frank?' I asked him when we were sitting together in the comfort of his front room at his home in Roswell.

'Forty-eight years! Yeah, forty-eight years and three months, twelve days!' he replied with a laugh.

'Why are you deciding that now is the time to tell the truth?' I asked.

'I haven't decided its time to tell the truth or not,' he answered in a more serious tone, 'but I feel something should come out and I think it would clear the air really and maybe tell some of the sceptics that there is truth in the matter, you know. Most of the people that were involved at that time, like Blanchard and Ramey and Jesse Marcel, Easley, Adair, Willbanks, Smith – all these fellas are gone. Pappy Henderson, one of the pilots who flew some of the bodies and debris out there, gone, and I think maybe we wouldn't be looked, some of us who are left, wouldn't be looked at as weirdos or something, that we are trying to concoct the story up, see. That's difficult to tell, let me put it that way, because the truth of the matter is not in our hands, the truth of the matter is in the files: find the files and the truth will come out.'

Where were the files, I asked.

'Your guess is as good as mine,' came the infuriating reply.

'I mean, the fact is there is no factual evidence, documentary evidence of any sort, to prove that your story is true?' I pressed.

'That's right,' admitted Kaufmann. 'You have to accept it. You either believe it or you don't. I mean, see, and . . .' He paused and thought for a moment, apparently genuinely trying to think of something that would help to substantiate his story. 'There's got to be some truth to this, not just from what I'm saying but other people involved, directly or indirectly, know and are able to corroborate what I'm saying; they have some fragments of information, that what you are doing, are being pieced together. The secrecy is still there, I sometimes feel that they are not ready to reveal that secret yet but they will – when, I don't know. And another thing too that makes this so difficult is that some of these people coming out of the woodwork, you know, claim they've been abducted by aliens, women claim they have been raped by aliens and given birth to aliens. Well, actually this adds to the difficulty of telling the truth too. But the most important thing you must remember, that at that time we were not allowed to keep anything, any piece of information, anything. Whatever reports we made, it was quickly turned over to an intelligence officer or security officer for filing. What he did with that file, I don't know, I haven't the slightest idea. I have an inkling but I don't know. The day will come when so to speak, the heavens will open up and the truth will be known, then they'll believe Jesse Marcel, they'll believe Major Easley, they'll believe Blanchard, they'll believe Adair, Willbanks, Kaufmann and some of the others. In the early days we were ridiculed, trying to concoct a story like this, but it's the truth; whether you believe it or not that's your business, but it will come out!'

I pointed out to him that many people will find it just too fantastic to be true.

'That's right,' agreed Kaufmann, immediately disarming my scepticism. 'It's always the way. The truth is always difficult, you know, unless you have something concrete.'

I pressed him one last time: 'But you are absolutely convinced what you've told us that you saw is one hundred per cent accurate?'

'I am, absolutely one hundred, one thousand per cent – it's the truth!'

'The whole truth and nothing but the truth . . . ?'

'That's right. As Ripley would say, "Believe it or not"!'

The Kaufmanns could not be more respectable. Polite, good-natured and hospitable, they are model citizens of Middle America. It is hard to conceive that Frank has deliberately set out to hoodwink the world's media with a carefully concocted story that purports to be the definitive solution to the Roswell mystery. However, if we assume that he has made it up, as many sceptics will undoubtedly conclude, there remains the question of motive. Kaufmann has never asked for money for any interview. Nor has he ever, as far as I know, sought out any publicity or press attention. On the contrary, he has appeared extremely reluctant to come forward with his version of events. As a former head of the Roswell Chamber of Commerce, could he be attempting to place the town on the map to develop its tourist potential? Possibly. But, given his character and that of his wife, it is extremely unlikely, and in any case any such benefit would be difficult to quantify and could hardly be guaranteed. Besides, the town already has a significant reputation in the folklore of the UFO world, certainly sufficient to attract numerous committed UFO travellers without any intercession from Frank Kaufmann.

In the absence of any clear motive for his spinning such a tall tale, we are left with the bleak possibility that Kaufmann is a pathological liar. Yet, if he is, then this appears to be the only event he has lied about, even though pathological liars tend to be found out sooner or later. In fact, there does not seem to be anything about the man's character to support the claim that Kaufmann is not telling the truth. He is intelligent enough to realize that most people will not believe him, and faced with that fact, it takes a certain amount of courage to tell the story that he has outlined for public consumption.

Even among those who make a living out of the study of Roswell and the UFO phenomenon there are some who are convinced that Kaufmann is a liar. I myself find it extremely difficult to countenance the idea that his story could be true. Yet I find almost as implausible the notion that he is deliberately deceiving a significant portion of the population with a fantasy skilfully woven out of half-truth and genuine events in which real people participated then and to which millions of people now look for the answers to abiding questions about a remarkable mystery.

Try to imagine yourself as a woman married to the same man for over forty years, living with him a relatively quiet life in a retirement community in a respectable suburb in New Mexico. Would it not be unconscionably strange to tolerate the sudden introduction of a fantastic story which you know to be a total lie and which is then repeated to a representative of the world's media, risking scorn, contempt and disbelief, all for no material gain in any shape or form? And would it not be equally strange to connive in this deception merely for the sake of confusing and bamboozling all those stupid and gullible enough to listen to the story and swallow it whole?

It's not impossible but it seems pretty damned unlikely!

Kaufmann's story would be more incredible were it not for the fact that there are many other witnesses whose accounts bear some relation to various aspects of his. There is the corroboration of his interpretation of the cover story perpetrated at the press conference conducted by General Ramey at Fort Worth, both by Jesse Marcel and his son. And there is the intriguing story of Glenn Dennis, the Roswell undertaker whom Kaufmann mentions *en passant* in respect of the bodies that were recovered at the crash site and the problem of the decomposition of the corpses. Dennis's story has a number of other salient features which add significantly to the mystery of the Roswell Incident and once again raise the twin spectres of truth and falsehood.

In 1947 Glenn Dennis was a young assistant at Ballard's Funeral Home, the local undertaker in Roswell. The firm enjoyed a close working and social relationship with the officers and men of the 509th Bomb Group. Dennis had graduated in the summer of 1946 from the San Francisco Mortuary College and was serving an apprenticeship at Ballard's Funeral Home, beginning as a car-washer, driver and general dogsbody. Later in his career Dennis would serve as Chairman of the New Mexico State Board of Funeral Directors and Embalmers and it was during his tenure that New Mexico demanded college study as a requirement for licensing to do business in the state.

It was as a young student that Dennis found himself one afternoon minding the shop and answering the phone in the front office. One call sticks in his mind in particular as it rang through just after lunch on a hot summer's day in July 1947. He picked up the phone to discover that it was the mortuary officer from the Roswell Army Air Field on the other end of the line. 'This is just a hypothetical situation,' said the voice at the other end of the line, 'but do you have any three feet or four feet long hermetically sealed caskets?'

'Yes . . .' replied Dennis, 'we have four feet . . .'

'How many have you got?'

'One . . .'

'How soon before you could get some more?' enquired the officer.

The apprentice undertaker made some quick calculations. 'If we called the warehouse in Amarillo, Texas, before 3 p.m. today, they can have them here tomorrow morning.'

As Ballard's Funeral Home had a standing arrangement with the base in the eventuality of an emergency such as an air crash and the contract to handle routine deaths at the base, Dennis assumed that perhaps there had been some sort of an accident. 'Is there some kind of crash?' he asked.

'No,' came the reply. 'This is just for our information.'

The mortuary officer rang off and Dennis went back to work until he was interrupted about an hour later by another call from the same man this time with a different query. 'How do you handle bodies that have been exposed to the desert for four or five days?' he asked, once again taking the trouble to reassure the civilian that there was no 'crash' but that this was a hypothetical situation where they needed to gather data for their files. The officer also wanted to know what embalming fluid was made of and what might happen when it reacted to human tissue; whether one could seal holes in a body that had been made by predators; and what was the best way to physically collect remains in such a condition. The apprentice answered each question with all the self-assurance of one who had recently completed a course in many of the areas in which information was being sought.

But the nature of the inquiry and the second call intimated something more than a mere exercise. 'Is there some kind of a crash?' Dennis asked again.

'No, no . . .' was the hasty reply. 'Just gathering information for our files.' Ballard's Funeral Home had handled up to twenty bodies at a time in crashes from the base and had constructed a special room next to the embalming area to handle just such emergencies, but it didn't seem like this was another occasion when the room might be called for.

In addition to acting as undertakers for the base, Ballard's also had a contract to run an ambulance service between it and the town. One hour after the second phone call, Dennis received a call for a transport job to take an injured airman back to the base from Roswell's hospital, where he had been treated for an injured hand. The airman sat in the front of the ambulance hearse as Dennis drove him to the base. The guards at the gate recognized Dennis and saw the uniformed airman in the front seat, and waved the ambulance through the barrier. Dennis was a familiar figure at the base, as were many of the townsfolk who had jobs there or who supplied groceries and other services to personnel of the 509th. Dennis was also an honorary member of the airbase's popular Officers' Club.

He drove his ambulance through the gates over to the hospital area, a building housed in a semicircular-roofed, corrugated-iron building and, as he normally did, reversed into the parking area. As he was manoeuvring into his parking position he noticed that there were two field ambulances in the spot that he normally parked in, so he pulled up alongside them. He got out of the vehicle to escort the injured airman into the hospital area, passing the field ambulances as he did so. Unusually these were being guarded by a military policeman. Curious, Dennis peered into the open back door of the vehicles and noticed that inside both lay a large pile of a thin, silvery, metallic material which seemed to be as thin as aluminium sheeting but not as flexible. His attention was drawn to two pieces of metal, each of which seemed to be two and a half or three feet high and which were curved like the bottom half of a canoe. He recalls that he also noticed strange markings in some sort of 'hieroglyphic' letters that seemed totally unfamiliar and yet were strangely reminiscent of Egyptian symbols to be found in the pyramids.

As Dennis made his way down the corridor of the hospital building towards the cold drinks machine he was confronted by an officer in uniform whom he didn't recognize.

'Looks like you've got an air crash,' remarked the funeral assistant. 'Should I go back to town and get my equipment ready?'

'Who the hell are you?' growled the officer, who, Dennis noticed, was red-haired. Somewhat taken aback, Dennis introduced himself and explained his role in the procedure for handling crash victims. The hostile officer promptly ordered the hapless young man to get out of the hospital and off the base. Dennis gladly complied and turned back down the hallway. On his way to the entrance he was startled to hear the same officer shout at him, 'Bring that sonofabitch back here!' Two MPs materialized, grabbed Dennis and marched him back to the officer, who told him, 'Now don't you go back to Roswell and start shooting your mouth off about how there's been a crash out here or . . .' A series of irate threats followed which really got Dennis's back up, particularly as what was happening was so contrary to the normal relations he and many others from the town enjoyed with those who served on the base. 'You can't talk to me like that!' he remonstrated. 'I'm a civilian. You haven't got any say over me.'

The officer was unimpressed by the young man's bravado and invocation of his citizen's rights. 'Listen, undertaker,' he hissed menacingly, 'somebody's gonna be picking your bones out of the sand!' With that the officer summoned two MPs to personally escort the intruder back to his ambulance and from there back to Ballard's Funeral Home. As they were heading back down the corridor a door to one of the supply rooms leading off the main corridor opened and there appeared a somewhat distraught female nurse with a towel covering the lower part of her face. Dennis's immediate thought was that she had been crying – certainly she appeared to be in a state of distress. He immediately recognized her as being one of the staff nurses assigned to the base. Both stopped in their tracks, surprised by their chance encounter. 'Glenn . . . !' exclaimed the nurse. 'What are you doing here? You're going to get shot!'

Taken aback by the nurse's shocked reaction, Dennis calmly informed her that he was on the point of trying to leave, pointing meaningfully at his burly armed escort. Then he realized that there were two other men following the nurse out of the room, both of whom were clutching towels to their faces. Peering past them, he was anxious to discover what lay in the room that might account for their strange appearance. He caught a glimpse of gurneys, the cast-iron wheeled beds used to ferry patients to and from the operating theatre, but was unable to see anything else.

The next day the nurse telephoned Dennis at his workplace and the two of them arranged to meet at the Officers' Club on the base.

There the young woman revealed an extraordinary story relating to the previous day's events. She claimed that a flying saucer had crashed in the desert and that the Army had recovered three corpses – purportedly alien beings. Two of the bodies were badly mangled by the crash and by predators while a third appeared to be in fairly good condition. As the nurse was telling her story, Dennis could see that she was becoming upset, and when she began to cry he thought it best to take her back to the nurses' quarters, which were nearby on the base. After dropping her off he never saw her again. He made frequent attempts to discover what had happened to her. On learning that she had been transferred overseas to England he obtained a forwarding address and wrote to her, only to have the letters returned intact with a stamp saying 'Addressee Deceased'. He was then informed that his friend had been killed in an air crash. Dennis was puzzled and somewhat upset, and though today he is coy about the relationship, it seems likely that there was a degree of romantic affection between them.

He recalls that at the Officers' Club she had given him a detailed description of what the creatures looked like. 'She said that they were little, smaller than an adult human. She said that the hands were different too, that they had only had four fingers, with the middle two protruding longer than the others. She saw no thumb and said that the anatomy of the arm was different; the bone from the shoulder to the elbow was shorter than the bone from the elbow to the wrist. She stated that the heads were larger than a human's, the eyes were large and had a concave shape, that all the features, the nose, the eyes and the ears were slightly concave.' The nurse even drew a sketch for him based on her recollection of what the bodies looked like, a rough drawing which she made on the back of a prescription pad which unfortunately does not seem to have survived. Dennis remembers that it showed that the bodies had four digits on each hand. The end of each digit consisted of a sort of pad 'like a suction cup'.

The nurse told Dennis that the two men who were with her when he bumped into them at the base were pathologists from the Walter Reed Hospital in Washington DC. As for the towels over their faces, she explained that 'until they got those bodies frozen, the smell was so bad you couldn't get within a hundred feet of them without gagging'. In order to get some fresh air she had stepped out of the room where she had been assisting the two doctors with the bodies, and it was then that she spotted Dennis. Apparently, the doctors were feeling nauseous and the odour had become so offensive that they had to turn off the air-conditioning to prevent it from spreading throughout the hospital. Soon they gave up trying to work under such conditions and completed the preparation of the bodies in a separate hangar.

This account, like so many of the other eyewitness statements, appears to be incredible and lacks any corroborating evidence. Not least, it seems inconceivable that two trained pathologists would have conducted any sort of medical examination on an entity from outer space without wearing protective clothing. Normal procedure would have required recognition of the risk that some unknown microbes or bacteria might be lurking in the alien corpses. The sceptic might point out that it is all too convenient that the source of Dennis's story, the nurse, has mysteriously disappeared from the face of the earth. Then again, if he was making it up, why introduce a nurse at all? He could have claimed that he saw the whole thing himself as the result of a chance encounter at the base hospital. But such a story, with the additional detail of the telephone calls from the mortuary officer at the base about the child-size coffins, might suggest the inventiveness of a science-fiction writer. Alternatively, the telling details could be seen as lending an air of authenticity to the whole account.

Dennis is an elderly, grey-haired man of ascetic appearance, tall and in good health. Like several of the other eyewitnesses of aspects of the incident, he is a sober and respectable individual about whom many members of the community speak highly. He tends to become somewhat irascible when he finds himself pestered by journalists and tourists, and this reluctance to repeat his story to all and sundry also counts in his favour. For, as with his fellow witnesses, he has no discernible motive for creating such a wild fantasy out of which he could, if he had wished, have made money.

While there is virtually no evidence to support his story – apart from minor details which accord with other witness accounts – his character and demeanour strongly suggest that he is relating a story which he sincerely believes occurred. In addition, he claims that he was sworn to secrecy by the nurse and honoured his promise by never revealing her name. Of course, there is the other possibility that Dennis is telling the truth but the nurse who told him the story was either lying or mistaken. Were it not that his own experience at the base lends the nurse's account some credence, either of these explanations could be used to undermine the whole story. It is indeed possible that the nurse was mistaken about what she saw or that she was lying, and, of course, it is possible that Dennis made the whole thing up. However, after meeting him in conjunction with all the others who have their own story to tell about the Roswell Incident, I came to the conclusion that the possibility of all these people lying is almost as equally implausible as the story they tell.

Two other witnesses whose experience adds to previous accounts and is equally mystifying is that of the Anaya brothers. Two likeable Hispanic men who have lived and worked in Roswell all their lives, they are of humble origin but seemingly honest and good-natured. Pete Anaya is a small, stout man with a flourishing grey moustache who lives on the outskirts of the town in a small, white-stucco bungalow close to the railway tracks and overlooking a large area of wasteland just across the road. Although in a poorer part of town, the Anaya house is well kept and homely, with a distinctive Mexican flavour and strings of chilli peppers hanging from the curved arches at the front. Mrs Anaya sits on the local council and as long-standing citizens of Roswell both she and her husband have a keen sense of civic duty and a patriotism that is often more heartfelt among first-generation immigrants than among native Americans.

Pete Anaya told me about his involvement in the Roswell Incident; despite his years in his adopted country he still speaks with a strong Hispanic accent which makes his words difficult to understand at times. 'My brother and I used to work at the base,' he explained. 'My brother was the only one with a pass for the car. Many times Senator Montoya used to come to Roswell. He was the Governor [of New Mexico] and we went to pick him up because we were the only ones who had the pass to go in the base.'

One afternoon the Anaya brothers got a telephone call to go and collect the Governor to drive him to the base. They drove on to the base after being checked through the main gate by the sentry and they parked close to a hangar. According to Pete Anaya, Montoya went inside the hangar only to emerge a few moments later looking positively shaken. 'He was real scared and he say he saw two little men and one was alive. And then the nurse came out and I went to see so I went up and tried to get in but they wouldn't let me in . . .' Pete Anaya remembers that the nurse said something to him about what was happening, then they drove out of the base compound and back to his house. When they arrived Governor Montoya was still extremely shaken up, so much so that they all had several stiff drinks.

'He was shocked, real shocked, because he had a drink, and I ain't kidding you, and then he left from here to Santa Fe. He drink a whiskey – don't think Coke or water or nothing – just straight out of the bottle. He was real scared! You can ask my wife! Anyway my wife won't lie and I don't think I am lying either . . . He said there was just two people – little people, big heads. Later on the sheriff come by and told us to lay off. I asked if he was going to run for sheriff again – but we were asked to lay off. I said, "Why?" and he said because the FBI threaten his life. That's all I know.'

The sheriff was George Wilcox, who had been involved at the beginning when Mac Brazel had brought a sample of the debris into town and deposited it at his office. His family have confirmed that he was himself threatened and ordered by military or police officers to keep quiet about what he knew. Pete Anaya's account also supported this: 'Sheriff Wilcox, he was scared, 'cos he was investigated. They investigate me and Ruben and the other ones. They didn't ask us nothing.' I asked him if he could remember exactly what Sheriff Wilcox had said, and he replied, 'He just told us to lay off 'cos we were going to get in trouble. And I said, for what? "'Cos what happen on the base with you and the Senator and Ruben."

'So I told him I don't know what happen; the only thing was I was there but I didn't see nothing. 'Cos I didn't see the little men, I'm not going to lie to you. I'm going by what the Senator said and what the nurse said.'

Pete Anaya himself was still nervous and confused about exactly what had happened, and it was difficult to discover exactly how 'the nurse' was involved. She was a potentially crucial detail as she may have been the nurse who figures in Dennis's account. (In fact, a later detail in the Anaya story strongly suggests that it could have been the same person.) I then asked Pete Anaya for a more detailed description of exactly what Governor Montoya had seen and his reaction to whatever it was that had confronted him when he ventured inside the hangar.

'Well, he came out of there – he came out scared,' he told me. 'He said he'd seen two little men with the big heads – one was alive, still alive. They had them laying down on the floor, he came out and told us they both was there and one was still alive. He was so scared when he came out but then they didn't allow me or Ruben or nobody to go in there. There were a lot of officers, MPs, but I didn't like to get close to it. Then the nurse came out 'cos I knew the nurse at the Officers' Club and I went to ask her if they'd let us go in. She said, "Pete, you don't wanna see that" and then I didn't see her no more.'

The detail about the nurse, that she frequented the Officers' Club and that she disappeared, are a close match to Dennis's story. Intrigued by the possibility that this could be the same nurse that the funeral assistant had spoken about at length in his account, I attempted to get Pete Anaya to remember more details about the young woman.

'She was a real nice person,' he recalled. 'She looks more like my wife, she had beautiful hair, because one time, on Halloween night, they had a big party and I danced with her at a Halloween party they had. That's before this happens. She was real friends with us. She used to come to the kitchen one time but I don't remember her name. A beautiful woman.'

Once again there is the possibility that this man is lying or has somehow heard Dennis's account and woven his fabrication around it. But again, this suggests a gift for fictional creation which just does not ring true. Nor is there any apparent motive, and Pete Anaya seems to be honest and straightforward. Although his wife was not at the base and was initially sceptical, she does not believe her husband would have invented the story.

'My wife didn't believe it, she said we were lying. And I said to her, "Uh uh, we're not lying." I saw it myself. They didn't see it but I did. And nobody want to believe us no more.

I also asked Mrs Anaya what she remembered about that day and she remembers her husband driving back with his brother and the Governor. 'He came in pretty excited and told me that the Senator was out here in the car and he wanted me to see him and talk to him – because we always visited with him when he came into town. So I came out and the Senator was shaking and scared like and he told me, "You know what? I have seen something I have never seen before" . . . [and] my husband had told me later on that the Senator had told him that he had seen two little men and that one of them was dead and the other one was alive.' I asked Mrs Anaya if she believed her husband and the Governor – after all, they had admitted having something to drink. Maybe they were all just a little drunk and the whole thing got exaggerated. She confirms that they had some drinks but is adamant that no one was drunk. 'Oh no, no, no, no! Oh no – he was not drunk.

No, no! He was completely sober when he got here, they were not drunk when he was here. That's when they started drinking when they were here.

'I believed him,' she adds supportively. ''Cos these guys were good friends and I knew they wouldn't lie and the Senator was a reliable man, I didn't doubt his word.' During the afternoon I spent with Mr and Mrs Anaya, Pete's brother Ruben drove up in his car. Despite a domestic crisis that was threatening to engulf the small Hispanic community, Ruben found time to give me his version of events.

'Well, number one, I was the only one who had a . . . because it was a very strict base, I was the only one who had a pass to go to the base. Senator Montoya, at that time he was the Lieutenant Governor, called me and told me to pick him up right away and he meant right away and I said, "Oh heck, why should I hurry?" He said, "You got to hurry up and get Pete to come with you." He was very excited on the phone and I came in and told Pete and then we pick up. I had two compadres – one lives right across the tracks over there about two blocks away. We went over there and the MPs were very strict and I told them what I came for and then these guys were with me, they could be with me in my car with my pass, I had security clearance. So I took them over there to pick up Lieutenant Governor Montoya, he was at the hangar, so the MPs just led us over there. I didn't park close to the hangar, I parked about half a block away and I said, what the hell's going on? And when they went over there I moved a little closer and that's when the hangar was open, the Senator came out and he said, "Let's get the hell out of here!" and he was even praying in his own way. And I said, "What's the problem?" and then the nurse came out running, big, heavy-set nurse, she was sort of a blonde, I guess one-sixty, one-seventy, and she says, "I can't believe it! I can't believe one is moving!"

'So naturally I wanted to see what was moving. There were two bodies covered with a white sheet but they were too small to be a man's body, you know . . . and then one was uncovered, he was moving. I said, what the hell's going on? And I asked the nurse, "Who are they?" She said, "They are not from this world" and that was it, you know. And then he got to the car, he was so scared he sat between the two guys in the back, which was me and my other compadre. At that time he was stricken . . . and he was just telling us what happened and we drove off the base. We got to the house here. I said you need a drink, you know, so I had a quart of Jim Beam, you know, square bottle, and he just gluggle it, glug, glug, glug, and he drink about two-thirds of that thing and he laid on the couch and passed out.'

Ruben Anaya's account differs from Pete's on a crucial aspect, namely the assumption that one of the bodies was still alive. Although there are other accounts that speak of a living survivor of the crash, they are all somewhat contradictory. It may be that Ruben is simply embellishing the story, but the important thing, leaving aside for one moment whether there were any living creatures inside the hangar, is that he confirms the broad outline of the story that is related by his brother. I pressed Ruben to tell me as much as he could about what the Senator had seen. 'Well,' he replied, 'he told me he didn't know what it was. He says a new word to me that they're not "Earthmans" or something like that. I said, "Who in the hell are they?" He says, "I don't know! They are about this small, smaller than me and I'm real small! But their eyes are like tears" – he moved his eyes like that – "and their nose is small and you can hardly see their mouths, that was when he was laying down." So I said, "What the hell are they?" He said, "I don't know, I don't know what they are. I don't know." He kept on very, very nervous.'

I asked Ruben if he really had seen inside the hangar and he repeated that he had. 'Yes, I saw into the hangar and there was two sheets with something under it. One was a little on the one side – the other was a little further away, you know. And the one that was this side, there wasn't no sheet but he was still moving.'

He may have exaggerated a little, but it seems unlikely that Ruben Anaya would make up a story which he must know could be confirmed or denied by his brother and to some extent by his sister-in-law. Maybe he did see something inside the hangar, although Frank Kaufmann has no recollection of anything surviving. (Could it be that, although the creatures appeared dead out in the desert, one was merely unconscious and later revived? After hearing these bizarre accounts you come to believe that almost anything is possible.)

Maybe everyone is telling a deliberately fabricated version of the same story; or maybe they are telling the same story but, as often happens, discrepancies have arisen from people's different perceptions and recollections and their varying ability to recall different aspects of the same event. Indeed when people tell what they hold to be the truth about an event their accounts differ in various respects. Furthermore, because of the subjective factors mentioned above, such variation is usually taken as an indicator of veracity rather than falsehood.

What is certain is that the more you hear different people telling different accounts of the same story with certain aspects that cross-relate and some that do not, the more difficult it becomes to conclude that they could all be deliberately lying. That one person is perhaps exaggerating or telling a total falsehood is easy to accept, but that a whole group should then follow that example and carefully research an existing version in order to embellish it, give credence to their own account and deliberately contradict some of the other versions which they may be aware of just does not make sense.

3

Of all the witnesses who claim some knowledge of the events surrounding the Roswell Incident none has a story to tell that is more outlandish than 'Colonel' Richard Tungate. His tale epitomizes the problems associated with the Roswell enigma – replete as it is with credible people recounting incredible stories and incredible people relating credible stories. Not only does Tungate confirm that the Roswell Incident happened and that it was a visitation by extraterrestrials; he also maintains that he was part of the cover-up that concealed all the documents relating to the incident and adds a detail so astonishing as to make one doubt the man's sanity.

Today Tungate lives on the outskirts of Roswell, where he runs a business converting and restoring classic American cars and pick-up trucks. A man of solid build with greying hair tied back in a pony-tail, he spends his days in a well-equipped workshop tinkering with the rusting hulks of derelict cars, metamorphosing them into beautifully revitalized American automobiles. Across the street from his garage is his single-storey house, which is guarded by two ferocious Rottweilers trained to kill. Next to the garage lies an overgrown and weed-filled patch of land where the carcasses of 1950s cars and trucks have been abandoned and cannibalized for spare parts or are awaiting transformation. Before making a living from his hobby, Tungate was, he claims, part of a US Special Forces unit known as Delta Force and that he served in undercover military operations in many parts of the world, including South America.

His exposure to the Roswell Incident allegedly began five years after the event. 'In 1952 I was sent here to reorganize, eliminate and reprocess the paperwork and the photography and documents that were left here and to transfer them to different areas. At that time I was First Lieutenant but was given temporary rank of Captain and during this process I had to go over the entire contents of the documents that were here: film that was here, destroy what needed to be destroyed and send the other documents to different areas. Part of the documents went to Maryland, part of the documents went to Texas and part of the documents went to Washington, along with photographs and film, and during this time there had been many duplications made of each copy and copies that were duplicated that had a certain person's name on it. I had to eliminate all of those documents regardless of what information was on it: if her name was involved those documents had to be destroyed.'

Tungate was only eighteen years old at the time and it is hard to believe that he could have been promoted to the rank of captain but, according to him, he was specifically selected by his commanding officer, a general, because he knew that Tungate possessed a photographic memory: 'that way it would not take that long to go through the documents. I could look at the document know what was on the document – whether it had to be filed or destroyed and which area it had to go to.'

Photographs and film which Tungate apparently saw left him in no doubt that a strange craft crashed near Roswell and he believes that there are documents which have survived as he was ordered to bury them in archives which could be publicly accessible if anyone knew where they were. Tungate states that as he sifted through the documents he made a startling discovery: 'I got to the pictures and found out that there was one still live being. That was when I was definitely surprised! And after going over the documents and stuff I called the general I was working under and told him to set up a meeting where I could see this being – that if I was going to continue this operation I had to see with my own eyes that this did exist. So he did – I saw the being that was still alive. I went to Los Alamos and first of all they let me see him through a glass.

'He was sitting in a room and I sat there and watched him for a while and he would move and came up to the glass and looked directly at me. And then I asked permission to go in the room where he was at. He was wearing a military fatigue jacket and pair of pants which they had altered because of his small stature.

'He was sitting there and I went in and sat down and he got up and walked around; I just sat there and he walked around me and came back around and sat down and you could look into his eyes. His eyes were as natural as your eyes are right now and he couldn't communicate directly voice-wise but things I wanted to know somehow I found out. I could ask him something and I would know the answer within, just as if the person was responding with the voice. There was no animosity: those were the most peaceful eyes I have ever seen and that was the first occasion that I saw him. Then I came back here and did some more paperwork and processing and I got further into the documents and film and I needed to go and have a second visit. This second visit, I felt as if he was elated that I came back to visit him; more or less just happy that there was a friendly face there. So that was probably a more peaceful session; the first one was a little edgy because you see something you've never seen before, but I got more at ease. I touched his skin, he touched my skin and we sat there for probably half an hour communicating some way. I have no idea how. He could make a rasping sound – that's all I ever heard.'

According to Tungate, the creature was given the acronym 'EBE' 'Extra-Terrestrial Biological Entity'. EBE was being held in a facility at Los Alamos under joint civilian and military control. Military photographers were apparently photographing him constantly, recording his movements. Tungate claims that he saw EBE a third time.

'I came back to Roswell and on the finishing of the paperwork that I had to send to different areas, I asked to go visiting one more time and this time this meeting was a more pleasant one than the other two had been. It was as if he was just joyous that I had come back to visit him again. I think the reason for that was all these other people were experimenting and trying to do things or ask him questions, trying to force him to maybe speak or to do something, but I didn't. I just went in with a calm attitude and he seemed just totally at ease. He felt really relaxed – I felt comfortable from what I could see in his eyes. But he never at any time showed any aggression or any animosity or anything towards where he was being kept, the way he was being kept, although I am sure he was uncomfortable the way he was being handled. But when I was there he seemed perfectly at ease and I felt the same way. It was just as if he was in the most peaceful setting that you could possibly find.' Bizarrely, if such an account can get more bizarre, Tungate claims that EBE was a male as he observed it using the lavatory to urinate in a standing position. As to where the creature hailed from, Tungate's quasi-telepathic contact with it never yielded anything as specific as a home address. Difficult though it is to give this story any credence, there can be little doubt of the sincerity with which Tungate imparts his account and in the process of a series of conversations he showed a marked reluctance to relate his story. As with Frank Kaufmann, this attitude does not sit easily with that of people who are eager to enthral the gullible listener with fantastic stories. And as with Kaufmann, Tungate is unable to produce anyone to corroborate his story or his background. He maintains that he had to swear an oath of loyalty and secrecy never to reveal the identities of those involved, and that his superior officer also visited the alien but is unwilling to divulge his name. According to Tungate, the General was equally awestruck: 'When he came back to the base he was quite astonished at what he had seen also. It was as if you see something that you don't believe it's there and as if you've never seen anything before in your life that even resembles that. There are hundreds of things you'd like to ask and get the answers. There's all kinds of things you would like to have known but you never found out that much.'

As for the craft, Tungate says: 'It was a craft of unknown origin, not of this planet.' He also claims to have handled some of the material from the craft: 'It had a small concave to it and was jagged where it had been broken in some way but it was a purplish violet colour, not real livid bright . . . and you could move it any way you wanted to and leave it alone and it would go back to its original position and the other piece of metal, I guess it was metal, had hieroglyphics on it that no one knew what they meant but they were very distinct and plain and well-lettered.' Tungate's descriptions of the properties of the strange material from the craft tallies with the descriptions from the other witnesses, although he could easily have read such accounts elsewhere.

He believes that the witnesses were threatened, as many others have claimed, and this would account for many of them remaining frightened and the lack of physical evidence in the form of debris. There has been a great deal of scepticism about the threats, not least from the USAF itself: a 1994 report acidly pointed to the discrepancy between the alleged threats that people received and their subsequent disclosures. Nevertheless, Tungate claims to have seen evidence in the documents themselves of the pressure that was put on some witnesses. 'I've read it on documents, of what some of the Military Police had said to people and there is still people around that were given these threats that will substantiate that.'

Furthermore, he says that not only were threats made, some of them were actually carried out. 'I'm certain they were. There were two gentlemen officers that met with fateful events and there was a nurse that disappeared . . . she never existed. All of her military documents were destroyed, all of her school records were destroyed; her birth certificate was destroyed . . . this person never was born.' Tungate confirmed that this is the same nurse as reported by Glenn Dennis, the one who participated in the hurried autopsy/medical examination at the base hospital and whom he never saw again. Tungate is convinced that she was executed – an astonishing claim with, it must be said, nothing to support it except that, according to Dennis's account, the nurse, whom he knew well, did apparently vanish.

It seems incredible that the United States government could have entertained the possibility of killing one of its own citizens, a young woman, to ensure her silence. The conspiracy theorists will nevertheless take this, together with the numerous accounts of dire threats that were made at the time, and conclude that such an occurrence is indeed possible. And it must be borne in mind that most of us would have reacted with equal incredulity to the notion that a democratically elected government could have conducted radiation experiments on human beings and joined forces with the Mafia in assassination conspiracies. For this reason we can at least countenance the possibility that, while it is unlikely and there is no evidence beyond the circumstantial, it could have happened. When pressed on this issue, Tungate responds with equanimity: 'I have no reason not to tell the truth. It's been many years . . . it's going to come out; the documents, some of them have already been found and once they've found part of them . . . they are searching very strongly now how the rest of them are filed. They think they have got the formula of the way the documents are filed but they don't have it. They found four of the documents, they felt if they found four then they can find all the rest of them but that's as far as they have got.'

The $64,000 question is whether any of this is true – on the surface it is too far-fetched to be credible. On certain points, what Tungate claims seems to be at best inaccurate and at worst wild fantasy. For example, when interviewed shortly before the General Accounting Office (the investigative branch of the US Congress and a Congressional Agency in its own right) was due to publish its report into the official records relating to the Roswell Incident, he claimed that he had spoken to the GAO and confidently predicted that it was going to report that an 'alien craft – crashed at Roswell but that there were no further documents'. In fact, the GAO concluded that there was no evidence to support the crash of any alien craft nor were there any official documents. The GAO did report that all records relating to the 'flying disc' had mysteriously disappeared. But, according to Tungate, the investigators had uncovered a document relating to the crash and had also retrieved a photograph of one of the bodies. He predicted that the evidence for the 'bodies' would be concealed – a prediction which was, to some extent, proved correct.

'They're not going to keep it classified probably for very long but they're going to say we're going to have to search further and maybe in a couple of months they are going to come up and say they have found a photo. They're going to just let it out in bits and pieces because if they let it out all at once, they'll say that it was a complete cover-up . . . it's not been covered up, it has been totally accessible except people just didn't know where to look.'

Further doubts were cast on Tungate's credibility when he responded to photographs taken from the autopsy footage of the alleged alien. On studying one of the pictures he responded by saying: 'The face, arms, hands are that of EBE: the one that I saw . . . this is one of the photographs and the pictures that I saw when I was classifying and directing the photos and paperwork to the departments.'

Confronted with the suggestion that the photographs from the autopsy footage were fake and that his whole story was at best disinformation and at worst fabrication, Tungate is unrepentant. 'They can't be proven false because they are actual pictures. I saw the films. I saw the pictures of all of that in 1952. All the documents describing where and when they were picked up, where they were taken, and there's been no one as I said before that I felt were genuinely interested in getting the true story to the people. There is a gentleman that they tracked for quite a while until they finally found me and they went through a lot of people and it took one gentleman about two years to locate me. He located me through an old staff sergeant and the staff sergeant called to let me know that they knew that I was here. So when they got here I knew who they were, what they were looking for. I am not a "disinformer". Everything is true.'

Tungate even claimed that there was an element of danger in revealing what he has so far revealed, although he is confident that 'they' will not try to silence him as it would merely add credence to his story. 'This is not the only incident I was involved in and if something happens to me now it wouldn't look very nice on record that at a stop sign I got ran over. This is almost like having an insurance policy. Because if something happens to me now it will directly go back to this interview and there will be another clue to look for if something happened to me.'

If even only half of what Tungate is telling is true then he is the custodian of secrets that must be of the highest value to the American government. He claims that he is in regular contact with a close-knit band of high-level military personnel, also initiated into the secret world of which he is part. In an attempt to check out the credentials of his military background and hence his veracity as a witness, the services of an independent investigator were enlisted. His task was to ascertain whether there was any basis for Tungate's Roswell story and any substance to his claims to have actively participated in clandestine military operations.

Retired FBI agent Earle Brandon, who now lives in Roswell, contacted Tungate on July 24, 1995 to arrange an interview intended to elicit details of his background. Brandon explained his own background and told Tungate that he wanted to check a few things out with him.

By coincidence, Brandon was also an aficionado of vintage cars and in a gesture designed to show that he and Tungate had something in common, he offered to drive his 1941 Chevy to the interview. 'This seemed to gain RT's interest and the time, place, and date was mutually agreed upon,' reported Brandon. Tungate agreed to see him the following day at 9 a.m. at his garage.

The next morning Brandon duly drove the Chevy to the garage, where Tungate was waiting as promised. However, one minute after the investigator arrived, and much to his surprise, a New Mexico State Police detective and two FBI agents appeared and began to question him. Tungate had called the police to advise them that a man posing as an FBI agent was coming to see him that morning. Brandon later noted in his report that, satisfied that he was who he said he was, 'the FBI and the State Police rather quickly departed and RT stated that one with his background can never be too careful when one has "the letter Q . . ." Supposedly a reference to a Top Secret clearance where "Q" represents one of the highest levels of security.'

Brandon continued his report by saying that: 'There is a federal government security clearance/access . . . designated as a "Q" clearance. Those who hold it do not mention that they have it.

Rick Tungate often remarked about the letter "Q" throughout the interview in an obvious effort to impress [me] who only concluded that Tungate probably never had a "Q" clearance. He did not even refer to it properly as was the case in many of his "mentionings." Those who do hold it, or have held it, do not mention it. The majority of this interview was discussed with a close friend who is in fact a retired Air Force Colonel who graduated from Annapolis in 1952, and went into the USAF to become a fighter pilot, and served in Korea at the end of the war. In short, this Colonel, referred to as "Col", feels Rick Tungate is sadly mistaken on several issues, and is short on truth and veracity.' (The author of the report adds that he feels he is being both reserved and kind.)

Brandon felt that Tungate was lying on a number of issues and that he was probably an enlisted mechanic or something similar in the USAF during the period 1951–71 or so, and probably retired from the Air Force, perhaps with a medical (i.e. psychological) discharge. 'Additionally, there were numerous questions that could have been asked,' commented Brandon, 'but RT had already impeached himself so the questions were not put.'

The former FBI agent's report continues: 'To prove the point, a few statements made by RT with comments are herewith set forth: RT is a white male, gray hair in pony tail, numerous tattoos; the tattoos are old. [Air Force officers do not normally have tattoos.]

'RT was asked if he would offer up his DD214. This is a record of separation which must be given to all service personnel upon discharge. [It does not indicate the level of security clearance held.] RT stated that he had to sign an oath at the bottom of the DD214 to the effect that he would not ever give a copy of it to anyone because of the letter "Q".' (This is untrue: the DD214 is for giving out for benefits, proof of service etc.)

Tungate claimed to have been given a direct commission after high school ROC and one year at the Virginia Military Institute, where he had trained as a pilot. Brandon telephoned the VMI to enquire if Tungate had in fact ever attended the school. The admissions office responded that there was no record of anyone of that name attending the institution since 1949. The admissions secretary even 'hand searched files to determine if anyone with that name had ever been dismissed from the institution, with negative results'.

In addition, Tungate had claimed that he went into the Air Force in 1951, receiving his commission at the age of twenty. Brandon's contacts informed him that the Air Force, in accordance with Federal law, commissioned no one under the age of twenty-one.

As mentioned earlier, Tungate maintained that he was awarded a commission so young because he had a photographic memory and did so well on his tests. Brandon himself attended the VMI in 1951. The institute is in Lexington, and its campus adjoins Washington and Lee University. A cadet must walk across the university's campus to get to town. Deciding that it would be advisable to put Tungate's self-proclaimed 'photographic memory' to the test, Brandon asked him a few basic questions about the geography of the Institute. Tungate did not recall the name of the town or the name or location of the Washington and Lee University. Nor did he know the name of the Commandant of Cadets at the VMI, which he claimed to have attended.

When Brandon offered a physical description of a fictitious Commandant at the Institute, Tungate agreed with him. (Similarly, when I suggested a fictitious name for an officer who might have been involved in the Roswell Incident, Tungate, on camera, responded in a positive manner.)

After the Roswell episode, Tungate's military career apparently continued to be out of the ordinary. He says that in 1952, while a pilot in the Korean War, he was shot down over that country and taken to a POW camp nine miles south of the border with China. He befriended a Chinese officer who gave him the run of the camp and let him come and go as he pleased. He acquired enough explosives to blow up the barracks housing the guards. He had broken his back and his neck, but on May 27, 1953 miraculously managed to escape, somehow succeeding in walking to Singapore and then catching a Norwegian freighter bound for the United States, to arrive in San Francisco on June 16 (or 18) that same year. No one else escaped! Brandon wrote in his report: 'EB: Why comment? Reader knows geography as well as EB! Colonel and EB had a good laugh!'

Tungate told Brandon that he was probably the most decorated hero in the United States Air Force and that despite his serious injuries he went on to fly with the CIA's proprietary airline in South East Asia, Air America, in Vietnam. (Brandon commented: 'You gotta be kidding!')

In Korea and Vietnam, Tungate said, he flew 'ground support for the marines . . .' (Brandon: 'God, I hope not!') The Air Force term is 'Close Air Support', and the description 'ground support' would never be used. Brandon wrote: 'EB wonders if this was put on for the sake of an old Marine Company Commander, and what would RT have said if EB had said he never was in the military?'

By now Brandon was convinced that Tungate was a complete hoaxer. His report concludes: 'There is more. The man is a sad case but at least he has no local police record. No other record checks have been conducted because it is felt there would be no point. It is felt Rick Tungate thinks he one-upped and snowed EB.

'EB feels the gent is harmless but is a real "loony-toon".

'Ergo, as we say, no further investigation is being conducted unless advised to the contrary.

'EB apologizes for the poor attempt at humour!'

At the time of writing, Tungate seems to have escaped the wilful and potentially lethal attention of the 'Men in Black', the generic name given to a paramilitary force supposedly linked to a super-secret US government department. UFO conspiracy theorists are convinced that this elite force is tasked to safeguard the 'Holy Grail' of extraterrestrial intelligence, which is jealously protected by the American government. The shadowy figures who make up this body appear in several 'eyewitness' accounts of UFO sightings and 'close encounters' of one sort or another. Inevitably they appear in a mysterious fashion, usually in unmarked cars, to harass witnesses and keep them under surveillance. Their trademarks are a sinister demeanour combined with a threatening attitude, and black helicopters with no markings which can often be seen hovering near the site of a UFO encounter.

Tungate's failure to supply any corroborating evidence for either his Roswell story or his career effectively rules him out as a credible witness. Yet, curiously, those who have met him find him to be sincere and highly believable, and I would almost include myself in that category. But until he is able to provide some evidence, whether it is another person or support for his account of his military exploits, his story can scarcely be credited with any significance.

While Tungate's paranoia about being threatened in connection with the Roswell Incident is a smokescreen, several accounts of threats made at the time have been given by people whose background and character make it likely that they are telling the truth. People such as Sheriff Wilcox's daughter Phyllis McGuire, the radio announcer and the owner of the station, Glenn Dennis from the funeral home and the daughter of the fire officer. That threats were made seems fairly certain . . . but what the threats were designed to keep quiet is open to conjecture. If the whole 'flying disc' affair was a genuine case of mistaken identity, then it is possible that the Air Force might have adopted a somewhat heavy-handed approach in an attempt at damage limitation. Or if there was a highly secret experiment of some kind, that too might have justified the use of threats. After all, the 509th's airbase was the only one in the world to be the centre for the storage of nuclear weapons and by 1947 the elation of Allied victory in the Second World War had dissipated, to be replaced by the mistrust and paranoia of the Cold War. It is reasonable to accept that threats were made and that, in the heat of the moment, these could conceivably have embraced the threat of violence or even murder. This evidence, circumstantial though it may be, is one of the main factors contributing to the conclusion that what happened at Roswell was far more important than the hasty cover-up of a balloon that had gone astray.

The memory of past threats continues to this day to disturb those citizens of Roswell who were involved at the time, and the situation has led some of them to campaign for greater disclosure by the government into what really happened. It was this concern among his own constituents, coupled with a genuine and wide-ranging curiosity about the events of 1947, that led Congressman Steven Schiff, the Republican representative for New Mexico, to ask questions in Washington on their behalf. 'In late 1993 I started getting letters from both within and without New Mexico by people interested in the Roswell Incident and expressing the common opinion that they felt the government had not exactly been forthcoming in explaining exactly what had happened back in 1947 and asking me to pursue getting further information.'

Schiff's first move was to forward a summary of the requests to the Department of Defense and a number of other agencies, thinking that it would be a fairly routine matter with a simple explanation. The Congressman was then surprised to receive a letter from a USAF colonel stating very briefly that he was forwarding the request to the National Archives. Schiff was taken aback at what appeared to be a cavalier response to a Congressional enquiry, since in his experience government agencies are usually helpful and tend not to 'pass the buck'. Annoyed, he wrote again to the Department of Defense, asking, 'Is this really how you meant to treat my request for information – just send it to another agency without any explanation or other offer of assistance?'. He then received a reply in the form of a letter from a Special Assistant to the Secretary of Defense which politely reiterated the original response: 'We are sending your request to the National Archives.'

Puzzled, the Congressman then contacted the National Archives, who wrote back to say that they had no information or records on the Roswell affair, while admitting that they had received many requests about Roswell in the recent past.

Schiff was distinctly unimpressed by what he interpreted as an unusually cavalier response. 'I felt like I had gotten the run-around. I thought, and am certain, that when the Defense Department got my request and sent it to the National Archives they knew very well at that point that the National Archives had no information. So basically it served no purpose except to frustrate my efforts just to get an answer. So it was at that point, in early 1994, that I met with officials of the General Accounting Office. I told them about this problem I was getting with the Defense Department, that I had tried to get information and basically that I had been stonewalled and asked if they could assist and they said they could and I turned the matter over to them.'

Schiff's curiosity was alerted by the lack of courtesy displayed by the Pentagon and, although no believer in little green men and flying saucers, he felt that in a democracy it was the wrong way to conduct the affairs of state. 'We are not trying to reconstruct from scratch the Roswell Incident, as you know that is nearly fifty years old and trying to reconstruct that to everyone's satisfaction is probably an impossibility. The issue is government records and providing to the public whatever records still exist – if any, and there may not be any . . . of the Roswell Incident, so people can make their own determination. This is the mission that I discussed with the General Accounting Office, so this is not a UFO hunt, it's a records hunt.' Schiff's initiative and a groundswell of popular interest from ordinary people and well-organized UFO pressure groups led to the USAF producing its own report on Roswell. The report, by Colonel Richard L. Weaver, was published in the autumn of 1994 and Schiff read it with great interest and a growing sense of mistrust. 'The Air Force has rather significantly changed its position in this review that they did,' says Schiff. 'Although they still say that the object that crashed was a balloon, they have changed completely the explanation of the balloon. The original explanation was that this was a "flying disc" – we would say "flying saucer" today. The Air Force changed that about eight hours later to say it was a weather balloon and that was their explanation for more than forty years. They changed that explanation when they came up with the new review. They said that although it was still a balloon, it was a highly classified radiation detection device trying to determine if the Soviet Union were setting off nuclear weapons in the atmosphere. Now I have to say that could well be the actual explanation.

'What has changed is the explanation: we have had three different explanations from the military about what crashed. The first explanation is it was a "flying disc" . . . They changed that and said "We've made a mistake, it wasn't a flying disc."

'I still find it amazing that the United States' top bomber wing, the only wing eligible to carry nuclear weapons at that particular time, would not know a weather balloon from a flying saucer but apparently someone didn't, according to them! So we then had this second explanation that this was a weather balloon and we now have the third explanation that this was part of a highly classified radiation experiment. So we have three separate explanations as to what crashed with no dispute that something crashed. In my mind there are two things about the Roswell Incident that are incontrovertible: the first is that something crashed. We know that. Second, the kind of handling the material received was not consistent with a weather balloon. There are many witnesses to high security in the area. There is no dispute about the fact that a special flight picked up whatever crashed and flew it to an Air Force base for examination. Those things are not consistent with a weather balloon. Now that does not mean that therefore it was a flying saucer and aliens that some people believe. It means it wasn't a weather balloon and the explanation that this was a highly classified mission at that time would fit the known circumstances. It then kind of just leaves open the question what took more than forty years to reveal that. And I don't think we'll ever get an explanation of that.

'The Cold War is long over, the Soviet Union has been testing or was testing nuclear weapons for many years so there was no reason to keep that experiment classified any longer. So I don't know that we'll be able to explain why the Air Force took till 1994 to give that explanation. But I think that if nothing else is accomplished here, the fact that the military changed its explanation after forty years is to me a remarkable event!'

4

In July 1994 the USAF released its official response to the Roswell Incident. It stated that the report was prepared as a result of the enquiries by Congressman Steven Schiff and the announcement that the GAO was launching its own investigation. Although widely dismissed by many ufologists, the report makes for interesting reading and is worth quoting at length.

The Air Force begins by revealing its methodology, stating that it 'initiated a systematic search of current Air Force offices as well as numerous archives and records centers that might help explain this matter. Research revealed that the "Roswell Incident" was not even considered a UFO event until the 1978–1980 time frame. Prior to that the incident was dismissed because the AAF originally identified the debris recovered as being that of a weather balloon. Subsequently various authors wrote a number of books claiming that, not only was debris from an alien spacecraft recovered but also the bodies of the craft's alien occupants. These claims continue to evolve today and the Air Force is now routinely accused of engaging in a "cover-up" of this supposed event.

'The research located no records at existing Air Force offices that indicated any "cover-up" by the USAF or any indication of such a recovery. Consequently, efforts were intensified by Air Force researchers at numerous locations where records for the period in question were stored. The records reviewed did not reveal any increase in operations, security, or any other activity in July 1947, that indicated any such unusual event may have occurred. Records were located and thoroughly explored concerning a then TOP SECRET balloon project, designed to monitor Soviet nuclear tests, known as Project Mogul. Additionally, several surviving project personnel were located and interviewed, as was the only surviving person who recovered debris from the original Roswell site in 1947, and the former officer who initially identified the wreckage as a balloon. Comparison of all information developed or obtained indicated that the material recovered near Roswell was consistent with a balloon device and most likely from one of the Mogul balloons that had not been previously recovered. Air Force research efforts did not disclose any records of the recovery of any "alien" bodies or extraterrestrial materials.'

The report readily admits that it was because Congressman Schiff was unhappy with its original response that the GAO was brought into the picture. Reading between the lines, the USAF's research is to some extent a pre-emptive strike. The official who oversaw the exercise was the Director, Security and Special Program Oversight, Office of the Secretary of the Air Force [SAF/AAZ]. This is his account of the background to the enquiry: 'On February 15 1994, the GAO officially notified Secretary of Defense William J Perry that it was initiating an audit of the Department of Defense policies and procedures for acquiring, classifying, retaining, and disposing of official government documents dealing with weather balloon, aircraft, and similar crash incidents. This notification was subsequently passed to the Department of Defense Inspector General who in turn officially notified the Secretaries of the Services and other affected parties of the audit in a February 23 1994 memo. This memorandum indicated that the "GAO is anxious to respond to Representative Schiff's request and to dispel any concerns that the DOD is being unresponsive". These were the first official US government documents that indicated the purpose of the GAO was to review "crash incidents involving weather balloons and unknown aircraft, such as UFOs and foreign aircraft, and . . . the facts involving the reported crash of an UFO in 1949 [*sic*] at Roswell, New Mexico and alleged DOD cover up".

'An entrance meeting of potentially concerned parties was held in the offices of the DOD Inspector General on February 28 1994. During this meeting it was learned that, while the audit officially would be reviewing the records of a number of DOD [and possibly other Executive Branch entities], the bulk of the effort would be focused on Air Force records and systems. The audit was officially given the GAO code 701034, and entitled "Records Management Procedures Dealing With Weather Balloon, Unknown Aircraft and Similar Crash Incidents".

'Although this official title appeared rather broad, there was no misunderstanding that the real purpose was to attempt to locate records and/or information on the "Roswell Incident". This incident, explained later in more detail, generally dealt with the claim that in July of 1947, the US Army Air Force (USAAF) recovered a flying saucer and or its alien occupants which supposedly crashed near Roswell, New Mexico. When the USAAF ultimately became the United States Air Force (USAF) in September 1947 the USAF inherited equipment, personnel, records, policies and procedures from the AAF. In this particular case, the Air Force also inherited the allegation that it had "covered up" the "Roswell Incident" and has continued to do so for the next 47 years. Within the Air Force, the Office of the Administrative Assistant to the Secretary of the Air Force (SAF/AA) is responsible both for information management procedures (SAF/AAI) and security policy and oversight (SAF/AAZ). Because of this organization, SAF/AA was the logical entity to assist the GAO in its audit and SAF/AAZ was officially named as the Central Point of Contact for this Endeavor. Subsequently, the then Administrative Assistant, Mr Robert J. McCormick, issued a tasking memorandum dated March 1, 1994, to a number of current Air Staff and Secretariat offices that might possibly have records related to such an incident if, indeed, something had actually occurred.

'This search for records was purposely limited to Air Force Records and systems since:
(a)   The Air Force had no authority to compel other agencies to review their records;
(b)   The Air Force would have no way to monitor the completeness of their efforts if they did; and
(c)   the overall effort was the task and responsibility of the GAO – not the Air Force.'

When we penetrate this maze of bureaucratese and acronyms designed to daze the mind and leave it confused, there emerges an interesting point. Although we are expected to have faith in the 'completeness' of the Air Force's response to the GAO enquiry, and believe that if any documents were discovered they would indeed be released, the Air Force admits that there would be no way for it to know if another agency was being less than 'complete' in its separate efforts. In other words, there could be no guarantee that, if information were found or already existed, it would be disclosed.

For the committed conspiracy theorists and hard-line ufologists there would be a tendency to dismiss the report anyway and in many cases there exists such a deep mistrust of the institutions of the State that they would regard all official claims to be part of the 'big lie', or at best 'disinformation'. The Air Force tends to be regarded by such people with the gravest of misgivings. For example, extremist ufologists are convinced that it has consistently lied to the American people about UFOs – from Project Bluebook through to Project Mogul. Thus no report is going to satisfy them, and yet with striking illogic they are ready to believe near-certain hoaxes such as MJ-12 (which is discussed later in this book).

It would be wrong to classify all members of the growing breed of ufologists as blind to reasoned argument. Nevertheless, there is among them an alarming tendency to mistrust anything official when it comes to a denial and believe anything, official or not, if it looks relatively convincing as evidence of a UFO, whether it be a witness, a sighting or a document obtained under the Freedom of Information Act. Provided there is some sort of official provenance there is a tendency to give such claims credence, and yet it stands to reason that if the government is such a mine of disinformation there can be no guarantee that 'official' statements are any more accurate than what is taken as disinformation. To be fair to the UFO research community, there is good reason for scepticism about official pronouncements and a great deal has been uncovered by the diligent research of a great many UFO experts. Indeed, the pioneering research of many in the field was responsible for exhuming the Roswell Incident from the archives of newspapers and the memories of witnesses who were alive in 1947.

The two most authoritative researchers, who have written more than one book on the affair, are Kevin Randle and Don Schmitt. They broke new ground by finding new witnesses and providing the most comprehensive account to date of the timetable of events, while Stanton Friedman, a UFO author from Canada, had been one of the first to realize the potential importance of the Roswell case.

The work of Randle and Schmitt receives the accolade of being referred to directly by Colonel Richard L. Weaver of the USAF, who bears the title of Director, Security and Special Program Oversight, and whose signature figures at the end of the Project Mogul report. This is what he says about the evidence uncovered by theirs and previous books and articles on Roswell: 'It was . . . decided, particularly after a review of the above popular literature, that no specific attempt would be made to try to refute, point by point, the numerous claims made in the various publications. Many of these claims appear to be hearsay, undocumented, taken out of context, self-serving, or otherwise dubious. Additionally, many of the above authors are not even in agreement over various claims. Most notable of the confusing and now ever-changing claims is the controversy over the date(s) of the alleged incident, the exact location(s) of the purported debris and the extent of the wreckage. Such discrepancies in claims made the search much more difficult by greatly expanding the volume of records that had to be searched. An example of trying to deal with questionable claims is illustrated by the following example: One of the popular books mentioned that was reviewed claimed that the writers had submitted the names and serial numbers of "over two dozen" personnel stationed at Roswell in July 1947 to the Veteran's Administration and the Defense Department to confirm their military service. They then listed eleven of these persons by name and asked the question: "Why does neither the Defense Department nor the Veteran's Administration have records of any of these men when we can document that each served at Roswell Army Air Field". That claim sounded serious so SAF/AAZD was tasked to check these eleven names in the Personnel Records Center in St Louis. Using only the names (since the authors did not list the serial numbers) the researcher quickly found records readily identifiable with eight of these persons. The other three had such common names that there could have been multiple possibilities. Interestingly, one of the listed "missing" persons had a casualty report in his records reflecting that he died in 1951, while the writers claimed to have interviewed him (or a person of the exact same name) in 1990.'

The careful reader will observe how the Air Force report rather skilfully glosses over the fact that the majority of the people mentioned do seem to have a genuine military record as claimed by the authors, while one person (whose name, frustratingly, is not revealed) turns out to be wrong. Thus aspersions are cast on the work of the researchers without acknowledging that they have actually got it more right than wrong.

In addition, no names are mentioned of those whose military service did check out, none of them appears to have been interviewed by those conducting the research for the Air Force report, and no attempt was made either to corroborate or demolish their claims about the incident. This is either bad research or reflective of a mind-set which assumes that any of those interviewed who support the conclusion that there may be an extraterrestrial dimension to the Roswell Incident are not worthy of investigation. This is as dangerous an approach to serious research as is the tendency of some researchers in the UFO field to accept evidence or hearsay too readily as being true. In fact, coming as it does from the USAF, an established body, the sin is compounded, as it devalues the confidence that the objective and open-minded reader should have in an official report. It suggests above all that the Air Force cannot take seriously any evidence contrary to the conclusion of its own report for no other reason than that it is too fantastic to consider. In this way it is playing straight into the hands of the conspiracy theorists and the Fox Mulders of this world.

It was precisely this mind-set that Congressman Schiff encountered, and it prompted him to set the wheels of officialdom turning to try to tease out some evidence which might resolve the Roswell mystery.

There is another interesting admission in this section of the report. The Air Force states that what it claims categorically are 'discrepancies' within the body of the research and claims of the UFO contingent have made their own 'document' search 'much more difficult by greatly expanding the volume of records that had to be searched'. This is a puzzling comment, since first of all, if these 'discrepancies' speak of a confusion based on the UFO researchers' acceptance of fabrication and hearsay, as the Air Force suggests, then this should narrow the field of documents available for investigation. How can it expand the extent of the enquiry? What are the documents that have to be searched, in addition to those which the Air Force might already be looking for?

The answer is not specified; but given that the discrepancies over the date of the alleged crash and its exact location are not that far apart – they span a few weeks and less than a hundred miles, why should this impact on the search for official documents? It is the same state, the same airbase, the same personnel, so either this is a protest with no basis in reality or it suggests that there are many records that relate in some way to this supposed event which have to be searched in addition to those that were being searched originally. As will be seen from later conclusions reached by the GAO, this second possibility turns out not to be the case. So what is the Air Force saying here? It is difficult not to conclude that this is some form of obfuscation or indirect evidence that documents are being withheld.

On the scope of the search, the report says that it 'was not limited to unclassified materials, but also would include records of the highest classification and compartmentation. The specific Air Staff/Secretariat offices queried included the following:

(a) SAF/AAI, Directorate of Information Management
(b) SAF/AQL, Directorate of Electronics and Special Programs
(c) AF/SE, Air Force Safety
(d) AF/HO, Air Force Historian
(e) AF/IN, Air Force Intelligence (including Air Force Intelligence Agency – AFIA, and the National Air Intelligence Center, NAIC)
(f) AF/XOW, Directorate of Weather
(g) [added later] The Air Force Office of Special Investigation.

'In addition to the above Air Staff and Secretariat Offices, SAF/AAZ also reviewed appropriate classified records for any tie-in to this matter. With regards to highly classified records, it should be noted that any programs that employ enhanced security measures or controls are known as Special Access Programs (SAPs). The authority for such programs comes from an Executive Order 12356 and flows from the Department of Defense to the Services via DoD Directive 5205.7. These programs are implemented in the Air Force by Policy Directive 16-7, and Air Force Instruction 17-701. These directives contain detailed requirements for controlling and reporting in a very strict manner, all SAPs. This includes a report from the Secretary of Defense (and ultimately to Congress) on all SAPs submitted for approval, and a certification that there are no "SAP-like" programs being operated. These reporting requirements are stipulated in public law.

'It followed then, that if the Air Force had recovered some type of extraterrestrial spacecraft and/or bodies and was exploiting this for scientific and technology purposes, then such a program would be operated as a SAP. SAF/AAZ, the Central Office for all Air Force SAPs, has knowledge of, and security oversight over, all SAPs. SAF/AAZ categorically stated that no such Special Access Program(s) exists that pertains to extraterrestrial spacecraft/aliens.

'Likewise, the Secretary of the Air Force and the Chief of Staff, who head the Special Program Oversight Committee which oversees all sensitive programs in the Air Force, had no knowledge of any such program involving, or relating to the events at Roswell or the alleged technology that supposedly resulted therefrom. Besides the obvious irregularity and illegality of keeping such information from the most senior Air Force officials, it would also be illogical, since these officials are responsible for obtaining funding for operations, research, development, and security.

'Without funding such a programme, operation, or organization could not exist. Even to keep such a fact "covered-up" in some sort of passive "caretaker status" would involve money. More importantly, it would involve people and create paperwork.

'The aforementioned March 1 1994 SAF/AA tasking generated negative responses from all recipients; i.e. all offices reported that they had no information that would explain the incident. Consequently, these negative responses led to an increase in the already on-going historical research at records centers and archives.

'The extensive archival and records center search was systematically carried out by the SAF/AAZD Declassification Review Team. This team is composed entirely of Air Force Reserve personnel who have extensive training and experience in large scale review of records. (Previous efforts include the Southeast Asia Declassification Review, declassification of POW/MIA records, and the review of the Gulf War Air Power Survey records.) The team members all had the requisite security clearances for classified information and had the authority of the Secretary of the Air Force to declassify any classified record they found that might be related to Roswell. SAF/AAZD conducted reviews at a number of locations, including the National Archives in Washington DC; the National Personnel Records Center, St Louis, MO; the National Archives, Suitland, MD; the National Records Center, Suitland, MD; Naval Research Laboratory, Washington DC; Federal Records Center, Fort Worth, TX; the INSCOM Archives, Ft Meade, MD; National Air and Space Museum, Washington, DC; Air Force Historical Research Agency, Maxwell AFB, AL; Center for Air Force History, Bolling AFB, DC; Phillips Laboratory, Hanscom AFB, MA and Kirtland AFB, NM; Rome Laboratory, Griffiths AFB, NY; and the Library of Congress, Washington, DC.

'The specific areas included all those subject areas logically believed to possibly contain any reference to activities at Roswell AAF during the period of time in question. It is anticipated that detractors from this effort will complain that "they did not search record group x, box y, or reel z, etc; that's where the real records are!" Such complaints are unavoidable and there is no possible way that the millions of records under Air Force control could be searched page by page. The team endeavoured to make logical searches in those places where records would likely be found. They were assisted in this task by archivists, historians, and records management specialists, including experienced persons who have continually worked in Army and Air Force records systems since 1943. The team also searched some record areas that were recommended by serious private researchers such as Robert Todd, who had independently obtained almost encyclopaedic knowledge of the complexities of Air Force records systems, particularly as related to this subject area.

'Not surprisingly the research team found the usual number of problems in many of the records centers (particularly St Louis) with misfiling, lost, or misplaced documents, mismatching of documents, or the breaking up of record groups over the years and refiling in different systems. This included, for example, a small amount of missing "decimal files" from the 509th Bomb Group at Roswell that covered the years 1945–49, that were marked on the index as "destroyed". The researchers noted that there was no pattern to any anomalies found and that most discrepancies were minor and consistent with what they had found in the past on similar projects.'

The separation of the Air Force from the Army Air Force in the same year as the Roswell Incident undoubtedly led to a certain amount of administrative chaos. As a result, there was probably confusion as to whether particular files should go to the new Air Force or should stay with the Army, which had been the controlling organization. Yet one is forced to share with the alleged conspiracy theorists just a twinge of die-hard scepticism on learning that some of the 509th Bomb Group's records from 1945–9 have mysteriously – some might say, conveniently – gone missing. Half a decade covering the most critical years of the formation and operational strategies of the 509th must represent a considerable body of paperwork – presumably enough papers, folders, files and memoranda to fill several trucks. How could such a large amount of documents go missing? Lost in a fire – that would be understandable – as, later, many of the Military Personnel records in fact were. Taken or stolen by an individual? Possible but unlikely. Deposited in a warehouse for onward dispatch to Washington or some other records centre? Possible, although likely to have been discovered. Deliberately filed in other areas so as to elude the gaze of dedicated archivists and researchers seeking out some information in future years? Possible but unlikely, although it is worth remembering that this is the precise claim of the mysterious Rick Tungate, who states that it was the specific task that he was assigned by a commanding officer in the early 1950s, with the sole objective of allowing the Air Force to claim in future times that there were no records available. Admittedly, Tungate claims responsibility only for the artful concealment of the Roswell Incident papers, but who is to say that there were not scores of other 'Tungates', also tasked with such concealment or the straightforward and wholesale destruction of an entire body of documents. Yet it must be admitted that this explanation is unlikely. But then consider this: how likely is it that records of what was historically and at that specific time the most important and strategically vital wing of the entire US military forces, the 509th Bomb Group – at the time the only military group in the world to have had experience of not only handling and flying with atomic bombs but also of delivering them and exploding them: over two Japanese cities at the end of the Second World War – should go missing in their entirety?

True, the planes that flew over Nagasaki and Hiroshima were based in Guam and flew their terrible missions from their base in the Far East, and many of those records survived, but it is at best somewhat suspicious that a large body of records should have been recorded as being 'destroyed' with no explanation as to what they were, how they came to be destroyed, who discovered their fate and what action was taken to either rectify the situation or hold to account those who were responsible for not safeguarding them. Presumably this loss would have been regarded as a serious matter. After all, the 509th should have been protected with the highest levels of security and personnel vetting deployed within the American military. Would not alarm bells have rung on the discovery that records for a five-year period of its history had disappeared? At the very least the security implications of such an event would have been potentially devastating – for example, the documents, or critical parts of them, might have been squirrelled away by a clerk in the pay of the Soviets. Such information would have been of tremendous value to the Eastern Bloc. Would the Americans not have been concerned about its loss? If they weren't or didn't know they had lost so many documents then it speaks of an alarming lack of security, although this, given that the Cold War was approaching its most paranoid stage, is equally unlikely. Even if we allow the benefit of the doubt and accept that records were going AWOL throughout the American military establishment, we might expect the USAF in its current report to offer some sort of explanation. But it doesn't.

There is no explanation, no rationale. Nothing. Consequently for the

Air Force to accuse its detractors of poor research, faulty methodology and unconvincing evidence rings somewhat hollow. At the very least it should offer some explanation for the nature of the documents that it admits are missing. It may well be that the Air Force is telling the truth about what exists, or does not exist, in the official archives about the Roswell Incident, but it hardly helps to instil confidence in its denials and claims about the story if it gives out such sketchy details of the lack of records available to support its own case.

Proceeding from this admitted lack of documentation, the report goes on to offer the Air Force's version of the Roswell Incident.

'WHAT THE ROSWELL INCIDENT WAS NOT

Before discussing specific positive results that these efforts revealed, it is first appropriate to discuss those things, as indicated by information available to the Air Force, that the "Roswell incident" *was not*:

'An Airplane Crash

Of all the things that are documented and tracked within the Air Force, among the most detailed and scrupulous are airplane crashes. In fact, records of air crashes go back to the first years of military flight. Safety records and reports are available for all crashes that involved serious damage, injury, death or a combination of those factors. These records also include incidents involving experimental or classified aircraft. USAF records showed that between June 24, 1947, and July 28, 1947, there were five crashes in New Mexico alone, involving A-26C, P-51N, C-82A, P-80A and PQ14-B aircraft; however none of these were on the date(s) in question nor in the area(s) in question.

'One of the additional areas specifically set forth by GAO in its efforts was to deal with how the Air Force (and others) specifically documented "weather balloon . . . and other crash incidents". In this area, the search efforts revealed that there are no air safety records pertaining to weather balloon crashes (all weather balloons "crash" sooner or later); however, there are provisions for generating reports of "crashes" as ground safety incidents in the unlikely chance that a balloon injures someone or causes damage. However such records are only maintained for five years.

'A Missile Crash

A crashed or errant missile, usually described as a captured German V-2 or one of its variants, is sometimes set forth as a possible explanation for the debris recovered near Roswell. Since much of this testing done at nearby White Sands was secret at the time, it would be logical to assume that the government would handle any missile mishap under tight security, particularly if the mishap occurred on private land. From the records reviewed by the Air Force, however, there was nothing located to suggest that this was the case. Although the bulk of remaining testing records are under the control of the US Army, the subject has also been very well documented over the years within Air Force records. There would be no reason to keep such information classified today. The USAF found no indicators or even hints that a missile was involved in this matter.

'A Nuclear Accident

One of the areas considered was that whatever happened near Roswell may have involved nuclear weapons. This was a logical area of concern since the 509th Bomb Group was the only military unit in the world at the time that had access to nuclear weapons. Again, reviews of available records gave no indication that this was the case. A number of records still classified TOP SECRET and SECRET – RESTRICTED DATA having to do with nuclear weapons were located in the Federal Records Center in St Louis, MO. These records, which pertained to the 509th, had nothing to do with any activities that could have been misinterpreted as the "Roswell Incident". Also, any records of a nuclear-related incident would have been inherited by the Department of Energy (DOE), and, had one occurred, it is likely DOE would have publicly reported it as part of its recent declassification and public release efforts. There were no ancillary records in Air Force files to indicate the potential existence of such records within DOE channels, however.

'The Air Force found absolutely no indication that what happened near Roswell in 1947, involved any type of extraterrestrial spacecraft. This, of course, is the crux of this entire matter. "Pro-UFO" persons who obtain a copy of this report, at this point, most probably begin the "cover-up is still on" claims. Nevertheless, the research indicated absolutely no evidence *of any kind* that a spaceship crashed near Roswell or that any alien occupants were recovered therefrom, in some secret military operation or otherwise. This does not mean, however, that the early Air Force was not concerned about UFOs. However in the early days, "UFO" meant Unidentified Flying Object, which literally translated as some object in the air that was not readily identifiable. It did not mean, as the term has evolved in today's language, to equate to alien spaceships. Records from the period reviewed by Air Force researchers as well as those cited by the authors mentioned before, do indicate that the USAF *was* seriously concerned about the inability to adequately identify unknown flying objects reported in American airspace. All the records, however, indicated that the focus of concern was not on aliens, hostile or otherwise, but on the Soviet Union. Many documents from that period speak to the possibility of developmental Soviet aircraft overflying US airspace. This, of course, was of major concern to the fledgling USAF, whose job it was to protect these same skies.

'The research revealed only one official AAF document that indicated that there was any activity of any type that pertained to UFOs and Roswell in July 1947. This was a small section of the July Historical Report for the 509th Bomb Group and Roswell AAF that stated: "The Office of Public Information was quite busy during the month answering inquiries on the 'flying disc', which was reported to be in possession of the 509th Bomb Group. The object turned out to be a radar tracking balloon." Additionally, this history showed that the 509th Commander, Colonel Blanchard, went on leave on July 8, 1947, which would be a somewhat unusual manoeuvre for a person involved in the supposed first ever recovery of extraterrestrial materials. [Detractors claim Blanchard did this as a ploy to elude the press and go to the scene to direct the recovery operations.]

'The history and the morning reports also showed that the subsequent activities at ROSWELL during the month were mostly mundane and not indicative of any unusual high level activity, expenditure of manpower, resources or security.

'Likewise, the researchers found no indication of heightened activity anywhere else in the military hierarchy in the July, 1947, message traffic or orders (to include classified traffic). There were no indications and warnings, notice of alerts, or a higher tempo of operational activity reported that would be logically generated if an alien craft, whose intentions were unknown, entered US territory. To believe that such operational and high level security activity could be conducted solely by relying on unsecured telecommunications or personal contact without creating any records of such activity certainly stretches the imagination of those who have served in the military who know that paperwork of some kind is necessary to accomplish even emergency, highly classified, or sensitive tasks.

'An example of activity sometimes cited by pro–UFO writers to illustrate the point that something unusual was going on was the travel of Lt. General Nathan Twining, Commander of the Air Materiel command, to New Mexico in July 1947. Actually, records were located indicating that Twining went to the Bomb Commanders' Course on July 8, along with a number of other general officers, and requested orders to do so a month before, on June 5, 1947.

'Similarly, it has also been alleged that General Hoyt Vandenberg, Deputy Chief of Staff at the time, had been involved in directing activity regarding events at Roswell. Activity reports, located in General Vandenberg's personal papers stored in the Library of Congress, did indicate that on July 7, he was busy with a "flying disc" incident; however this particular incident involved Ellington Field, Texas and the Spokane (Washington) Depot. After much discussion and information gathering on this incident, it was learned to be a hoax. There is no similar mention of his personal interest or involvement in Roswell events except in the newspapers.

'The above are but two small examples that indicate that if some event happened that was one of the "watershed happenings" in human history, the US military certainly reacted in an unconcerned and cavalier manner. In an actual case, the military would have had to order thousands of soldiers and airmen, not only at Roswell but throughout the US, to act nonchalantly, pretend to conduct and report business as usual, and generate absolutely no paperwork of a suspicious nature, while simultaneously anticipating that twenty years or more into the future people would have available a comprehensive Freedom of Information Act that would give them great leeway to review and explore government documents.

'The records indicate that none of this happened (or if it did, it was controlled by a security system so efficient and tight that no one, US or otherwise, has been able to duplicate it since). If such a system had been in effect at the time, it would have also been used to protect our atomic secrets from the Soviets, which history has showed obviously was not the case. The records reviewed confirmed that no such sophisticated and efficient security system existed.

'WHAT THE ROSWELL INCIDENT WAS

As previously discussed, what was originally reported to have been recovered was a balloon of some sort, usually described as a "weather balloon," although the majority of the wreckage that was ultimately displayed by General Ramey and Major Marcel in the famous photos in Ft. Worth, was that of a radar target normally suspended from balloons. This radar target, discussed in more detail later, was certainly consistent with the description of a July 9 newspaper article which discussed "tinfoil, paper, tape, and sticks." Additionally, the description of the "flying disc" was consistent with a document routinely used by most pro-UFO writers to indicate a conspiracy in progress – the telegram from the Dallas FBI office of July 8, 1947. This document quoted in part states: ". . . The disc is hexagonal in shape and was suspended from a balloon by a cable, which balloon was approximately twenty feet in diameter . . . the object found resembles a high altitude weather balloon with a radar reflector . . . disc and balloon being transported . . ."

'Similarly, while conducting the popular literature review, one of the documents reviewed was a paper entitled "The Roswell Events" edited by Fred Whiting, and sponsored by the Fund for UFO Research (FUFOR). Although it was not the original intention to comment on what commercial authors interpreted or claimed that other persons supposedly said, this particular document was different because it contained actual copies of apparently authentic sworn affidavits received from a number of persons who claimed to have some knowledge of the Roswell event. Although many of the persons who provided these affidavits to the FUFOR researchers also expressed opinions that they thought there was something extraterrestrial about this incident, a number of them actually describe materials that sounded suspiciously like wreckage from balloons. These included the following:

'Jesse A. Marcel, MD (son of the late Major Jesse Marcel; eleven years old at the time of the incident). Affidavit dated May 6 1991. ". . . There were three categories of debris: a thick, foil like metallic grey substance; a brittle brownish-black plastic like material, like Bakelite; and there were fragments of what appeared to be I-beams. On the inner surface of the I-beam, there appeared to be a type of writing. This writing was a purple violet hue, and it had an embossed appearance. The figures were composed of curved geometric shapes. It had no resemblance to Russian, Japanese, or any other foreign language. It resembled hieroglyphics, but it had no animal like characters . . ."

'Loretta Proctor (former neighbour of rancher W.W. Brazel). Affidavit dated May 5 1991: ". . . Brazel came to my ranch and showed my husband and me a piece of material he said came from a large pile of debris on the property he managed. The piece he brought was brown in color, similar to plastic . . . 'Mac' said the other material on the property looked like aluminum foil. It was very flexible and wouldn't crush or burn. There was also something he described as tape which had printing on it. The color of the printing was a kind of purple . . ."

'Bessie Brazel Schreiber (daughter of W.W. Brazel; fourteen years old at the time of the incident). Affidavit dated September 22 1993: ". . . The debris looked like pieces of a large balloon which had burst. The pieces were small, the largest I remember measuring was about the same as the diameter of a basketball. Most of it was a kind of double sided material, foil-like on one side and rubber-like on the other. Both sides were grayish silver in color, the foil more silvery than the rubber. Sticks, like kite sticks, were attached to some of the pieces with a whitish tape. The tape was about two or three inches wide and had flower-like designs on it. The flowers were faint, a variety of pastel colors, and reminded me of Japanese paintings in which the flowers are not all connected. I do not recall any other types of material or markings, nor do I remember seeing gouges in the ground or any other signs that anything may have hit the ground hard. The foil-rubber material could not be torn like ordinary aluminum foil can be torn . . ."

'Sally Strickland Tadolini (neighbour of W.W. Brazel; nine years old in 1947). Affidavit dated September 27 1993: ". . . What Bill showed us was a piece of what I still think was fabric. It was something like aluminum foil, something like satin, something like well-tanned leather in its toughness, yet was not precisely like any of those materials . . . It was about the thickness of very fine kidskin glove leather and a dull metallic grayish silver, one side slightly darker than the other. I do not remember it having any design or embossing on it . . ."

'Robert R. Porter (B-29 flight engineer stationed at Roswell in 1947). Affidavit dated June 7 1991: ". . . On this occasion, I was a member of the crew which flew parts of what we were told was a flying saucer to Fort Worth. The people on board included . . .

and Maj Jesse Marcel. Capt. William E Anderson said it was from a flying saucer. After we arrived, the material was transferred to a B-25. I was told they were going to Wright Field in Dayton, Ohio. I was involved in loading the B-29 with the material, which was wrapped in packages with wrapping paper. One of the pieces was triangle shaped, about 2 1/2 feet across the bottom. The rest were in small packages, about the size of a shoe box. The brown paper was held with tape. The material was extremely lightweight. When I picked it up, it was just like picking up an empty package. We loaded the triangle shaped package and three shoe box-sized packages into the plane. All of the packages could have fit into the trunk of a car . . . When we came back from lunch, they told us they had transferred the material to a B-25. They told us the material was a weather balloon, but I'm certain it wasn't a weather balloon."'

In addition to those persons above still living who claim to have seen or examined the original material found on the Foster ranch, there is one additional person who was universally acknowledged to have been involved in its recovery: Sheridan Cavitt, Lieutenant Colonel, USAF (Ret). Cavitt is credited in all claims with having accompanied Major Marcel to the ranch to recover the debris, sometimes along with his Counter Intelligence Corps (CIC) subordinate, William Rickett, who, like Marcel, is deceased. Although there does not appear to be much dispute that Cavitt was involved in the recovery of the material, other claims about him prevail in the popular literature. He is sometimes portrayed as a closed-mouth (or sometimes even sinister) conspirator who was one of the early individuals who kept the 'secret of Roswell' from getting out. Other things about him have been alleged, including the claim that he wrote a report of the incident at the time that has never surfaced.

Since Cavitt, who had first-hand knowledge, was still alive, a decision was made to interview him and get a signed sworn statement from him about his version of the events. Before the interview, the Secretary of the Air Force provided him with a written authorization and waiver to discuss classified information with the interviewer and release him from any security oath he may have taken. Subsequently, Cavitt was interviewed on May 24, 1994 at his home. He provided a signed, sworn statement of his recollections in this matter. He also consented to having the interview tape-recorded. In this interview, Cavitt related that he had been contacted on numerous occasions by UFO researchers and had willingly talked with many of them; however, he felt that he had oftentimes been misrepresented or had his comments taken out of context so that their true meaning was changed. He stated unequivocally, however, that the material he recovered consisted of a reflective sort of material like aluminum foil, and some thin, bamboo-like sticks. He thought at the time and continued to do so today, that what he found was a weather balloon and has told other private researchers that. He also remembered finding a small 'black box' type of instrument, which he thought at the time was probably a radiosonde. Cavitt also reviewed the famous Ramey Marcel photographs of the wreckage taken to Fort Worth (often claimed by UFO researchers to have been switched and the remnants of a balloon substituted for it) and he identified the materials depicted in those photos as consistent with the materials that he recovered from the ranch. Cavitt also stated that he had never taken any oath or signed any agreement not to talk about this incident and had never been threatened by anyone in the government because of it. He did not even know the 'incident' was claimed to be anything unusual until he was interviewed in the early 1980s.

Similarly, Irving Newton, Major, USAF (Ret), was located and interviewed. Newton was weather officer assigned to Fort Worth, who was on duty when the Roswell debris was sent there in July 1947. He was told that he was to report to General Ramey's office to view the material. In a signed sworn statement Newton related that 'I walked into the General's Office where this supposed flying saucer was lying all over the floor. As soon as I saw it I giggled and asked if that was the flying saucer ... I told them that this was a balloon and RAWIN target ...' Newton also stated that 'while I was examining the debris, Major Marcel was picking up pieces of the target sticks and trying to convince me that some notations on the sticks were alien writings. There were figures on the sticks, lavender or pink in color, appeared to be weather faded markings, with no rhyme or reason [*sic*]. He did not convince me that these were alien writings.' Newton concluded his statement by relating that 'During the ensuing years I have been interviewed by many authors, I have been quoted and misquoted. The facts remain as indicated above. I was not influenced during the original interview, nor today, to provide anything but what I know to be true, that is, the material I saw in General Ramey's office was the remains of a balloon and a RAWIN target.'

Major Newton is a sprightly and spirited American of military bearing and forthright opinion. While not wishing to speak ill of the dead, he is less than generous in his estimation of the mental capability of Jesse Marcel and severely sceptical about his powers of analysis that day in the office with the 'wreckage' strewn over the floor in front of them. Newton is a down-to-earth character, full of common sense who laughs with a full-throated guffaw at the whole notion that the 'Roswell Incident' could conceivably be a flying saucer. Certainly, if anyone could identify a weather balloon, Major Irving Newton would be the man, which was precisely why his Commanding Officer, General Roger Ramey, summoned him to his office that day in July 1947.

'I'm a meteorologist,' Newton told me, 'and I had been at this time a weather forecaster for approximately five years and I was working at Fort Worth base weather station as well as flight service; we had two separate operations and I was the only person on duty at this time of the afternoon. Normally, we would have forecasters in both places and possibly more than two. But things had quieted down and I was operating both operations and I got a call from out of the blue and they asked me to come over to the general's office. They wanted me to look at something. And I told them I couldn't possibly get over there, because I was the only one qualified forecaster on duty and finally the general called and said, "Get your ass over here to my office. We've got something here we want you to look at." And [I said] "Aye, aye, sir" and he says, "If you've got a car, fine; if you haven't, get one. Get the first means of transportation and get over to my office." Nobody told me they had a flying saucer or anything at this time. I got over to his office and some colonel, I don't know who it was [most probably Colonel Thomas Dubose, Ramey's Staff Officer] met me at the door and he says that someone in Roswell had picked up what they thought was a flying saucer and they brought it over there and they had it in the general's office and the general thought maybe it was part of some meteorological equipment. That's all they said – they didn't say, "We want you to go in there and identify this weather balloon" – nothing like that; they didn't tell me a thing!

'So they ushered me into the general's office and there is all that crap laying on the floor. And when I saw that I says, "Is that your flying saucer?" And they said, "Yeah." And I said, "Well, hell no! That's a RAWIN target and balloon and if it isn't I'd eat it without salt or pepper!" "Are you sure?" "Yes, I'm sure! I know what that is."

And there were six or eight people in there at the time, the general, a couple of aides and Major Marcel and some photographers and regular reporters.'

Newton is unshakeable as to what he saw, although by implication he cannot address the possibility put forward by Marcel's son and implied by Jesse Marcel himself that there was a switch of the material. The 'cover-up' which Frank Kaufmann claims was that 'beautiful' piece of disinformation. Right or wrong, Newton's assessment of the situation is invaluable, not least because he was able to form a good impression of the character and ability of Major Marcel himself.

'Now if I may, I would put out here what I think is the simple facts as I know them,' offers Newton, by way of his own interpretation of what had been going on. 'The facts are that in the middle of June, this Western rancher, Brazel, was riding or walking through his pasture with his son, I think, and he saw some suspicious-looking debris over there, some shiny metallic stuff and he went away and didn't think anything about it. But then, like the following month, there was started some speculation there about flying saucers and someone mentioned, "Well, I think there's a reward if we can find a flying saucer!" And so Brazel, being a good, intelligent fellow, says, "Well, hell, maybe I got just what they want!" So he went out in the pasture and he collected up a bunch of stuff. Let's see now if I can get what he picked up. He says, "Yeah, there was this area covered about a two hundred yard diameter and it was blown around there and the rubber was a smoky grey and the tin foil paper, tape and sticks, made up a bundle about three feet long and about seven or eight inches thick. While the rubber made a bundle of about eighteen to twenty inches long and about eight inches thick." In all he estimated the entire lot would have weighed maybe five pounds. This is what he had in the field. Now this balloon, when we send them up, is like eight to twelve feet in diameter, when it gets up to altitude, the high altitude, it expands probably to twenty or thirty feet even, and then it will deteriorate in the sun and come down for some reason or other, and if you can imagine a great big balloon like that, with a target whipping around in the desert for God knows how long – nobody saw this thing come down, nobody has any idea how long it was laying in there but after it had been ripping through the sage bush and everything else it would cover all this crap and deteriorate and that's what happened to that rubber or neoprene, whatever it was – it just deteriorated. Anyway, he reported this to the sheriff and the sheriff reported it to the base.

And Major Marcel, an intelligence officer, well, here we've got an intelligence project, so he would be a likely man to get it. So they invited him in to look at it and he looked at all this stuff too, and then some PR guy got in there, and I don't know how he got in there, but someone showed it to him, and boy! Just like that! He released the information: "We have a flying disc." This went out over all of the papers. And these people were just climbing all over themselves to get in on this information 'cause they had a "flying disc"! Nobody thought about "We might have a flying disc or we're going to check on this. We have a flying disc . . ." Anyway, they bundled this great big thing up and flew it to Fort Worth – that's where I came in. They flew it in to General Ramey's office and they spread it around and his suspicion is that it might be some meteorological stuff so he got the first guy that might know what it was – and he got me! Fortunately, I knew what it was, because I had been on several projects where we used a similar thing like this, now – this was not used normally in the weather business, just on special projects for upper air information for guns and for aircraft operation. But I knew what it was, I saw what it was, and I identified it as such.'

Newton's confidence is not unsettled by the assertion that the material could have been switched. It is based on his clear memory of how Major Jesse Marcel behaved while they were together in General Ramey's office. The men had never met before – nor did they ever meet again. 'While we were in the office,' remembers Newton, 'he kept following me around with those sticks, those sticks had some hieroglyphic-looking things on there. He said, "Have you ever seen this?"

'Well, I had never seen that, I had never seen that on any target that I had seen before; but it was on there. But this strongly indicated to me that he was trying to convince me that he had picked up this flying disc and this was an alien source and that I hadn't seen that; but all the rest I had seen.'

The other point upon which Irving Newton is clear – with a certain amount of support, both indirectly from Marcel, and, as we have seen from the Air Force report, with the backing of several of the eyewitnesses themselves – is the exact nature and properties of the 'strange material', which is described with an unusual degree of similarity by so many different observers. This is perhaps the strongest element of witness evidence in favour of the Air Force explanation concerning the 'balloon' versus the 'flying disc'. Even those who cast doubt on the Air Force at this stage can hardly claim that a 'flying disc' would be constructed of materials which bear an uncanny resemblance to balsa-wood, tape, tin foil and a rubber-like material. Even if we accept that a flying saucer could contain materials similar to these we would have to concede that it is beyond any coincidence that an earth-bound balloon and a celestial flying saucer could be constructed from raw materials which are either basically the same or exhibit near-identical physical and chemical properties. To sustain the 'flying disc/extraterrestrial' hypothesis and Air Force cover-up in the face of this argument, we would have to conclude, and produce something in the way of evidence to support the conclusion, that the Air Force at that time concocted the weather balloon cover story and deliberately planted this and some of the descriptions in the minds of those who saw and heard about the material that was recovered. It would not have been difficult to say to cooperating witnesses, or to witnesses who were threatened, as many suggest they were, 'Others have suggested that this strange material was almost like foil, balsa-wood, aluminium etc . . .' to easily elicit answers which would then later exhibit a high degree of unanimity. Leading questions could account for the way in which these descriptions corroborate each other on a number of points. But the evidence is that most of these accounts were given to interviewers who, if anything, were predisposed to an extraterrestrial solution to the Roswell mystery. Therefore the descriptions which lend credence to a more earth-bound solution should be valued even more highly.

Even if we accept that they are true but relate to material and debris which came from an alleged extraterrestrial craft, it seems barely credible that this vehicle could have been constructed with such flimsy components, let alone bits and pieces which are very similar to those known to form part of a weather balloon, however exotic such a balloon might be. One further, admittedly far-fetched explanation, which might serve to explain the confusion between the descriptions of the materials from a 'flying saucer' and its close resemblance to those used in balloons, is the notion that the object which did crash in New Mexico in 1947 could have been some sort of UFO which became entangled with a balloon. It must be emphasized that this is rather unlikely, but there is an FBI document, obtained under the Freedom of Information Act, and dated the same day as the USAF press release was reported in the newspapers, which gives sufficient grounds for at least entertaining this notion:

'TELETYPE
FBI DALLAS 7-8-47 6.17PM
DIRECTOR AND SAC, CINCINNATI URGENT FLYING DISC, INFORMATION CONCERNING. HEADQUARTERS EIGHTH AIR FORCE TELEPHONICALLY ADVISED THIS OFFICE THAT AN OBJECT PURPORTING TO BE A FLYING DISC WAS RECOVERED NEAR ROSWELL NEW MEXICO, THIS DATE. THE DISC IS HEXAGONAL IN SHAPE AND WAS SUS-PENDED FROM A BALLOON BY CABLE, WHICH BALLOON WAS APPROXIMATELY TWENTY FOOT IN DIAMETER.

[*Censored*]. FURTHER ADVISED THAT THE OBJECT FOUND RESEMBLES A HIGH ALTITUDE WEATHER BALLOON WITH A RADAR REFLECTOR, BUT THAT TELEPHONIC CONVER-SATION BETWEEN THEIR OFFICE AND WRIGHT FIELD HAD NOT BORNE OUT THIS BELIEF. DISC AND BALLOON BEING TRANSPORTED TO WRIGHT FIELD BY SPECIAL PLANE FOR EXAMINATION. INFORMATION PROVIDED THIS OFFICE BECAUSE OF NATIONAL INTEREST IN CASE AND FACT THAT NATIONAL BROADCASTING COMPANY, ASSOCI-ATED PRESS AND OTHERS ATTEMPTING TO BREAK STORY OF LOCATION OF DISC TODAY. [*Censored*] ADVISED WOULD REQUEST WRIGHT FIELD TO ADVISE CINCINNATI OFFICE RESULTS OF EXAMINATION. NO FURTHER INVESTIGA-TION BEING CONDUCTED.
WYLY END'

The above is a genuine FBI document which has been declassified and was written on the same day as the celebrated article appeared in the *Roswell Daily Record*. Remarkably, it refers to both a flying disc and a balloon. Thus, either it is evidence that there were two separate objects – a 'disc', described as 'hexagonal', and a balloon, described as 'approximately twenty foot in diameter'. It is a curious document, for supposing that the object described is indeed a balloon, then it is unlikely to resemble a disc. Equally, if it was a 'flying disc' it would have been unlikely to resemble a balloon. The report does not solve the mystery, but it does at least legitimize the confusion. It is known that weather balloons were recovered fairly frequently from remote areas and on ranches, and people were reasonably familiar with what they looked like. Yet few of these craft can have been the subject of urgent teletyped messages from the FBI. Assuming it was a balloon, it raises the question of how it could have been so easily mistaken for a 'flying disc' and provoke such excitement among ranchers, townsfolk, intelligence officers and the Air Force itself. Such a mistake can only have arisen if either they were all taken in or, gripped by the hysteria of the saucer sightings, they collectively suffered a wave of self-delusion sufficient to suspend their normal judgement.

Major Newton thinks it is possible that, once the rumour started that a flying saucer had been retrieved, no one was sufficiently objective to then identify the debris as a mere weather balloon. 'As soon as that cowboy said, "We have a flying saucer, I'm sure they clamped down on it . . . Now, if they had gone to a weather person at Roswell, he may have identified it, but I'm sure they weren't inviting any weather forecaster over there, or anyone else. I'm sure they put this security all around it and that's where you start breeding this stuff where they said, on the threat of death, "Don't you mention this, don't talk about it." Well, I can see where they were trying to squelch this story, but I don't think they were really trying to get anyone not to tell the facts.' There still remains the question as to how the 509th could have so spectacularly misidentified what was nothing more than a balloon as a flying saucer. Again, Newton believes that Marcel could have been both mistaken and misguided. 'Now, no reflection on Marcel and his intelligence capabilities,' he says pulling his punch before delivering one, 'he did not know that it was a weather balloon. He didn't know anything. Now, I think he, with all of these dignitaries here, and the general, and the newspapers, I think he's embarrassed as crazy and he would like to do anything to make that turn into a flying saucer and I think he would push anything he could to make that into . . . but it wasn't going to change nothing, see, because it wasn't a flying saucer. And there's no doubt in my mind, and again there's a remote possibility that I could be wrong, but what Brazel described picking up and what I saw on the floor, and Marcel trying to show me how that writing came from outer space, there is no doubt in my mind that that's one and the same stuff.'

A new balloon story is essentially the explanation offered now by the Air Force. Colonel Weaver's report refers to the fact that they discovered records of balloon tests taking place at Alamogordo (now Holloman AFB) and White Sands during June and July 1947. It refers to '. . . testing "constant level" balloons and a New York University/Watson Laboratories effort that used "meteorological devices

. . . suspected for detecting shock waves generated by Soviet nuclear explosions"' – a possible indication of a cover story associated with the NYU balloon project. Subsequently a 1946 HQ AMC memorandum surfaced that described the constant-level balloon project and specified that the scientific data be classified 'TOP SECRET Priority 1A'. Its name was Project Mogul.

Project Mogul was a then sensitive, classified project whose purpose was to determine the state of Soviet nuclear weapons research. This was the early Cold War period and there was serious concern within the US government about the Soviets developing a weaponized atomic device. Because the Soviet Union's borders were closed, the US sought to develop a long-range nuclear explosion detection capability. Long-range, balloon-borne, low-frequency acoustic detection was proposed to General Spaatz in 1945 by Dr Maurice Ewing of Columbia University as a potential solution. (Atmospheric ducting of low-frequency pressure waves had been studied as early as 1900.)

As part of the research into this matter, AAZD personnel located and obtained the original study papers and reports of the NYU project. Their efforts also revealed that some of the individuals involved in Project Mogul were still living. These persons included the balloon Director of Research, Dr Athelstan F. Spilhaus; the project engineer, Professor Charles B. Moore; and the military Project Officer, Colonel Albert C. Trakowski.

All of these persons were subsequently interviewed and signed sworn statements about their activities . . . These interviews confirmed that Project Mogul was a compartmented, sensitive effort. The NYU group was responsible for developing constant-level balloons and telemetering equipment that would remain at specified altitudes (within the acoustic duct) while a group from Columbia University was to develop acoustic sensors. Dr Spilhaus, Professor Moore and certain others of the group were aware of the purpose of the project, but they did not know of the project's nickname at the time. They handled casual enquiries and/or scientific enquiries and papers in terms of 'unclassified meteorological or balloon research'. Newly hired employees were not made aware that there was anything special or classified about their work; they were told only that their work dealt with meteorological equipment.

An advance ground team, led by Albert P. Crary, preceded the NYU group to Alamogordo AAF, New Mexico, setting up ground sensors and obtaining facilities for the NYU group. On their arrival, Professor Moore and his team experimented with various configurations of neoprene balloons, the development of balloon 'trains' and automatic ballast systems and the use of naval sonobuoys (as the Watson Laboratories acoustical sensors had not yet arrived). They also launched what they called 'service flights'. These were not logged nor fully accounted for in the published Technical Reports generated as a result of the contract between NYU and Watson Laboratories. According to Professor Moore, the service flights were composed of balloons, radar reflectors and payloads specifically designed to test acoustic sensors (both early sonobuoys and later Watson Laboratories devices). The 'payload equipment' was expendable and some carried no 'REWARDS' or 'RETURN TO . . .' tags because there was to be no association between the flights and the logged constant-level flights, which were fully acknowledged. The NYU balloon flights were listed sequentially in their reports – i.e. A, B, 1, 5, 6, 7, 8, 10 . . . yet gaps existed for Flights 2–4 and Flight 9. The interview with Professor Moore indicated that these gaps were the unlogged service flights.

Professor Moore, who was the on-scene Project Engineer, gave detailed information concerning his team's efforts. He recalled that radar targets were used for tracking balloons because they did not have all the necessary equipment when they first arrived in New Mexico. Some of the early developmental radar targets were manufactured by a toy or novelty company. These targets were made up of aluminium foil or foil-backed paper, balsa-wood beams that were coated in an 'Elmeer's-type' glue to enhance their durability, acetate and/or cloth reinforcing tape, single-strand and braided nylon twine, brass eyelets and swivels to form a multifaceted reflector somewhat similar in construction to a box kite. Some of these targets were also assembled with purplish-pink tape with symbols on it.

According to the log summary of the NYU group, Flight A through Flight 7 (November 20, 1946–July 2, 1947) were made by neoprene meteorological balloons (whereas later flights were made with polyethylene balloons). Professor Moore stated that the neoprene balloons were susceptible to degradation in the sunlight, turning from milky white to dark brown. He described finding remains of balloon trains with reflectors and payloads that had landed in the desert. 'The ruptured and shredded neoprene would almost look like dark grey or black flakes or ashes after exposure to the sun for only a few days. The plasticizers and anti-oxidants in the neoprene would emit a peculiar acrid odor and the balloon material and the radar target material would be scattered after returning to earth, depending on surface winds.' Upon review of the local newspaper photographs from General Ramey's press conference in 1947 and descriptions in popular books by individuals who supposedly handled the debris recovered on the ranch, Professor Moore opined that the material was most likely the shredded remains of a multi-neoprene balloon train with multiple radar reflectors. The material and a 'black box' described by Lieutenant Colonel Cavitt was, in Moore's scientific opinion, most probably from Flight 4, a service flight that included a cylindrical metal sonobuoy and portions of a weather instrument housed in a box, which was unlike typical weather radiosondes, which were made of cardboard. Additionally, a copy of a professional journal maintained at the time by A.P. Crary, and provided to the Air Force by his widow, showed that Flight 4 was launched on June 4, 1947 but was not recovered by the NYU group. It is very probable that this TOP SECRET project balloon train, made up of unclassified components, came to rest some miles north-west of Roswell, became shredded in the surface winds and was ultimately found by Mac Brazel some ten days later. This possibility was supported by the observations of Cavitt, the only living eyewitness to the actual debris field and the material found. He described a small area of debris which appeared 'to resemble bamboo-type square sticks one quarter to one half-inch square, that were very light, as well as some sort of metallic reflecting material that was also very light . . . I remember recognizing this material as being consistent with a weather balloon.'

If this is an accurate reflection of the analysis of the material that was recovered from the ranch – both the material that Brazel had handed to Sheriff George Wilcox and the remains that the two Army Air Force officers discovered when they visited the site themselves – then it seems reasonable that there would have been a cautious preliminary account to the effect that the material was in all probability a terrestrial weather balloon of some description. This certainly seems to have been the recollection of Cavitt, and he must have discussed it with Major Jesse Marcel. If the latter disagreed, then there would have been an argument, discussion and some sort of debate which, if serious enough, would then have come to the attention of the base commander, Colonel Blanchard. Yet there appears to be no record of any such argument or difference of opinion, whereas there was a fairly serious divide if one considers that the competing alternative explanations were between a balloon and a flying saucer. Nor is there even any recollection of any dispute arising from the divergence of opinions on the nature of what might have crashed before it reached the attention of the 509th to be brought back to the Roswell airbase. Therefore the question remains: what could have possibly prompted a sensational press release referring to the recovery of a 'flying disc'?

The official USAF report addresses this conundrum as follows: 'Concerning the initial announcement, "RAAF Captures Flying Disc," research failed to locate any documented evidence as to why that statement was made. However, on July 10, 1947, following the Ramey press conference, the Alamogordo News published an article with photographs demonstrating multiple balloons and targets at the same location as the NYU group operated from at Alamogordo AAF. Professor Moore expressed surprise at seeing this, since his was the only balloon test group in the area. He stated, "It appears that there was some type of umbrella cover story to protect our work with Mogul." Although the Air Force did not find documented evidence that General Ramey was directed to espouse the notion of a weather balloon in his press conference, he may have done so either because he was aware of Project Mogul and was trying to deflect interest from it, or he readily perceived the material to be a weather balloon based on the identification from his weather officer, Major Newton. In either case, the materials recovered by the AAF in July, 1947, were not readily recognizable as anything special (only the purpose was special) and the recovered debris itself was unclassified. Additionally, the press dropped its interest in the matter as quickly as it had jumped on it. Hence there would be no particular reason to further document what quickly became a non-event.

'The interview with Colonel Trakowski also proved valuable information. Trakowski provided specific details on Project Mogul and described how the security for the programme was set up, as he was formerly the TOP SECRET control officer for the programme. He further revealed that many of the original radar targets that were produced around the end of World War Two were fabricated by toy or novelty companies using a purplish-pink tape with flower and heart symbols on it. Trakowski also recounted a conversation that he had with his friend and superior military officer in his chain of command, Colonel Marcellus Duffy, in July, 1947. Duffy formerly held Trakowski's position on Mogul, but had subsequently been transferred to Wright Field. He stated: "Colonel Duffy called me on the telephone from Wright Field and gave me a story about a fellow that had come in from New Mexico, woke him up in the middle of the night or some such thing with a handful of debris, and wanted him, Colonel Duffy, to identify it . . . He just said, 'It sure looks like some of the stuff you've been launching at Alamogordo' and he described it, and I said, 'Yes, I think it is.' Certainly Colonel Duffy knew enough about radar targets, radiosondes, balloon-borne weather devices. He was intimately familiar with all that apparatus."

'Attempts were made to locate Colonel Duffy but it was ascertained that he had died. His widow explained that, although he had amassed a large amount of personal papers relating to his Air Force activities, she had recently disposed of these items. Likewise, it was learned that A.P. Crary was also deceased; however his surviving spouse had a number of his papers from his balloon-testing days, including his professional journal from the period in question. She provided the Air Force researchers with this material.

'During the period the Air Force conducted this research, it was discovered that several others had also discovered the possibility that the "Roswell Incident" may have been generated by the recovery of a Project Mogul balloon device. These persons included Professor Charles Moore, Robert Todd and, coincidentally, Karl Pflock, a researcher who is married to a staffer who works for Congressman Schiff.

'Some of these persons suggested where documentation might be located in various archives, histories, and libraries. A review of Freedom of Information Act (FOIA) requests revealed that Robert Todd, particularly, had become aware of Project Mogul several years earlier and had doggedly obtained from the USAF, through the FOIA, a large amount of material pertaining to it; long before the AAZD researchers independently seized on the same possibility.

'Most interestingly, as this report was being written, Pflock published his own report of the matter under the auspices of FUFOR, entitled "Roswell in Perspective" (1994). Pflock concluded from his research that the Brazel ranch debris originally reported as a "flying disc" was probably debris from a Mogul balloon; however, there was a simultaneous incident that occurred not far away, that caused an alien craft to crash and that the AAF subsequently recovered three alien bodies therefrom. Air Force research did not locate any information to corroborate that this incredible coincidence occurred, however.

'OTHER RESEARCH

In the attempt to uncover additional information, a number of other steps were taken. First, assistance was requested from various museums and other archives to obtain information and/or examples of the actual balloons and radar targets used in connection with Project Mogul and to correlate them with the various descriptions of wreckage and materials recovered. The blueprints for the "Pilot Balloon Target ML307C/AP Assembly" (generically the radar target assembly) were located at the Army Signal Corps museum at Fort Monmouth and obtained. This blueprint provides the specification for the foil material, tape, wood, eyelets and string used and the assembly instructions thereto. An actual device was also obtained for study with the assistance of Professor Moore. (The example actually procured was a 1953-manufactured model "C" as compared to the Model B which was in use in 1947. Professor Moore related the differences were minor.) An examination of this device revealed it to be simply made of an aluminum colored foil like material over a stronger paper like material, attached to balsa wood sticks, affixed with tape, glue, and twine. When folded, the device is in a series of triangles, the largest being four foot by two feet ten inches. The smallest triangle section measures two feet by two feet ten inches. [Compare these figures with descriptions provided by Lieutenant Colonel Cavitt and others, as well as photos of the wreckage.] Additionally, the researchers obtained from the Archives of the University of Texas–Arlington (UTA), a set of original [i.e. first-generation] prints of the photographs taken at the same time by the Fort Worth Star Telegram that depicted Ramey and Marcel with the wreckage. A close review of these photos [and a set of first-generation negatives also subsequently obtained from UTA] revealed several interesting observations.

'First, although in some of the literature cited above, Marcel allegedly stated that he had his photograph taken with the "real" UFO wreckage and then it was subsequently removed and the weather balloon wreckage substituted for it, a comparison shows that the same wreckage appeared in the photos of Marcel and Ramey. The photos also depicted that this material was lying on what appeared to be some sort of wrapping paper [consistent with the affidavit of crew member Robert Porter, above]. It was also noted that in the two photos of Ramey, he held a piece of paper in his hand. In one it was folded over so nothing could be seen. In the second, however, there appears to be text printed on the paper. In an attempt to read this text to determine if it could shed any further light on locating documents relating to this matter, the photo was sent to a national level organization for digitizing and subsequent photo interpretation and analysis. This organization was also asked to scrutinize the digitized photos for any indication of the flowered tape (or "hieroglyphics," depending on the point of view) that were reputed to be visible to some of the persons who observed the wreckage prior to it getting to Fort Worth. This organization reported on July 20, 1994, that even after digitizing, the photos were of insufficient quality to visualize either of the details for analysis. This organization was able to obtain measurements from the 'sticks' visible in the debris after it was ascertained by an interview of the original photographer what kind of camera he used. The results of this process are provided in Atch 33, along with a reference diagram and the photo from which the measurements were made. All these measurements are compatible with the wooden materials used in the radar target previously described.

'CONCLUSION

The Air Force did not locate or develop any information that the "Roswell Incident" was a UFO event. All available official materials, although they do not directly address Roswell per se, indicate that the most likely source of the wreckage recovered from the Brazel Ranch was from one of the Project Mogul balloon trains. Although that project was TOP SECRET at the time, there was no specific indication found to indicate that an official pre-planned cover-story was in place to explain an event such as that which ultimately happened. It appears that the identification of the wreckage as being part of a weather balloon device, as reported in the newspapers at the time, was based on the fact that there was no physical difference in the radar targets and the neoprene balloons (other than the numbers and configuration) between Mogul balloons and normal weather balloons. Additionally, it seems that there was over-reaction by Colonel Blanchard and Major Marcel, in originally reporting that a "flying disc" had been recovered when, at that time, nobody knew for sure what that term even meant since it had only been in use for a couple of weeks.

'Likewise there was no indication in official records from the period that there was heightened military operational or security activity which should have been generated if this was in fact the first recovery of materials and/or persons from another world. The post-war US military (or today's, for that matter) did not have the capability to rapidly identify, recover, coordinate, cover-up, and quickly minimize public scrutiny of such an event. The claim that they did so without leaving even a little bit of a suspicious paper trail for 47 years is incredible.

'It should also be noted here that there was little mention in this report about the recovery of the so-called "alien bodies". This is for several reasons: First, the recovered wreckage was from a Project Mogul balloon. There were no "alien" passengers therein. Secondly, the pro-UFO groups who espouse the alien bodies theories cannot even agree among themselves as to what, how many, and where, such bodies were supposedly recovered. Additionally, some of these claims have been shown to be hoaxes, even by other UFO researchers. Thirdly, when such claims are made, they are often attributed to people using pseudonyms or who otherwise do not want to be publicly identified, presumably so that some sort of retribution cannot be taken against them (notwithstanding that nobody has been shown to have died, disappeared or otherwise suffered at the hands of the government during the last 47 years). Fourth, many of the persons making the biggest claims of "alien bodies" make their living from the "Roswell Incident". While having a commercial interest in something does not automatically make it suspect, it does raise interesting questions related to authenticity. Such persons should be encouraged to present their evidence (not speculation) directly to the government and provide all pertinent details and evidence to support their claims if honest fact-finding is what is wanted. Lastly, persons who have come forward and provided their names and made claims, may have, in good faith but in the "fog of time," misinterpreted past events. The review of Air Force records did not locate even one piece of evidence to indicate that the Air Force had any part in an "alien" body recovery operation or continuing cover-up.

'During the course of this effort, the Air Force has kept in close touch with the GAO and responded to their various queries and requests for assistance. This report was generated as an official response to the GAO, and to document the considerable effort expended by the Air Force on their behalf. It is anticipated that they will request a copy of this report to help formulate the formal report of their efforts. It is recommended that this document serve as the final Air Force report related to the Roswell matter, for the GAO, or any other inquiries.'

The report is signed by Richard L. Weaver, Colonel, USAF, Director, Security and Special Program Oversight.

While the Project Mogul explanation is convincing at a number of levels, not least the correspondence between the various eyewitness descriptions of the nature of the material and the components of the balloon assembly relating to foil, balsa-wood, rubber materials etc, the Air Force points out that the balloon itself was no different, in the materials it contained, from any other balloon. Marcel and anyone else at the base must have been familiar with weather balloons. Major Marcel, when interviewed, stated that he was and his son is scornful of the notion that his father would not have recognized one. Either they were so mistaken as to have made a misidentification bordering on negligence, or they did indeed recover something else and the Air Force is either continuing a cover-up or is itself not privy to documents and intelligence that provide an alternative explanation for the Roswell Incident. It is also worth noting that the Air Force has been fairly selective in its choice of witnesses. This is understandable, but it does not appear to have interviewed any of those people who have supplied other descriptions of the material or ordinary people such as Phyllis McGuire, the daughter of Sheriff Wilcox, who recalls her mother describing the recovery of bodies from a craft.

Nor has the Air Force bothered to deal with the claims of former personnel such as Frank Kaufmann. It would have surely been in its interests to discredit him, yet it does not refer to his statements, which should have been available, although it is possible that it was unaware of them. In addition, those who are sceptical about the truth-telling records of government institutions may detect an ambiguity about the repeated reference to the inability to 'locate' documents. If the whole incident revolves around nothing more than a balloon, it seems strange that in an environment where reports and memoranda are the daily routine of military life, nothing should have been 'located' to either prove or disprove what occurred in Roswell in the summer of 1947.

If the Air Force was unable to discover any documents about Roswell, then perhaps the GAO would fare better. Its brief was, after all, far more wide-ranging and it had the ability to search archives of not only the Air Force but other agencies which might have been involved. After a year of what must have been exhaustive enquiries the General Accounting Office published the results of its investigation.

5

Following the disappointing, at least for ufologists, USAF report, an eager sense of anticipation preceded publication of the findings of the General Accounting Office. In the weeks before the GAO was ready to release its report, rumours were flying as to what might have been discovered. These ranged from suggestions that, at last, proof would emerge that the US government had been engaged in a massive cover-up and conspiracy to keep secret from the American public the fact that for nearly half a century they had been sitting upon incontrovertible proof of existence of life-forms from another planet, that bodies were kept in a special form of cryogenic suspension in a secret hangar on the Wright Patterson airbase, in a location known as the 'Blue Room', to rumours that the GAO would report that there was no evidence of anything at all having happened at Roswell in the summer of 1947.

The GAO's findings were finally made public in a slim document in July 1995. The cover stated that it was a 'United States General Accounting Office Report to the Honorable Steven H. Schiff, House of Representatives: Government Records Results of a Search for Records Concerning the 1947 Crash near Roswell, New Mexico.' The first page consisted of a letter from the 'National Security and International Affairs Division to the Honorable Steven H. Schiff'. This stated: 'On July 8 1947, the Roswell Army Airfield (RAAF) public information office in Roswell, New Mexico, reported the crash and recovery of a "flying disc". Army Air Forces personnel from the RAAF's 509th Bomb Group were credited with the recovery. The following day, the press reported that the Commanding General of the US Eighth Air Force, Fort Worth, Texas, announced that RAAF personnel had recovered a crashed radar tracking (weather) balloon, not a "flying disc".

'After nearly fifty years, speculation continues on what crashed at Roswell. Some observers believe that the object was of extraterrestrial origin. In the July 1994 Report of the Air Force Regarding the Roswell Incident, the Air Force did not dispute that something happened near Roswell, but reported that the most likely source of the wreckage was from a balloon-launched classified government project designed to determine the state of Soviet nuclear weapons research. The debate on what crashed at Roswell continues.

'Concerned that the Department of Defense (DOD) may not have provided you with all available information on the crash, you asked us to determine the requirements for reporting air accidents similar to the crash near Roswell and identify any government records concerning the Roswell crash.

'We conducted an extensive search for government records related to the crash near Roswell. We examined a wide range of classified and unclassified documents dating from July 1947 through the 1950s. These records came from numerous organizations in New Mexico and elsewhere throughout DOD as well as the Federal Bureau of Investigation (FBI), the Central Intelligence Agency (CIA), and the National Security Council. The full scope and methodology of our work are detailed at the end of this report.

'RESULTS IN BRIEF
In 1947 Army regulations required that air accident reports be maintained permanently. We identified four air accidents reported by the Army Air Forces in New Mexico during July 1947. All of the accidents involved military aircraft and occurred after July 8, 1947 – the date the RAAF public information office first reported the crash and recovery of a "flying disc" near Roswell. The Navy reported no air accidents in New Mexico during July 1947, there was no requirement to prepare a report on the crash of a weather balloon.

'In our search for records concerning the Roswell crash, we learned that some government records covering RAAF activities had been destroyed and others had not. For example, RAAF administrative records (from March 1947 through Dec. 1949) were destroyed. The document disposition form does not indicate what organization or person destroyed the records and when or under what authority the records were destroyed.

'Our search for government records concerning the Roswell crash yielded two records originating in 1947 – a July 1947 history report by the combined 509th Bomb Group and RAAF and an FBI teletype message dated July 8, 1947. The 509th–RAAF report noted the recovery of a "flying disc" that was later determined by military officials to be a radar tracking balloon. The FBI message stated that the military had reported that an object resembling a high altitude weather balloon with a radar reflector had been recovered near Roswell.

'The other government records we reviewed, including those previously withheld from the public because of security classification, and the Air Force's analysis of unidentified flying objects sightings from 1946 to 1950 (Project Blue Book Special report No.14), did not mention the crash or the recovery of an airborne object near Roswell in July 1947. Similarly, executive branch agencies' responses to our letters of inquiry produced no other government records on the Roswell crash.

'According to press accounts from July 1947, Army Air Forces personnel from RAAF were involved in the recovery of an airborne object near Roswell. Therefore, if an air accident report was prepared, it should have been prepared in accordance with Army regulations. According to an Army records management official, in 1947 Army regulations required that air accident reports be maintained permanently. An Air Force official said there was no similar requirement to report a weather balloon crash. According to an Air Force official who has worked in the records management field since the mid-1940s, air accident reports prepared in July 1947 under Army regulations should have been transferred to Air Force custody in September 1947, when the Air Force was established as a separate service.

'The Air Force Safety Agency is responsible for maintaining reports of air accidents. We examined its microfilm records to determine whether any air accidents had been reported in New Mexico during this time period. All of the accidents involved military fighter or cargo aircraft and occurred after July 8, 1947 – the date the RAAF public information office first reported the crash and recovery of a "flying disc" near Roswell. According to the Army Air Forces' Report of Major Accident, these four accidents occurred at or near the towns of Hobbs, Albuquerque, Carrizozo, and Alamogordo, New Mexico. Only one of the four accidents resulted in a fatality. The pilot died when the aircraft crashed during an attempted take-off.

'In searching for government records on the Roswell crash, we were particularly interested in identifying and reviewing records of military units assigned to RAAF in 1947 – to include the 509th Bomb Group, the 1st Air Transport Unit, the 427th Army Air Force Base Unit, and the 1395th Military Police Company (Aviation).

'Document disposition forms obtained from the National Personnel Records Center in St Louis, Missouri, indicate that in 1953, the Walker Air Force base (formerly RAAF) records officer transferred to the Army's Kansas City records depository the histories of units stationed at Walker Air Force Base. These histories included the 509th Bomb Group and RAAF for February 1947 through October 1947; the 1st Air Transport Unit for July 1946 through June 1947; and the 427th Army Air Force Base Unit for January 1946 to February 1947. We could not locate any documentation indicating that records of the 1395th Military Police Company (Aviation) were ever retired to the National Personnel Records Center or its predecessor depositories.

'The July 1947 history for the 509th Bomb Group and RAAF stated that the RAAF public information office "was kept quite busy . . . answering inquiries on the 'flying disc' which was reported to be in [the] possession of the 509th Bomb Group. The object turned out to be a radar tracking balloon."

'By his signature, the RAAF's commanding officer certified that the report represented a complete and accurate account of RAAF activities in July 1947.

'In addition to unit history reports, we also searched for other government records on the Roswell crash. In this regard, the Chief Archivist for the National Personnel Records Center provided us with documentation indicating that (1) RAAF records such as finance and accounting, supplies, buildings and grounds, and other general administrative matters from March 1945 through December 1949 and (2) RAAF outgoing messages from October 1946 through December 1949 were destroyed. According to this official, the document disposition form did not properly indicate the authority under which the disposal action was taken. The Center's Chief Archivist stated that from his personal experience, many of the Air Force organizational records covering this time period were destroyed without entering a citation for the governing disposition authority. Our review of records control forms showing the destruction of other records – including outgoing RAAF messages for 1950 – supports the Chief Archivist's viewpoint.

'During our review of records at FBI headquarters, we found a

July 8, 1947 teletype message from the FBI office in Dallas, Texas to FBI headquarters and the FBI office in Cincinnati, Ohio. An FBI spokesperson confirmed the authenticity of the message. According to the message, an Eighth Air Force headquarters official had telephonically informed the FBI's Dallas office of the recovery near Roswell of a hexagonal shaped disc suspended from a large balloon by cable. The message further stated that the disc and balloon were being sent to Wright Field (now Wright-Patterson Air Force Base, Ohio) for examination. According to the Eighth Air Force Official, the recovered object resembled a high-altitude weather balloon with a radar reflector. The message stated that no further investigation by the FBI was being conducted.

'To follow up on the July 8 message, we reviewed microfilm abstracts of the FBI Dallas and Cincinnati office activities for July 1947. An abstract prepared by the FBI Dallas office on July 12, 1947 summarized the particulars of the July 8 message. There was no mention in the Cincinnati office abstracts of the crash or recovery of an airborne object near Roswell.

'Because the FBI message reported that the debris from the Roswell crash was being transported to Wright Field for examination, we attempted to determine whether military regulations existed for handling such debris. We were unable to locate any applicable regulation. As a final step, we reviewed Air Materiel Command (Wright Field) records from 1947 to 1950 for evidence of command personnel involvement in this matter. We found no records mentioning the Roswell crash or the examination by Air Materiel Command personnel of any debris recovered from the crash.

'We sent letters to several federal agencies asking for any government records they might have concerning the Roswell crash. In this regard, we contacted DOD, the National Security Council, the White House Office of Science and Technology Policy, the CIA, the FBI, and the Department of Energy.'

Not surprisingly, all of the above federal agencies replied that (with the exception of the FBI document previously mentioned) there were no documents or records in their files. The GAO admits, 'We did not independently verify the information provided to us in their written responses.' While it appears all too convenient that any records that might have offered some illumination have disappeared or been destroyed, the GAO points out that this was not an uncommon practice.

One can't help but conclude that even if the 'flying disc' never existed, there would have been some form of report, still existing in some archive somewhere, concerning how a balloon could have been mistaken for a 'flying disc'. Someone somewhere must have been concerned that someone somewhere else alerted the world's press to the recovery of a 'flying disc' only for it to turn out to be a balloon.

It raises the question of how such a press release could have been issued with such scant regard for checking the facts. The public information officer who released the report in 1947 is still alive and, although he does not feature in the official Air Force Report of 1994, he is highly approachable and spoke at length about the few days that he was involved with the story.

Walter Haut still lives in Roswell. He and his wife have a green, wooden-fronted house in a smart suburb of Roswell, not far from the house where Jesse Marcel lived in 1947. Haut is a devout Christian and he and his wife are loyal supporters of their local church. One could not expect to meet a more normal and average American than this retired military officer.

One of the first questions I asked Haut was about the levels of security at the base itself. 'It was a very tight security out at the base,' he remembers. 'To give you an example, I was a bombardier and navigator, I flew thirty-eight missions against Japan. I dropped the glass-gauged instruments into the explosion at Bikini and I could not get near any aircraft that had a configuration to handle an atomic bomb in its bomb bay. With my experience, my whole background, I still didn't have clearance enough to get near an aeroplane that could carry an atomic weapon, so I could not see what ever kind of armament they had, how the bomb racks were and what the whole of the inside of the bomb bay was. It was a very tightly run operation. If you needed to know you were told; if you didn't need to know, don't bother to ask because they wouldn't tell you! Everybody had to have a pass to get on to the base. You needed further passes to get on to the flight line and then you needed a further pass in order to get near the aircraft. It was amongst the highest classifications as far as security was concerned.'

Despite the strict security, there were areas of the base that were accessible to traders and wives of serving personnel, such as the commissary and the hospital. More secure areas were heavily fenced, with military police standing guard.

One of Haut's duties was to foster good relations with the local people. 'One of Colonel Blanchard's first duty assignments when he got out of West Point was to serve as a Public Relations Officer. He understood the relationship between a community and base. He told me to get involved with the community. If they needed a truck for a parade or, you know, most anything they wanted, we could supply it to them within reason . . . if they were having a Fourth of July production down Main Street, could we send our planes to kind of buzz their parade. There were a lot of things that we could do that normally didn't come under public relations. We were striving to get a whole mingling between the civilians and the military and break down the barriers that you have in so many communities that have military and civilian thrown together and it worked real well.'

Part of the job involved relations with the local newspapers and radio stations. 'Anything that we were doing that appeared to be newsworthy, it was up to me to get it put on to the two newspapers and turned over to radio stations. That was the extent of our news media. Two radio stations, two newspapers, and that's what we did: we turned out press releases, we had their personnel come out to the base on special occasions and let them shoot a lot of pictures and do what ever they wanted to do within certain areas. We didn't let them go out and take pictures of the bomb base or B–29s, for example. We were working very hard to get a good relationship going and ultimately that's what we got . . . I could pick up the phone and call the Mayor and tell him, "I wanna do this, can you get it cleared with the City Council?" "Go ahead." They wanted something, they called myself or Colonel Blanchard and said, "Gosh, we could use a . . ." "You got it." It became a very close working relationship between the community and the base.'

Amid the routine of maintaining good relations between town and base, Haut remembers clearly a day that was out of the ordinary for him: the day the release went out about the 'flying disc'. 'I would have to say it was the morning of July 8, when I was told to put out a press release stating that we had in our possession a flying saucer and that Major Marcel, the Group Intelligence Officer, was flying parts of it to Fort Worth. I have to smile when I say that because in the press release we stated that Major Marcel flew the material to Fort Worth. The first phone call I got when I got back to the base after delivering this release to the foreign news media happened to come from London, England and this fella in this typical very heavy English accent: "How did he know how to fly it?" and I had to explain to him they put the pieces in an airplane and the airplane was flown to Eighth Air Force – just one of those little slips you make and you don't look at the exact words. Oh, he was all ready to jump all over me and ask me a bunch of questions about who knew how to fly it? What kind of propulsion? All that . . . !'

I tried to discover from Walter Haut how exactly the press release had originated and who had written it. He answered, 'I was instructed by Colonel Blanchard to put out a press release which in effect stated that we had in our possession a flying saucer and that it was being flown to Eighth Air Force Headquarters, Fort Worth, and that was around noon time of July 8.' I was also curious to know who exactly had written the actual release, Haut or Blanchard? 'I can't honestly answer that,' replied Haut. 'In a lot of instances Colonel Blanchard would have it all typed and say, "Here's what I want . . ." At times he would call me on the phone and say, "Haut, here's what I want you to put in the press release, I want you to get it out right now" or whatever circumstances happened to be surrounding it. It's possible that he had it typed up in his office and I went by and picked it up . . . basically, Colonel Blanchard had the authority to put out just about anything he wanted. I say almost anything he wanted. He could not put out information relative to the fact that we had three atomic weapons on the base – things of a secret nature, he would have had to clear that with the Eighth Air Force and they in turn, depending on how important it was, could either say go ahead or we've gotta keep on going up the chain until we can find out a yes or a no answer.'

This invites the question of whether a press release which reported the capture of a 'flying disc', a matter which even in 1947 would have had national security implications and international repercussions, would have been issued on the authority of Blanchard without being referred higher up the chain of command. Haut thinks it is quite possible that it was not Blanchard who sanctioned the press release. 'I honestly don't think that Colonel Blanchard was the one that authorized the press release. My feeling is that material had gone to General Ramey's office and probably to Higher Headquarters, beyond Eighth Air Force, and this whole thing was an orchestrated plan to have the local base commander in all his naïveté say, "We have in our possession a flying saucer" and then the next higher ranking officer, General Ramey, says, "Oh! You're wrong. It was a weather balloon." They had seen this material prior to the eighth [of July], so I feel that they had time to, as I said, orchestrate a plan to how best present it to the public and then be able to come back and say, "Oh no, a mistake was made" and this is my own feeling as to what happened. They just felt that they could go ahead and broadcast the fact that we had it and then come back and say, "Oh, they didn't know any better. That's a new type of weather balloon" and that's everybody off. Nobody got excited about a weather balloon crashing out there.'

There is certainly some logic to Haut's theory. Given the normally cautious and secretive approach of the military, it is unlikely that it would issue any press release without first making absolutely sure that it was approved and was what it intended to say. This would apply whether it was a genuine 'flying disc' or whether it was a balloon. What seems less likely, yet is what we are expected to believe, is that a press release would be issued about something the Air Force had in its possession, without someone somewhere being fairly sure that what was being said was correct. In other words, the material that was collected by Jesse Marcel, whatever it was, would surely have been studied and examined and analysed *before* any press release, not after. Haut remembers the description that he heard from Jesse Marcel about the nature of the material that had been picked up.

'The material has been described to me by Major Marcel and his son: material that you could wrinkle up in your hand and let go of it and it'd go back out in exactly the same condition it was when you first started. I don't think in 1947 that we had anything like that in our possession, materials that had ability to return to normal form. I don't think we've got anything like that today – a piece of foil that you can wrinkle up and let go and it goes back to a flat surface. Maybe there is something in one of the laboratories someplace in some highly technical organization, but I really don't think that we have this type of material as Major Marcel described to me. And I-beams: about three-eighths to a half-inch beam that they hit with a twelve-pound sledge. They put it on one of these concrete car stops and a fella wound up and hit that with a twelve-pound sledge hammer and the sledge hammer bounced off. That's pretty potent material, and as far as weight was concerned it had a strength beyond anything that they could imagine.'

Haut is convinced that the materials described could not have been anything that America had in existence at the time. He says that he discussed this point with both Major Marcel and his son. 'I talked to both of 'em, quite some length. They both come up with almost the same stories. I feel very strongly about the fact that they do tell a little different stories. Like one says it was a light lavender, the other one says it was a light orchid colour, a three-eighth inch I-beam, or a half-inch I-beam . . . that to me is convincing.' Haut thinks that the discrepancies between their accounts, and presumably those of other participants as well, adds credibility to the story they are telling. But I wondered what he made of the Air Force report confirming that it was a balloon from Project Mogul and that therefore Marcel must have been mistaken or somewhat mentally unstable. Although a retired Air Force officer who fought for his country in the Second World War, Haut is sceptical. 'Well, all they've really done is give us a new balloon or different balloon. Insofar as his mental capacity, he was the Intelligence Officer out at the base; he was not taken off that duty assignment. His son who was a rather precocious twelve-year-old, has pretty much the same remembrance of the physical properties of this material. I think that probably when we start getting closer to the fiftieth anniversary of this crash we'll probably have another balloon or something; they'll find another thing that they can come out and try to refute. The two of them were friends who I could place a lot of confidence in. I know other witnesses. Loretta Proctor up at Corona handled the material. There are a number of them, and they all come up with about the same explanation as to the physical properties of the material. If they all came up with exactly the same we'd have reason to be suspect but if there are differences, as you would have with any group of people that had seen something happen forty-eight years ago, they're not going to remember everything exactly the same.'

I pointed out to Haut that exactly the same point could be made, and was made quite effectively in the Air Force Report, to support the balloon theory. 'Ah,' he replied. 'Did they in that report state that the foil-like material could not be pierced with a sharp knife, a sliver could not be taken off the I-beam? They just come out with those things that fit their story.'

Although Haut readily admits that he has little direct knowledge from the time of the incident, he has spoken to many people, some of whom were directly involved, since the whole episode first began. 'I believe from all I can gather,' he concludes, 'the crash actually occurred about 11.30 or so on the night of the Fourth of July. The military got out on the fifth and cleaned up the debris of the crash site. Everything would have been fine until Mac Brazel come into the sheriff's office with a whole bunch of material that was so unique, light in weight and they had to come up with something so they just figured that they'd have a good scenario here and just admit that, yes, we have this crashed saucer in our possession and that all this emanates from our base and five hours later the people on high say, "Oh no! You're wrong: it's a weather balloon." That's a way to cover it up. Had they initially stated this is a weather balloon it would be hard to convince these people that went out there and picked up material. The rancher said he'd showed it to them in the light, it'd be real difficult for them to accept it, but when you come out with a story admitting to it and then saying from a Higher Headquarters, coming back and saying, "We know actually about this type of weather balloon. It's part of operation such and so . . ." or whatever excuses they gave – it was a real sleight of hand trick almost.'

Curiously, Haut says that he did not speak to Jesse Marcel at the time about whatever it was that he had recovered but that he did talk to him about it in 1980, thirty-three years later! He told Haut that 'in essence the material that he picked up was not of this earth. Very adamant. I started to ask him questions like, "Are you sure, Jess?" There were lots of progress going on during those years where things were happening so fast that we had developed an atomic weapon . . . And he would get to a point where – he was a relatively small man – I thought he was gonna crawl on my frame if I kept questioning his integrity and he was very very definitive about it: "This was not of this earth."'

Haut remembers meeting Jesse Marcel on two occasions. Both times Marcel had been brought back to Roswell by TV stations filming reports on Roswell. 'After they finished out at the crash site, he and I went to the Roswell Inn – that's where he was staying – and we sat and talked for about three hours and another outfit brought him back in about two years later and we went through the same routine. He never changed his attitude about it.

'He was very, very definitive, there was no doubt in his mind about it: this is what happened, this is what I saw, this is what it was like, and he'd just get uptight and you start pushing him into a corner: "Oh, Jesse, it was probably something that they'd built up at Sandia or someplace else and they were playing around with it down there." "No, it wasn't . . ." And we used to almost fight about it!'

Haut also remembers that Marcel told him that the material featured in the photograph with General Ramey was definitely not what he found and had flown to Fort Worth. 'General Ramey had Major Marcel in his office and had him get down on a knee and hold pieces of a weather balloon and say this is what I found out on the ranch and Jesse says, "This is not what I brought in; that was a weather balloon," he said. "I knew what a weather balloon is." But that was the picture that went out.'

The former public information officer recalls that Marcel told him that he felt he had been put in an untenable position by having to pose with something that he knew to be false. He is convinced that Marcel was telling the truth. 'I think it was a cover-up just to bury the whole thing,' claims Haut, who also believes that the reports of the bodies of aliens are also probably true, even though he has no direct evidence. He trusts the account given by Glenn Dennis.

Although Jesse Marcel is dead, most of those who knew him, including Haut and his son, are adamant that he could not have made such a basic mistake as to erroneously identify a weather balloon, whether it was the radar target section or anything else attached to it, as being material from outer space. It certainly seems highly unlikely, as does the fact that no one else appears to have examined the find before the press release. Fortunately, Marcel was interviewed by both television stations and researchers before he died, so it is possible to get an idea of what he remembered about the incident.

By all accounts Marcel had a good service record both before and after the Roswell Incident. He had entered the US Army Air Force in 1942, serving as an aide to a general, before enrolling at Air Intelligence School in Harrisburg, Pennsylvania under Commanding Officer Colonel Egmont Koenig. His expertise was then used in mapping and photographic reconnaissance and interpretation and he stayed on as an instructor before being assigned to combat duties in the South Pacific, where he served as the Squadron Intelligence Officer. Marcel had been flying since 1928 and undertook several combat missions in B-24s. He was promoted to Group Intelligence Officer and sent back to America shortly before the atomic bomb was dropped on Hiroshima. He was taking part in a radar navigation course at Langley Field when the 509th dropped the bomb, and then reassigned to the Eighth Air Force and to Roswell as the Intelligence Officer for the Bomb Group. One of his first assignments was as an observer of the atomic bomb tests at Bikini. He remembers the Roswell Incident well enough but was unclear on the dates in one interview with a local television station: 'It was in July 1947. I was in my office when I got a call from the sheriff in Roswell.' This was Sheriff Wilcox, who told Marcel that he had been contacted by Mac Brazel, who had come to town to sell wool from the sheep he had just sheared but had visited the sheriff about something that had crashed on the Foster ranch either the day before or a few days before. The sheriff wondered whether Major Marcel would be interested in investigating what might have happened. 'Well, fine,' said Marcel. 'Where can I meet him?' The sheriff told Marcel that Brazel was in his office at that very moment and that he was going to leave about 3.30 or 4 p.m. and invited the major over. Marcel spoke to Brazel and ascertained that there was quite a large amount of debris, so he returned to the base to report the matter to Colonel Blanchard, who recommended that he take one of the CIC (Counter Intelligence Corps) agents with him to explore the area. Marcel was unable to recall the name of the officer who accompanied him but they set off in a jeep carry-all following Brazel's pick-up truck across country before arriving at the ranch shortly before dusk, by which time it was too dark to do anything, so they spent the night in a small shack and set out the following morning. 'We started picking up fragments,' said Marcel, 'which was foreign to me. I'd never seen anything like that. I didn't know what we were picking up. To this day, I still don't know what it was and I brought as much of it as I could back to the base and some ingenious young GI thought he'd try to put a few pieces together and see if he could match something. I don't think he ever matched two pieces, it was so fragmented it was strewn over a wide area. I guess maybe three quarters of a mile long and a few hundred feet wide, so we loaded and came back to the base. In the meantime we had an eager-beaver public relations officer, he found out about it, he calls AP about it then that's when it really hit the fan. I probably got telephone calls from everywhere, new reporters were trying to come in to talk to me – but I had nothing for them, I couldn't tell them anything. They wanted to see the stuff, which I couldn't show them. My CO early the next morning sent me to Carswell.'

It was at Carswell that the famous photo–opportunity took place. Despite evidence from others that he was 'set up', there appears to be no comment from Marcel himself about exactly what happened. Nor does he appear to have made any statements regarding either the recovery of aliens or the actual craft. In his later television interview, Marcel implies that it could have been the hasty overreaction of Walter

Haut that precipitated the 'flying saucer' legend. Yet Haut himself confirms that the press release would have to have been approved by the Commanding Officer, Colonel Blanchard, or even that it was dreamt up by 'Higher Headquarters' as the first shot in a campaign of disinformation. Doubts have also been raised about Marcel's war record and the number of missions that he flew, although any discrepancies may be due to misreporting rather than not telling the truth. Nevertheless, one of the frustrations of the story is that Marcel is no longer around to be interviewed.

6

Ufologists who researched the story in the late 1970s also unearthed several other witnesses of bright lights in the sky and, more importantly, came to the conclusion that there were two sites: the debris site and the crash site. The debris site was where the wreckage was recovered from the Foster ranch and the crash site was where the craft itself finally came to rest – possibly at the location described by Frank Kaufmann. This would then mean that there were two separate military operations to collect the material from both sites and bring them back to the base.

Another possibility, and again there is some circumstantial evidence for this (in the accounts of Kaufmann and the conjecture of Haut) is that the crash site was chanced upon almost immediately by a military recovery team from the 509th base, possibly augmented by teams from Alamogordo and/or military police units who could have been drafted in from anywhere – for example, Los Alamos or Sandia, the top-secret research establishment just outside Albuquerque. This would have the recovery team sweeping everything up from the desert site near Roswell and, as Kaufmann claims, bringing it all back to the base. While this was being done, towards the middle of June (Brazel's date for first finding the debris was June 14) or the beginning of July, there would have been time to concoct an elaborate disinformation campaign to protect the secret of the recovery of the craft from the crash site. The plan would have been to announce the recovery of debris from the Foster ranch, which would allay the suspicions of all those who were involved in the recovery from the crash site and others who had picked up rumours and gossip along the way; only to then put into operation the second stage of the plan, which was simply to display the balloon fragments in General Ramey's office at Carswell Air Force base in Forth Worth, Texas, the HQ of the Eighth Air Force. Admittedly rather far-fetched, this theory has nevertheless found fairly wide acceptance in the UFO community. But whether it is true or false, there is no doubt that the Air Force was capable of mounting such an exercise at that time. After all, it had just come out of the Second World War, where skilful propaganda and disinformation were at an absolute premium in its efforts to save lives and deceive the enemy.

This theory would also explain the lack of records, as it is unlikely that such an overt act of deception would be committed to paper, for the object of the exercise was to cover up the incident and create a degree of confusion. Additional support is lent to this idea by Marcel's own account, told over thirty years later to the *American Reporter* for its piece on the Roswell Incident.

Marcel is asked how far along the ground the actual debris stretched into the distance. 'About as far as you could see,' the 509th Intelligence Officer recalled. 'Three quarters of a mile long and two hundred to three hundred feet width. One thing I did notice,' he added significantly, 'nothing actually hit the ground, bounced on the ground. It was something that must have exploded above ground and fell . . . scattered all over. Just like you'd explode something above the ground and just fall to the ground. One thing I was impressed with was that it was obvious you could just about determine which direction it came from and which direction it was heading. It was travelling from north-east to south-west, it was in that pattern, you could tell where it started and where it ended by how it thinned out. Although I did not cover the entire area this stuff was in, I could tell that it was thicker where we first started looking and it was thinning out as we went south-west and *I learned later that farther west, towards Carrizozo, they found something like that, too.*' (author's italics)

Marcel's recollection is echoed by many other accounts of a separate crash site. Some are credible, such as Kaufmann's chronicle of events, while others veer towards the outlandish, many feeding off the account that has gone before to add detail and a veneer of credibility. But even the existence of two sites still does not add up to incontrovertible evidence or even a strong suggestion of a visitation from outer space.

Fortunately Marcel, along with other witnesses, was asked about alternative scenarios for the crash site and the subsequent events.

When asked about the possibility that they could have mistaken the debris for some sort of experimental craft or a V-2 rocket from White Sands, Marcel was adamant: 'Oh no! Unh unh! I've seen rockets sent up at White Sands Testing Grounds; it definitely wasn't part of an aircraft nor a missile or a rocket. I was pretty acquainted with most of the things that were in the air at the time, not only from my own military aircraft but also in a lot of foreign countries, and I still believe it was nothing from this earth. The biggest mistake I ever made, of course, I couldn't, was not able to keep a piece of it, but in all fairness to my work and the service I couldn't . . . the one thing that I kept wondering: Why no publicity was given about that by the Air Force. They probably got something they wanted to sit on, that's my opinion. There had been a lot of reports about "flying saucers" in that area. In fact, I'm not sure I would swear to this but one night about 11.30, I lived in town, the Provost Marshal called me and said, "You better come out here in a hurry." He wouldn't elaborate on the telephone what it was, so I got in my car and put my foot on the accelerator and going as fast as I could go, and it was a straight road, something caught my attention. It was a formation of lights moving from north to south, but it was so . . . I mean, we had nothing that travelled that fast anyway. I knew that! We had no aircraft that travelled at that speed because it was visible maybe only three or four seconds from overhead to the horizon . . . bright lights flying a perfect "V" formation, and I hesitated to open my mouth about that because I knew nobody would believe me but two or three days later some GI said, "I saw something in the skies the other night" and he described exactly what I had seen!'

This is an intriguing additional detail because there is no doubt that several of the local people in and around Roswell in late June and early July 1947 did spot strange lights in the sky. And it was not just in Roswell: there were sightings, extensive and multiple, all over New Mexico at around the same time. Nor was it just New Mexico, for there were myriad observations, sightings, reports, incidents and encounters with strange objects in the sky. As they built up and produced their own momentum in terms of the interest being shown by the press and radio, these occurrences rapidly became news. Eventually the crescendo of sightings and eyewitness accounts set the first wave of 'flying saucer' hysteria sweeping across the nation.

A few years later this hysteria was to be repeated, and thereafter it recurred intermittently for at least a decade. At times public excitement reached such a pitch that it was considered by the White House to pose a threat to national security. The government's response was to order the CIA and other federal agencies to report on a phenomenon that was gripping the nation like a phantom and instilling an anxiety that was all the greater because its source vanished as soon as one tried to get close to it.

The first wave of public frenzy about alien visitations, and indeed the birth of the term 'flying saucer', occurred by coincidence in the same year as the Roswell Incident.

On Tuesday June 24, 1947 a pilot who flew for both business and pleasure took off on a mission to search for the wreckage of a missing airplane in the vicinity of Chehailis and Yakima in Washington State. The pilot was Kenneth Arnold, who earned a living by selling fire-fighting equipment. Earlier that same day he had been installing some of his equipment for the Chehalis Central Air Service and got into conversation with their chief pilot, Herb Critzer, who had informed him about the mysterious case of a C-46 Marine Transport aircraft which was believed to have crashed in the vicinity of Mount Rainier but which had so far not been discovered. Arnold learned that a $5000 reward was being offered by the relatives of the crew for the discovery of the aircraft. Intrigued by what he heard, and no doubt attracted by the prospect of what in those days was a generous reward, Arnold had plotted a flight path which would take him into the area above Yakima.

At first the flight was uneventful: 'I simply sat in my plane observing the sky and the terrain . . . when a bright flash reflected on my plane.' Startled, Arnold thought that he must have flown too close to another aircraft and had encountered the reflection from its fuselage. Momentarily distracted from his mission to locate the crash area, he searched the skies. According to his own account which he later wrote down: 'I looked every place in the sky and couldn't find where the reflection had come from until I looked to the left and the north of Mount Rainier where I observed a chain of nine peculiar aircraft flying from north to south at approximately 9500 foot elevation and going, seemingly, in a definite direction of about 170 degrees.' Initially, as any pilot would, Arnold assumed that they must be a squadron of jet aircraft. He was certain that they were the source of the reflected light because 'two or three of them every few seconds would dip or change their course slightly, just enough for the sun to strike them at an angle that reflected on my plane'.

As they were at a considerable distance, Arnold was unable to identify the aircraft clearly, but as they flew in front of the snowcapped peaks of Mount Rainier, the contrasting light of the white snow enabled him to get a better picture and make out more precisely the outline and shape of the aircraft. What he saw amazed him and continued to puzzle investigators for years afterwards. 'I thought it was very peculiar that I couldn't find their tails but assumed they were some type of jet planes.' Arnold was somewhat alarmed to realize that the planes were flying so close to the top of the mountains and even more astonished to see that against the white background 'when the sun reflected from one or two or three of those units, they appeared to be completely round'.

Difficult though it is for pilots to measure size and distance in such circumstances, as an experienced pilot Arnold estimated that the objects were between twenty and twenty-five miles away. If this was correct, it meant that they would have to be fairly large in order to register within his field of vision. Comparing the objects to a bonnet fastener on his plane, he compared their size to a DC-4 on his left. The craft appeared to be smaller: 'their span would have been as wide as the furthest engines on each side of the fuselage of the DC-4.'

In an attempt to work out the speed at which they were flying, Arnold noted the time it took for them to pass between Mounts Rainier and Adams. 'As the last unit of this formation passed the southernmost high, snow-covered crest of Mount Adams, I looked at my sweep second hand and it showed that they had travelled the distance in one minute and forty-two seconds. Even at the time this timing did not upset me as I felt confident that after I would land there would be some explanation of what I saw.' In total, the flight path of the mysterious craft was in Arnold's sight for approximately three minutes. After they had disappeared from view, the intrepid pilot continued his quest for the C-46 for fifteen or twenty minutes, but his mind was no longer on the original purpose of his flight, for 'while searching for this Marine plane, what I had just observed kept going through my mind. I became more disturbed, so after taking a last look at Tieton reservoir I headed for Yakima.'

The incentive of the $5000 reward had been overtaken by the events of his memorable flight, and now Arnold was eager to return to the landing strip at Yakima Airport and discuss his adventure with the ground staff there. Perhaps, he thought, the pilots there would be able to cast some light on the mystery and review his own rough calculation of the trajectory of the craft; after all, as he recalled, 'Around airports pilots are continually arguing about how fast our Army and Navy jets and missiles really can go.'

At around four o'clock that same afternoon, Arnold arrived back at Yakima and headed for the office of Al Baxter, the general manager, to tell him the complete story. Arnold later recalled that he thought Baxter probably didn't attach much credence to his encounter and during their meeting had invited one of the pilots present to listen to Arnold's account. The pilot had remarked that he thought they could have been guided missiles from a nearby base at Moses Lake, Washington.

Arnold refuelled his Cessna and set course for Pendleton, where he discovered that his story had also taken flight and landed in advance of its author, along with a party of interested onlookers. The people at Yakima had contacted Pendleton with their version of Arnold's story and had fuelled an excited curiosity. Arnold recalled that he noticed a group of people: 'No one said anything. They just stood around and looked at me . . . before very long it seemed everybody around the airfield was listening to the story of my experience.'

Taking advantage of the gathered expertise, Arnold recalculated the likely speed of the objects he had seen. Using detailed maps of the surrounding area, he went back over his original estimates. 'When it kept coming out in excess of 1700 miles per hour I thought, "Holy smoke! We're taking the measurement of distance far too high up on both Mount Rainier and Mount Adams." So we took a measurement of the very base, as closely as it could be determined, and which I knew from the map was far below the snow line. The distance was thirty-nine point eight miles.' Despite this, 'we still had a speed of over 1300 miles per hour.' Arnold was forced to conclude that the craft were 'guided missiles, robotly controlled', for the simple reason that 'the human body simply could not stand [such speeds], particularly considering the flipping erratic movements of these strange crafts. They didn't fly like any aircraft I had seen before . . . they flew in a definite formation but erratically . . . their flight was like speedboats on rough water or similar to the tail of a Chinese kite that I once saw blowing in the wind . . . they fluttered and sailed, tipping their wings alternately and emitting those very bright blue-white flashes from their surfaces.'

Satisfied that he had analysed and reviewed the incident as thoroughly as he could, Arnold gathered up his calculations and his maps and set off for the local FBI office. 'I thought it was my duty to report these things,' he recalled later. 'I kind of felt I ought to tell the FBI because I knew that during the war we were flying aircraft over the pole to Russia, and I thought these things could possibly be from Russia.' Unfortunately the FBI office was shut.

Undeterred, his next port of call was the offices of the local newspaper. At the offices of the *East Oregonian*, he met the editor of a weekly column called 'End of the Week', Nolan Skiff, to whom he proceeded to relate the entire adventure. Skiff, naturally sceptical, was gradually convinced of Arnold's honesty. It was apparently during the course of this conversation that Arnold drew the comparison between the flight path of the objects he had seen and a stone thrown across an expanse of water. The objects had been flying 'like a saucer would if you skipped it across the water'.

One of Skiff's fellow journalists, Bill Becquette, spotted that the story had national potential and sent off an Associated Press dispatch which was written as follows: 'PENDLETON, Ore, June 25 (AP) – Nine bright saucer-like objects flying at "incredible speed" at 10,000 feet altitude were reported here today by Kenneth Arnold, Boise, Idaho, pilot who said he could not hazard a guess as to what they were.

'Arnold, a United States Forest Service employee engaged in searching for a missing plane, said he sighted the mysterious objects yesterday at three p.m. They were flying between Mount Rainier and Mount Adams, in Washington State, he said, and appeared to weave in and out of formation. Arnold said that he checked and estimated their speed at 1200 miles an hour.

'Enquiries at Yakima last night brought only blank stares, he said, but he added he talked today with an unidentified man from Utah, south of here, who said he had seen similar objects over the mountains near Ukiah yesterday. "It seems impossible," Arnold said, "but there it is."'

It was this AP dispatch that propelled the Arnold story into the national news arena. In the media frenzy that it generated, the story inevitably gathered distortion and exaggeration as journalists and headline writers sought to outdo one another and sensationalize the bare facts in an attempt to exploit the story for more than what it was worth. Before long, Arnold found himself under siege from reporters. Many of them were aware of only the sketchiest outlines of his story, but lost little time in getting one or two quotes from the horse's mouth before rushing into print with a new version. Arnold said after the event, 'Many of these stories were distorted and inaccurate, and I didn't share the general excitement. I can't begin to estimate the number of people, letters, telegrams, and phone calls I tried to answer. After three days of this hubbub I came to the conclusion that I was the only sane one in the bunch.'

It was the publication of Arnold's sighting that precipitated the first wave of 'flying disc' sightings and indeed ushered in the flying saucer era. The American north-west's evening papers of June 25, 1947 were the first to contain details following on from the AP release.

The next day the *Chicago Tribune* reported another sighting, attributed to a couple living in Pendleton, in turn based on a sighting they had made on June 24, the very same day as Arnold's! On June 26, the *Republic* of Phoenix, Arizona and the *Baltimore Sun* recycled an AP dispatch from the previous day relating a sighting by one F. Johnson, a prospector from Portland, who had seen five or six discs near Cascade Mountains on the same morning as Arnold's historic sighting of June 24. Then, on June 26, the *Oklahoma City Times* reported an observation by one Byron Savage which was over four weeks old, while the *Kansas City Star* got in on the act by reporting yet another sighting, in West Davenport. 'Saucermania' had arrived just a few days before the greatest sighting of them all, at Roswell.

These scattered incidents were followed by a whole succession of additional sightings and reports which flooded into the newspapers over the next few days. Confronted by this sudden wave of flying saucers, Arnold noted drily, 'From then on, if I was to go by the number of reports that came in of other sightings, of which I kept a close track, I thought it wouldn't be long before there would be one of these things in every garage. In order to stop what I thought was a lot of foolishness, and since I couldn't get any work done, I went out to the airport, cranked up my plane, and flew home to Boise!'

Although many of the reports were absolutely genuine, some of the more respectable newspapers steered well clear of the controversial subject. For example, the *New York Times* made no mention of the 'flying saucer' stories before July 4, ignoring the multiple accounts that had surfaced in the previous three weeks. On Independence Day, the first article on the 'saucers' appeared in that newspaper. The piece, dealing with the Army's position on the question, quoted an Army Air Force spokesman in Washington to the effect that the sightings reported to date had 'not produced enough facts to warrant further investigation'. The same spokesperson went on to say that 'we don't have a thing that would give any realism [to the] report made last week by a flying Boise (Idaho) businessman ... Air Forces people are inclined to believe either that the observers just imagined they saw something, or that there is some meteorological explanation for the phenomenon.' The standard weather phenomena explanation was cited by the *Times* when it reported that 'solar reflections on low hanging clouds produced "spectral flashes" which might have appeared like moving objects . . . a small meteor might have broken up . . . and icy conditions in high clouds produced "large hailstones" which might have flattened out and glided a bit.' (This account overlooked the irony that such artificial weather conditions were probably even more unlikely than the 'flying saucers'!) By July 6, any inhibitions that the newspaper may have felt about losing its respectability in covering the sightings seemed to have vanished. That day's edition carried reports of well-documented sightings from 'such reliable men as Captain E.J. Smith of United Airlines and co-pilot Ralph Stevens' and referred to the 'first photograph' of a 'flying saucer', taken by a US coastguard, Frank Ryman, on July 4. 'Military and civilian meteorologists were said to have shrugged their shoulders when first asked for an explanation,' commented the *Times* somewhat cryptically.

Although the venerable organ may have shed its scruples about reporting such a dubious phenomenon – no doubt influenced by the circulation increase of some of its more populist rivals – it was extremely careful to adopt a tone of sober caution by devoting a great deal of space to 'sightings' that could be explained by the misinterpretation of natural phenomena. The curator of the Hayden Planetarium was quoted as saying that the first reports were 'entirely authentic' but the later ones were in his opinion a 'mild case of meteorological jitters' mixed in with a case of 'mass hypnosis'! Apparently the curator, Gordon A. Atwater, had found himself inundated with requests for explanations of sightings. The favoured response was that they were 'ice crystals formed by nature high in the sky'. Natural crystals, much larger than those obtained in the laboratory, 'could reflect the sun's rays like a small mirror and make the phenomena visible', while 'some here have suggested that the flying saucers might be meteorites, but we are inclined to believe they are neither meteorological or astronomical in origin . . . no meteorites are disc-shaped, and they vary from a pinhead in size to one weighing thirty-six tons.'

The *New York Times* reporter had also canvassed several other scientists for possible explanations. The astronomer Dr Jan Schilt, a professor at Columbia University, was quoted as saying, 'the true answer would be found from some phenomena seen during the two last wars, when speeding airplanes churned up the atmosphere and caused distortion of light rays'. He continued this bizarre train of thought by proposing that this effect might be largely electrical in nature, caused by the turmoil of the propeller and wings creating something like 'smoke-rings'!

The less exotic explanations of birds in flight or the reflection of headlights in the clouds were also put forward.

The wave of sightings continued to spread across the country – if it was a case of 'mass hypnosis' then it was a mental ailment that was proving to be highly contagious. Additional sightings were reported in Oregon, Michigan, Louisiana and Pennsylvania, this time eliciting the dry comment from a researcher from the US Weather Bureau's Division of Synoptic Reports and Forecasts that 'I'll have to see one before I make a guess what they are.' A representative from the Bureau of Standards in Washington, DC remarked with considerable prescience, 'It is like one of these Loch Ness Monster stories. Once the reports get about, everyone thinks they see it.'

The *New York Times* does not appear to have given much contemporary coverage to Roswell, an omission explained perhaps by the fact that most of the press readily accepted the Army Air Force dismissal at the Fort Worth press conference. Yet, coming as it did in the middle of the saucermania of the summer of 1947, it is surprising that there do not seem to be any in-depth accounts of the incident. If it had been a genuine mistake, one would have expected a gleeful press to have made something more of it, yet apparently it didn't. (The theory that efforts were made to squash reports on the radio is well documented, but nothing similar seems to have occurred with the press.) In fact, the *New York Times* journalist did file a report during the same period about an object that had been found near a farmhouse in Ohio but was 'declared by the Army Air Forces to be a radiosonde', part of an observation balloon. Intriguingly, the article also included a comment from an unidentified 'scientist in nuclear physics' at the California Institute of Technology, stating that the saucers 'might be the result of "transmutation of atomic energy" experiments'. This in turn led to a denial in an AP dispatch from Denver quoting David Lilienthal, the Chairman of the Atomic Energy Commission, who swore that the phenomenon was in no way linked to atomic tests, adding that 'of course, I can't prevent anyone from saying foolish things'.

A second article on flying saucers in the July 6 edition of the *New*

York Times cast more light on the photograph taken by the coastguard, which showed 'bright little specks in perfect formation . . . the only trouble with the photograph is that it was taken at five thirty p.m. on July the Fourth. Bright little specks are apt to appear in the sky almost any time on the Glorious Fourth . . . we have no disposition, however, to laugh this phenomenon off.' Perhaps mindful that its previous tone had been a touch too dismissive about something on which practically the entire population of the United States now had an opinion, the newspaper conceded that 'A lot of people have seen the discs, and one and all dismiss the thought that they were sun-spots – not the whirling spots on the sun itself but the after images of light on the human eye. The flying saucer could be real.' The paper's 'flying saucer' correspondent finally admitted what the rest of the country was excitedly contemplating: 'They may be visitants from another planet launched from spaceships anchored above the stratosphere'!

Despite its earlier rather terse dismissal, which was in fact completely untrue, in that the Air Force was taking a very active interest in the sightings as many of them had been made by its own pilots and radar operators, the *Times* published a San Francisco AP report announcing that military planes, equipped with cameras and other photographic instruments, had been launched on a mission to track down the saucers in the skies above Oregon and California as well as other locations. The search had apparently not yielded any results but a spokesman was quoted as saying that while they did not know what the saucers were, they did not believe that 'anyone in this country or outside this country, has developed a guided missile that will go 1200 miles an hour as some reports have indicated'. On the same day that the *Roswell Daily Record* was exclaiming in banner headlines 'RAAF captures Flying Saucer on ranch in Roswell region' the *New York Times* was reporting that 'The Associated Press said that thirty nine states, plus the District of Columbia and a part of Canada were playing host to the heavenly discs . . . Despite the humorous scepticism of scientists and military experts, the latest flock of rumours showed increasing imagination. No longer, for example, were the discs just white. In some cases, they were in technicolor, with orange the predominant hue.' The same article quoted an experiment by a physiology professor from Sydney designed to demonstrate how easy it was for people to see 'flying saucers play tag amongst the stars'.

The professor asked 450 students to 'stare fixedly at a point in the sky about a mile distant', with the result that 'within ten minutes twenty-two students were back with findings'. They even drew pictures to prove that they had seen 'flying discs'. The physiologist concluded that 'It was all due to the effect of red corpuscles of blood passing in front of the retina. This is well recognized and anybody interested can draw his own conclusions.'

Other explanations now began to jostle for attention as saucermania reached new heights. Reports came in that one alleged saucer was a balloon that had hit an aeroplane, while another that had inadvertently landed in a courtyard and been denounced to the FBI rematerialized as a circular saw!

On July 9 General Ramey's pouring of cold water on Walter Haut's press release was virtually lost in the flurry of sightings that had preceded and were continuing, merely mentioning a flying disc that had crashed near an atomic test site and had turned out to be a weather probe. The *New York Times* found greater significance the following month in a Gallup opinion poll that revealed that whereas only one out of two Americans had heard of the 'Marshall Plan', nine out of ten had heard about the saucers. Whatever else had happened, Kenneth Arnold had unwittingly given birth not only to the phenomenon of flying saucers but also to what has become a perennial media preoccupation. He had instilled in journalists and newspaper editors across America the realization that flying saucers could be happily exploited to sell newspapers to fascinated readers. A new age had been born and along with it a topic which would help to satisfy the insatiable appetite of the mass media for sensation and mystery; an appetite which in America has reached its apogee in the demented reporting of tabloid newspapers like the *National Enquirer* and *World News*. While Europe has never experienced anything to match America's nationwide saucermania, a steadily growing band of enthusiasts and amateurs have formed a variety of societies and study groups to analyse the phenomenon. At the same time their formerly eccentric hobby has become increasingly mainstream, to the point of being assimilated into popular dramatic entertainment such as the massively successful film *Independence Day* and the more cultish Columbia Television series *Dark Skies*.

This all goes to remind us how far the popular perception of the subject has shifted in the past fifty years, from a minority interest shared by obsessive and like-minded individuals to an activity whose aficionados are now so numerous that it is surprising no politicians have latched on to it as a surefire way of winning several million voters to their cause. (In this respect, former Presidents Carter and Reagan may have been ahead of their time in claiming to have had irrefutable encounters with UFOs!)

Back in 1947, as we have seen from the changing response of the reporters on the *New York Times*, there was still considerable disquiet about openly admitting to the belief that we might be playing unwitting host to an invasion of uninvited alien travellers.

As the controversy escalated around the nation, its hapless author, Kenneth Arnold, was relieved to get a telephone call from a friend, Dave Johnson, the aviation editor of the *Idaho Statesman*, whom Arnold already knew as a 'man of respected ability and intelligence in matters related to military and civilian aviation'. Arnold was glad of the opportunity to discuss what he had seen with an expert in the field who could probably suggest a solution to the mystery. The confidence he placed in his friend was revealed when he later commented, 'The doubt he displayed of the authenticity of my story told me, and I am sure he was in a position to know, that it was not a new military guided missile and that if what I had seen was true, it did not belong to the good old USA. It was then that I really began to wonder.' Johnson confided in him that his own contacts within the Air Force had let it be known that the Wright Field airbase in Ohio was keen to get the full story of exactly what had happened – not least because the nationwide hysteria over flying saucers had coincided with, or been fuelled by, Arnold's original encounter. Pressmen from all over America were converging on the unlikely location of the modest dwelling of Kenneth and Doris Arnold in Boise. The innocent couple were under siege and, lamented the beleaguered Mr Arnold, beginning 'to feel like we were living in Grand Central Station!'

Adopting the drastic step of abandoning his home, Arnold gave the newshounds the slip by escaping with his friend Colonel Paul Wieland on a clandestine fishing expedition to Sekiu. During the flight, they naturally discussed the sighting that had caused all the trouble and when Arnold expressed doubts that he could have seen anything travelling at such a high speed, his military friend reassured him by pointing out that artillery shells, travelling at seven hundred miles per hour, despite their relatively small size, could also be seen by the naked eye if a person was in the right position. Arnold was relieved to hear that perhaps his calculation of the speed of the objects was, after all, not completely impossible – although that had been one of the issues that the newspapers had seized upon to cast doubts on the accuracy of his observation. The following day the two men flew from Sekiu to Seattle, where, by a strange coincidence, they encountered the United Airlines team that had also figured prominently in the national press for their sighting of several flying discs.

Curious and ever hopeful that their experience would confirm his own and corroborate the reality of the phenomenon, Arnold met up with Captain E.J. 'Big' Smith and Ralph Stevens in a local coffee shop, where he impatiently beseeched them to relate the smallest detail of what had happened to them on their flight. He was eager to discover additional clues to explain what he still considered to be an extraordinary phenomenon which he had inadvertently flown into while on his search-and-rescue mission. The three men exchanged recollections about their shared experience of having witnessed 'flying saucers', which, while not unique, was at the time endowed with such a strong sense of mystery that it was understandable that they all felt nervous and under considerable pressure. In the heady mix of public interest and media obsession that had catapulted ordinary people like Arnold into an unprecedented limelight, it was not surprising that he in particular needed to get away from the press pack to gather his thoughts.

Captain Smith began to tell Arnold the story of the United Airlines sighting. It was just before take-off, he recalled, that someone, prompted no doubt by recent newspaper headlines, had asked him if he believed in 'flying saucers'. He had replied that he would believe in them the day he saw one. Amazingly, eight minutes later, as they were flying over Emmet, Idaho, Smith and his crew managed to see not just one but nine 'flying saucers': first a group of five, then a group of four. The captain remembered them as being circular with a flat underbelly, rough on top and comparable in size to an aeroplane of the stature of a DC-3. To Arnold, this description seemed literally incredible. 'When Big Smith got through telling me this, and in spite of my own experience, I kept repeating to myself, "It's just amazing – simply amazing! Positively amazing!" Big Smithy's sighting somehow made mine small and insignificant.'

When he returned home, Arnold loyally sorted through the copious correspondence that had arrived as a result of his original sighting, and he was able to record that 'not one letter that I recall had even a note of criticism. This to me was rather surprising, since most of the newspapers were having a terrifically good time trying to make the public believe that we were crazy, seeing visions, or recording corpuscles on the retinas of our eyeballs.' As panic over the 'flying disc' at Roswell was quietly growing in New Mexico, Arnold and his aviation editor friend Dave Johnson, accompanied by a photographer for the Statesman Newspapers, flew over the area where the original June 24 sighting had occurred. Unfortunately, their attempt to capture one of the mysterious flying saucers on film failed.

In direct contradiction of its earlier public statement, the Army Air Force displayed considerable interest in this and other sightings, with Wright Field requesting information to be filed on the sighting. Arnold, who had been desperate for the expression of some official concern, gratefully wrote a detailed account for them which even included the feelings expressed by pilots with whom he had served in the Second World War, who had assured him that he had not been seeing things! They had confided in their friend that they had received warnings that they might see such craft during their combat missions. Arnold couldn't resist also referring to another veteran pilot of his acquaintance who had told him that the flying discs were experimental craft undergoing test flights by the American government or some other country.

Arnold made it equally clear that he was not some cheap publicity seeker, saying, 'I reported something that I know any pilot would have reported.' He was even somewhat indignant that the Army or the FBI, 'these two important protective forces of our country', had not seen fit to hold an enquiry. He patriotically volunteered to sit any physical or mental examination 'for any determination they [the military] might wish to make as to the capabilities of my five senses'.

A few days later Arnold did indeed receive a visit from the Army Air Force, in the shape of two Air Force intelligence officers from Hamilton Field, California. 'I was very happy to see them,' he admitted. 'I couldn't figure out why such an efficient body as Military Intelligence hadn't called on me before.' Arnold's faith in his country's intelligence capabilities was quickly deflated when the two officers, Lieutenant Frank M. Brown and Captain William Davidson, invited him and his wife to dinner and hastily confessed that they had no answers to the mystery. 'They said, frankly and openly, they didn't know what the flying saucers were. They had never seen one, they told us, but ever since my first report they were practically bug-eyed from watching the sky themselves!' After dinner Arnold suggested that the officers should meet Captain Smith of United Airlines, who could give them his testimony about their July 4 sighting. The intelligence officers were delighted to accept Arnold's offer with its prospect of two saucers for the price of one (or nearly a dozen in the two cases!) and subsequently headed off to the Boise Municipal Airport, where Arnold bumped into his ubiquitous friend from the *Idaho Statesman*, Dave Johnson. Apparently, Brown and Davidson also wanted to interview Johnson, as by now he too had had a sighting of some saucers; this had occurred on July 9, the same day as General Ramey's Fort Worth press conference on the Roswell Incident.

After the discussion, during which, said Arnold, 'Everybody was talking at the same time . . . [and] none of us found out much', he and his wife invited the Army Air Force officers to their home, where they could talk in private. Arnold then proceeded to answer all their questions. 'I stuck absolutely to the facts. I didn't consider my opinion important. I drew pictures for them and recounted my original observation as accurately as I could.'

Before leaving, Brown and Davidson looked over the mail that Arnold had received, scrutinizing the letters from various groups who had asked for written reports of his sighting. 'I was happy they did go through my mail,' said Arnold in retrospect, 'as I didn't feel capable of evaluating much of the contents of the letters I had received.'

Curiously, given that they themselves had confessed to knowing nothing that might shed any light on the sighting, the officers advised Arnold not to talk too much about it and to contact them if anything strange should turn up.

Brown and Davidson had earlier carried out a check on Arnold himself, presumably to assess how credible his account was and explore the remote possibility that he was a foreign agent. To this end they had telephoned Dave Johnson, who had told them that 'as far as he was concerned anything Mr Arnold said could be taken very seriously and that he, Mr Johnson, actually believed that Mr Arnold had seen the aforementioned flying discs'. To their credit, after meeting Johnson in person Brown and Davidson were of the same opinion.

The two officers compiled an official report which was then sent to Allen Hynek, the astronomer to the Air Force. Hynek had asked to study the report so as to avoid any possible confusion with astronomical phenomena. In the Arnold case Hynek would eventually conclude that there did not appear to be any 'astronomical explanation for this classic incident which is the prototype of many of the later flying saucer stories'. He was at a loss to explain the case but he did pick up some inconsistencies in Arnold's report.

'Arnold made drawings of objects showing definite shape and stated that objects were about twenty times as long as wide, estimating them as forty five to fifty feet long. He also estimated the distance as twenty to twenty five miles and clocked them as going forty seven miles in 102 seconds (1700 mph). If the distance was correct then in order for details to be seen, objects must have been closer than six miles to have shown the detail indicated by Arnold. At this distance, angular speed observed corresponds to a maximum speed of 400 mph. In all probability therefore, objects were much closer than thought and moving at definitely sub-sonic speeds.'

Hynek's conclusion was that Arnold had seen some aircraft. However, it is unlikely that such a formation could have been anything other than military and the Army Air Force has never offered an explanation for the presence of any fighters in the area. Hynek himself went on to become one of the world's leading scientific researchers into UFOs, founding the Center for UFO Studies [CUFOS] and acting as an adviser to the USAF in their Project Blue Book study of the phenomenon.

7

As some of the witnesses from Roswell recalled in their interviews, the wave of 'flying saucer' sightings in the summer of 1947 was common knowledge and may well have encouraged Mac Brazel to bring the debris he had discovered to Sheriff Wilcox's office. Marcel himself had recalled seeing strange lights some days before his expedition to the Foster ranch. Yet there remains some doubt as to how accurate Marcel's recollections were; he was curiously vague about the exact nature of the debris recovered and refers only in passing to the existence of another site, which, if Frank Kaufmann is to be believed, was where the main craft, whatever it was, actually crashed. Although in reference to another crash site Marcel admitted, 'I don't know anything about', he did provide the vague detail that the 'other incident' was something like sixty to eighty miles west of the Foster ranch and that it had occurred at roughly the same time. Hazy on any details, Marcel thought that it had been discovered by 'some surveyor'.

In his interview with the television reporter, Marcel's recollection of another site is a puzzling though tantalizing aside. For it raises the fundamental question, if it is true, of what happened there and why did Marcel not know anything about it? One possible explanation is that a different search and recovery team was dispatched with orders to maintain absolute levels of secrecy which included not telling any other personnel at the base. (There is some evidence for this 'compartmentalization of intelligence', not least in Kaufmann's account of procedures for the shipping of the remains of the craft back at the base, which he claims was the responsibility of another team and he knew nothing about it.) Once it became apparent that the crash site was the real centre of attention, then it would make sense to throw a tight security cordon around that area and play down the Marcel site at the ranch. Yet it seems strange that Marcel, as Intelligence Officer for the 509th, would be kept out of the loop. If, on the other hand, Colonel Blanchard, as has been suggested, referred to Higher Headquarters at an early stage, to report the existence of a crashed craft of a highly unusual nature (leaving aside for the moment whether it contained aliens or was from outer space), headquarters and, in turn, the commanding officers from Washington would have certainly identified the incident as an extremely serious intrusion over sensitive military airspace with obvious implications for America's national security. One can easily imagine that there would have been a security clamp-down, pending further enquiries, and that could well have included Marcel. Equally, at the stage that it was known that some craft had violated US airspace and crashed, the priority would have been to recover the evidence as soon, and as secretly, as possible.

If the object was extraterrestrial, then oddly enough, the same sort of security blanket would have existed, and once this was confirmed it would undoubtedly have been emphasized repeatedly that no word of the news that the Americans had got hold of a 'flying disc' should be broadcast to anyone at all. For even at this stage, the potential for technological and scientific advantage, as well as the scientific prestige, was of unimaginable proportions and the secret would be one to conceal at all costs from all personnel with the minute exception of those few who needed to know.

Acute sensitivity as to what the press and radio might publish or broadcast would have been of paramount importance. The experience of the proprietor of the local radio station in Roswell lends a certain credibility to this scenario.

In 1947 Jud Roberts was the part owner of KGFL, the local broadcaster in Roswell. He is now in his eighties and although not in the best of health still remembers receiving a telephone call warning him about the story. 'I got a call from Washington, from one of the offices of one of the senators, saying, "Look, if you put out any stories on this thing, you're gonna lose your licence, and it's not gonna be over a period of time, it's gonna be the same day that we tell you that you're off the air."' Roberts also remembers that the military had cordoned off the whole area around the debris site. 'If it was a weather balloon, what were they doing with all these little blue cars from security running around and keeping anybody from getting out.

All you had to do was go out there and you found out that everything was blocked off. There wasn't any question in anybody's mind that in a ranching country where weather balloons are lost on ranches every place, that's one thing you can't mistake. It's like a worn-out tyre.'

Roberts recalled that the radio station had many contacts at the Roswell airbase and had done various broadcasts with officers serving there. He remembers from conversations between personnel from the base and people working at the radio station that there seemed to be a lot more to the story than the official version. But then a marked change became apparent: 'We knew that the guys who flew things back to Wright Patterson and so forth, they never mentioned a word from that time on. They were completely close-mouthed on it so there weren't any question about the thing: it was not from this universe.'

The stories about threats, muzzling of the press and the close eye being kept on Mac Brazel all indicate that the Army Air Force was attempting to control the release of information. If an extraterrestrial craft had landed at Roswell, then the priority would have been to keep everything under the tightest security and as quickly as possible put the whole matter in the hands of an elite group of military and scientific leaders who could evaluate the problem. If that had happened, it seems highly unlikely that no word of the operation would ever leak out. In December 1984 evidence emerged that seemed to confirm the existence of exactly this type of top-secret scenario and provide sensational confirmation of what had really been discovered at Roswell.

In one of the most controversial episodes within the field of UFO research, a document emerged which claimed that a group had been formed with the express purpose of evaluating the technology of 'crashed discs'. On December 11, 1984 Jaime Shandera, a television producer, received a heavily sealed envelope containing an undeveloped strip of 35mm photographic film, which was found to be a record of a series of pages from a supposed top-secret document which has become known as 'MJ-12' or 'Majestic'. The document referred to a high-level group of scientists and military figures engaged in the secret analysis of recovered saucers and aliens.

At the time Shandera was working with UFO researcher William Moore, co-author of an earlier book on Roswell. Since its appearance, MJ-12 has divided the UFO research community into those who are convinced that it is a fake, those who believe it to be absolutely genuine and those who believe that while the document may be fake, the events and the people described did exist.

The first page of the document is headed 'EYES ONLY' and under this appears the classification 'TOP SECRET' and:
'SUBJECT: OPERATION OF MAJESTIC-12 PRELIMINARY BRIEFING FOR PRESIDENT ELECT EISENHOWER DOCUMENT PREPARED 18 NOVEMBER 1952.
BRIEFING OFFICER: ADM. ROSCOE H. HILLENKOTTER (MJ-1)
NOTE: This document has been prepared as a preliminary briefing only. It should be regarded as introductory to a full operations briefing intended to follow.

'OPERATION MAJESTIC-12 is a TOP SECRET Research and Development/Intelligence operation responsible directly and only to the President of the United States. Operations of the project are carried out under control of the Majestic 12 (Majic-12) Group which was established by special executive order of President Truman on 24 September 1947, upon recommendation by Dr Vannevar Bush and Secretary James Forrestal. (See attachment "A".)'

The document goes on to list the twelve members of the group, among them the top scientists and military officers of the day, including General Nathan Twining, the head of the Air Materiel Command at Wright Field and General Hoyt Vandenberg, Chief of Staff for the Air Force. On the second page the report goes on to detail the background of 'Majestic'.

'On 24 June 1947 a civilian pilot flying over the Cascade mountains in the State of Washington observed nine flying disc shaped aircraft travelling in formation at a high rate of speed. Although this was not the first known sighting of such objects, it was the first to gain widespread attention in the public media. Hundreds of reports of sightings of similar objects followed. Many of these came from highly credible military and civilian sources. These reports resulted in independent efforts by several different elements of the military to ascertain the nature and purpose of these objects in the interests of national defense. A number of witnesses were interviewed and there were several unsuccessful attempts to utilize aircraft in efforts to pursue reported discs in flight. Public reaction bordered on near hysteria at times.

'In spite of these efforts, little of substance was learned about the objects until a local rancher reported that one had crashed in a remote region of New Mexico located approximately seventy-five miles North-West of Roswell Army Air Base (now Walker Field).

'On 7 July 1947 a secret operation was begun to assure recovery of the wreckage of this object for scientific study. During the course of this operation, aerial reconnaissance discovered that four small human-like beings had apparently ejected from the craft at some point before it exploded. These had fallen to earth about two miles east of the wreckage site. All four were dead and badly decomposed due to action by predators and exposure to the elements during the approximately one week time period which had elapsed before their discovery. A special scientific team took charge of removing these bodies for study. (See Attachment "C".) The wreckage of the craft was also removed to several different locations. (See Attachment "B".) Civilian and military witnesses in the area were debriefed, and news reporters were given the effective cover story that the object had been a misguided weather research balloon.

'A covert analytical effort organized by Gen. Twining and Dr Bush acting on the direct orders of the President, resulted in a preliminary consensus (19 September, 1947) that the disc was most likely a short range reconnaissance craft. This conclusion was based for the most part on the craft's size and the apparent lack of any identifiable provisioning. (See Attachment "D".) A similar analysis of the four dead occupants was arranged by Dr Bronk. It was the tentative conclusion of this group (30 November, 1947) that although these creatures are human-like in appearance, the biological and evolutionary processes responsible for their development has apparently been quite different from those observed or postulated in homo-sapiens.

'Dr Bronk's team has suggested the term "Extra-terrestrial Biological Entities", or "EBEs", be adopted as the standard term of reference for these creatures until such time as a more definitive designation can be agreed upon.

'Since it is virtually certain that these craft do not originate in any country on earth, considerable speculation has centered around what their point of origin might be and how they get here. Mars was and remains a possibility, although some scientists, notably Dr Menzel, consider it more likely that we are dealing with beings from another solar system entirely.

'Numerous examples of what appear to be a form of writing were found in the wreckage. Efforts to decipher these have remained largely unsuccessful. (See Attachment "E".)

'Equally unsuccessful have been the efforts to determine the method of propulsion or the nature or method of transmission of the power source involved. Research along these lines has been complicated by the complete absence of identifiable wings, propellers, jets, or other conventional methods of propulsion and guidance, as well as a total lack of metallic wiring, vacuum tubes, or similar recognizable electronic components. (See Attachment "F".) It is assumed that the propulsion unit was completely destroyed by the explosion which caused the crash.

'A need for as much additional information as possible about these craft, their performance characteristics and their purpose led to the undertaking known as U.S. Air Force Project SIGN in December, 1947. In order to preserve security, liaison between SIGN and Majestic-12 was limited to two individuals within the Intelligence Division of Air Materiel Command whose role was to pass along certain types of information through channels. SIGN evolved into Project GRUDGE in December 1948. The operation is currently being conducted under the code name BLUE BOOK, with liaison maintained through the Air Force officer who is head of the project.

'On 06 December, 1950, a second object probably of similar origin, impacted the earth at high speed in the El Indio-Guerrero area of the Texas-Mexican border after following a long trajectory through the atmosphere. By the time a search team arrived, what remained of the object had been almost totally incinerated. Such material as could be recovered was transported to the AEC facility at Sandia, New Mexico, for study.

'Implications for the National Security are of continuing importance in that the motives and ultimate intentions of these visitors remain completely unknown. In addition, a significant upsurge in the surveillance activity of these craft beginning in May and continuing through the autumn of this year, has caused considerable concern that new developments may be imminent. It is for these reasons as well as the obvious international and technological considerations and the ultimate need to avoid a public panic at all costs, that the Majestic-12 Group remains of the unanimous opinion that imposition of the strictest security precautions should continue without interruption into the new administration. At the same time, contingency plan MJ-1949-04P/78 (Top Secret-Eyes Only) should be held in continued readiness should the need to make a public announcement present itself. (See Attachment "G".)

'NUMERATION OF ATTACHMENTS
ATTACHMENT "A".........Special Classified Executive Order #092447. (TS/EO)
ATTACHMENT "B".........Operation Majestic-12 Status Report #1, Part A. 30 Nov '47 (TS-MAJIC/EO)
ATTACHMENT "C"..........Operation Majestic-12 Status Report #1, Part B. 30 Nov '47 (TS-MAJIC/EO)
ATTACHMENT "D" Operation Majestic-12 Preliminary Analytical Report.
19 Sep '47 (TS-MAJIC/EO)
ATTACHMENT "E" Operation Majestic-12 Blue Team Report #5 TS 30 Jun '52 (TS-MAJIC/EO)
ATTACHMENT "F" Operation Majestic-12 Status Report #2. 31 Jan '48 (TS- MAJIC/EO)
ATTACHMENT "G" Operation Majestic-12 Contingency Plan MJ-1949=04P/78. 31 Jan '49 (TS-MAJIC/EO)
ATTACHMENT "H" Operation Majestic-12, Maps and Photographs Folio (Extractions). (TS-MAJIC/EO)'

At last, here was irrefutable proof of the government conspiracy so long alleged by the die-hard ufologist researchers who had for so long been battering at the seemingly impenetrable walls of officialdom. The keepers of the key to the Holy Grail of the 'flying saucer' debate would finally be forced to admit that they had wilfully kept secret, from the American public and the world, the evidence that would confirm the reality of extraterrestrial existence and the retrieval of 'flying saucers' and their occupants.

This new evidence would lay to rest the controversy of the Roswell Incident and blow apart the various cover stories offered by the Air Force in response to Roswell and succeeding UFO events which had been consistently denied. For a few heady weeks the 'MJ-12' documents were hailed as a triumph of indefatigable research over bureaucratic stonewalling and downright deception. It was only the sober analysis and questioning, much of it from within the arena of ufology itself, that demonstrated that MJ-12 was almost certainly a hoax.

Since the documents' discovery, thousands of dollars have been spent on attempts to prove them true and further large amounts to prove the opposite. True or false, MJ-12 became a major issue to which rival ufologists could devote acres of newsprint, and make arcane references to obscure events, in order to prove their case or discredit their opponents, or both.

Outside the circle of ufologists, journalists and professional sceptics, such as Philip Klass, the renowned correspondent for *Aviation Week*, had a field day, pouring scorn on their opponents and seizing the opportunity to proclaim MJ-12 an elaborate hoax which merely served to bring further discredit on the pseudo scientific researchers who for so long had challenged the orthodoxy of the scientific establishment with the minimum of facts and the maximum of conviction. Undeterred, the ufologists maintained that the MJ-12 documents were genuine and Stanton Friedman, a veteran ufologist, was given a grant by the Fund for UFO Research to investigate their authenticity exhaustively.

As it turned out, the facts concerning the MJ-12 documents were not wholly encouraging in supporting their authenticity. Considerable doubts have been raised about the numbers for the Executive Orders, which apparently do not correspond to those that would have been in use at the time, as well as the typography and the presidential signature, which appears to be a copy of a genuine one taken from another document. Klass made a number of telling observations about the set of documents relating to the style and use of words, as well as the form of dates used – it being highly unusual to use commas and the prefix 01, 02, etc before the month. Klass even commented that it was a form of dating that was identical to the way that ufologist William Moore prefixed his own correspondence. Another suspicious indicator was that Moore and Shandera had sat on the documents for two years before releasing them and that when they did they had originally contained many blacked-out sections, common to genuinely declassified documents but in this case apparently added by the authors of the discovery. The case for authentication seemed to take a leap forward with the surprise discovery of another document in a file in the National Archives in Maryland which has become known as the 'Cutler–Twining memorandum'. Purporting to be a memo from Robert Cutler, the special assistant to President Eisenhower, to General Nathan Twining, it concerns the scheduling of a secret Majestic meeting.

The document had been conveniently discovered by Moore and

Shandera on a visit to the National Archives, where they had requested the files from Record Group 341 and after copious searching finally alighted on Box Number 189, which contained a folder of documents: T4-1846. Picking the document up, Shandera read the following: 'The President has decided that the MJ-12/SSP briefing should take place during the already scheduled White House meeting of July 16 rather than following it as previously intended. More precise arrangements will be explained to you upon arrival. Please alter your plans accordingly. Your concurrence in the above change of arrangements is assumed.'

The document was headed 'July 14, 1954 NSC/MJ-12 Special Studies Project'.

MJ-12 appeared to be vindicated and Moore now felt justified in proclaiming that the memorandum 'unquestionably verifies the existence of an "MJ-12" group in 1954 and definitely links both the National Security Council and the President of the United States to it.' It followed, he added, that if the MJ-12 group was real then so were flying saucers!

The Cutler–Twining memorandum revived the bitter debate between rival ufologists and the debunker Klass. Robert Todd, a level-headed UFO researcher, wrote to the Eisenhower Library and received the following reply:

'1. President Eisenhower's Appointment Books contain no entry for a special meeting on July 16, 1954 which might have included a briefing on MJ-12. Even when the President had "off-the-record" meetings, the Appointment Books contain entries indicating the times of the meetings and the participants.

2. The classification marking on this memorandum is one we have never seen on an Eisenhower Administration document. "Top Secret" and "Restricted" are two different levels of classification. There neither is, nor ever was, a classification level known as "Top Secret Restricted". The use of "Restricted" as a classification marking was discontinued in November 1953.

3. TheDeclassificationOfficeoftheNationalSecurityCouncilhasinformed us that it has no record of any declassification action having been taken on this memorandum or on any other documents on this alleged project.

4. No additional documentation on MJ-12 has been located at either the National Archives or the Eisenhower Library.

5. Finally, Robert Cutler, at the direction of President Eisenhower,

was visiting overseas installations on the day he supposedly issued this memorandum – July 14 1954.'

The Administration Series in Eisenhower's Papers as President contains Cutler's memorandum and report to the President upon his return from the trip. The memorandum is dated July 20, 1954 and refers to Cutler's visits to installations in Europe and North Africa between July 3 and July 15. Furthermore, Cutler's name does not appear on the roster for the regular NSC meeting on July 15. Also, within the NSC Staff Papers is a memorandum dated July 3, 1954 from Cutler to his two subordinates, James S. Lay and J. Patrick Coyne, explaining how they should handle NSC administrative matters during his absence. One would assume that if the memorandum to Twining were genuine, Lay or Coyne would have signed it.

Additional confirmation of doubts about the authenticity of the Cutler–Twining memorandum surfaced in a public rebuttal from the National Archives itself. Jo Ann Williamson, the Chief of the Military Reference Branch, Military Archives Division, pointed out that the document did not bear a 'Top Secret' register number, unlike the other papers in the Record Group 341, and that the document did not bear an official government letterhead or watermark. A specialist also examined the memorandum and determined that it was 'a ribbon copy prepared on dictation onionskin. The Eisenhower Library has examined its collection of the Cutler papers. All documents created by Mr Cutler while he served on the NSC staff have an eagle watermark in the onionskin carbon paper. Most documents sent out by the NSC were prepared on White House letterhead paper. For the brief periods when Mr Cutler left the NSC, his carbon copies were prepared on "prestige onionskin".' All in all, it looked as if whoever had created the Cutler–Twining memorandum had overlooked some critical period detail, thus ensuring a fairly short shelf life for the forgery. There was also the mystery about how Moore could have alighted on the document itself – the explanation that he had received an anonymous postcard with cryptic clues about where to look did little to allay suspicions that he might have created and planted the document himself. Despite strict procedures at the National Archives, it would not be impossible to insert something in a file.

The doubts provoked by the memorandum, taken in concert with the anomalies over the MJ-12 papers, provided an almost overwhelming case against the documents' alleged authenticity, although there are still those who maintain that either the case is not proven or that the MJ-12 group did really exist and that what has since emerged is all part of the continuing cover-up. Apart from this stubborn minority, almost everyone else who has studied the evidence, including most of the reputable UFO research groups, has concluded beyond a shadow of doubt that the whole thing is an elaborate hoax. Stanton Friedman has continued to maintain somewhat unconvincingly that the documents are real, countering objections about Dr Donald Menzel, who was always debunking the flying saucer phenomenon, by discovering that Menzel was engaged in many top-secret projects and therefore could well have been a natural choice to serve on MJ-12. This may be true but unfortunately it did not yield any evidence that he had.

As to the source of the forgery, many have pointed a finger at those who actually produced the documents, namely William Moore and his colleague from television Jaime Shandera. Certainly, they stood to gain the most from the appearance of the documents, but it should be stated that there is no evidence, merely suspicion, that they did actually fake the documents. It has been pointed out in their favour that they waited a considerable time before releasing the documents.

Another name which has figured in the search for a hoaxer is that of Richard L. Doty, who was a former USAF sergeant with the intelligence division known as the Air Force Office of Special Investigations (AFOSI) and whose name had surfaced in earlier encounters with researchers from the world of UFO study. Doty was at one time stationed at Kirtland Air Force base in New Mexico and had already, in 1980, passed to Moore a document containing a reference to MJ-12. The document was denounced as a hoax by the Air Force and after leading another UFO researcher astray (film-maker Linda Moulton Howe, who was apparently led on a wild-goose chase and promised all sorts of definitive proof about flying saucers and aliens by Doty), Doty was removed from the USAF in 1988 for allegedly faking reports of contacts with communist agents while stationed in West Germany. He was also rumoured to be the identity behind an alleged 'high level' contact known as 'Falcon' who was the conduit for top-secret intelligence about UFOs and aliens that was passed on to Moore and who appeared in a subsequent television programme in which Falcon claimed first-hand knowledge of captured aliens and pronounced that their favourite food was strawberry ice cream! If, as people like Moore are so fond of proclaiming, the UFO phenomenon is classified at the highest levels of secrecy within America's intelligence community, then it is highly unlikely that a mere Air Force sergeant would be privy to the innermost secrets held by the US government and successfully kept under wraps for the past fifty years. The notion of aliens eating ice cream speaks for itself.

Doty has denied that he was the unidentified speaker who appeared with his voice and appearance disguised on the television show *UFO Cover-Up . . . Live!* that was broadcast in the United States on October 18, 1988. He claimed in a letter that he was still working for 'a government agency' and that, despite being asked to leave AFOSI voluntarily after an incident in which he was engaged in counter-espionage activities in West Germany (allegedly part of an entrapment mission to catch foreign agents), he has retained his top security clearance. As for being privy to the innermost secrets of the USAF's knowledge about UFOs, Doty wrote: 'My own personal beliefs regarding the subject of UFOs is this: I think Earth is not the only planet in the Universe that supports intelligent life. Whether Earth has been visited in the past by visitors from other planets I simply don't have enough information to make a personal decision. If I should base my decision on information that I had access to during my government service, I would have to say, yes, Earth has been visited. However I am not 100% certain that the information I had access to was entirely accurate.'

Doty may be telling the truth, but some believe that the former sergeant may still be part of a deliberate disinformation programme comprising a motley collection of former and serving intelligence personnel who have been ordered to spread half-truths and hoaxes in order to discredit and confuse the tireless efforts of individual UFO researchers and the organizations that they work for.

8

Although the MJ-12 documents are almost certainly a hoax, there are hundreds of fascinating official papers relating to the UFO phenomenon which have genuinely been declassified. Many of these were once deemed to be 'top secret' and have been released under America's relatively liberal Freedom of Information Act. Although nothing emerged from the General Accounting Office enquiry, research by other organizations, including some of the pioneering UFO research groups, has yielded some rewarding information.

What the documents show as a body is that the US government has treated the UFO phenomenon very seriously and that its intelligence agencies have at various times undertaken fairly exhaustive investigations into the phenomenon. Both the CIA and the NSA (National Security Agency, the USA's much larger equivalent of Britain's GCHQ, Government Communications Headquarters) still have documents in their secret archives which they have refused to release on grounds of national security, but those which have reached the public domain make fascinating reading. It comes as a surprise to most people to learn that organizations such as the Central Intelligence Agency and the USAF have made official studies of the UFO phenomenon. But the only reason it appears strange is that today UFOs have become virtually synonymous in people's minds with 'flying saucers' and 'extraterrestrial vehicles'. As a result, the official response tends to be to ridicule and play down reported sightings, in most cases attributing them to balloons, geese or Venus seen in an unusual light.

Most UFO sightings probably can be explained away by such mundane factors. Nevertheless, there is a substantial body of sightings, recorded observations, radar returns, testimony from pilots both military and civilian and encounters by reputable observers such as police officers and scientists that defy rational explanation. It is these cases which have attracted the interest of the intelligence community and left even them baffled as to their origin. Also, when the phenomenon began to receive serious attention, after the Second World War, UFOs were genuinely 'Unidentified Flying Objects': they were something seen in the sky by someone who could not explain what they were. It was only later that the extraterrestrial hypothesis gained widespread currency and attracted official ridicule.

As we have seen, it was largely due to Kenneth Arnold's sighting and the wave of 'saucermania' in 1947 that the UFO phenomenon really took off. Of course, there had been many sightings before then and many references throughout history which can be interpreted as visits by UFOs: from references in the Bible, through cave paintings of prehistoric times, to the phantom objects reported by many Second World War pilots and known as 'Foo Fighters'. This wave of sightings reached its zenith in 1946, when there were over two thousand reports from the Scandinavian countries of Finland, Norway, Sweden and Denmark of 'ghost rockets'. At the time it was thought that these objects could have been either some new fearsome weapon invented by the Germans or strange meteors. But pilots' accounts that described them as manoeuvring around their fighters and bomber aircraft seemed to discount that possibility. When this was followed by the wave of sightings in 1947 which gave rise to the terms 'flying discs' and 'flying saucers', the Air Force began (as we have seen with the Arnold case), to take serious notice of the phenomenon. Arnold had submitted an official report to the Air Force:

'PENDLETON ORG JULY 12 1233A
COMMANDING GENERAL
WRIGHT FIELD DAYTON OHIO
DEAR SIR: YOU HAVE MY PERMISSION TO QUOTE GIVE OUT OR REPRINT MY WRITTEN ACCOUNT AND REPORT OF NINE STRANGE AIRCRAFT I OBSERVED ON JUNE 24TH IN THE CASCADE MOUNTAINS IN THE STATE OF WASHINGTON. THIS REPORT WAS SENT TO YOU AT REQUEST SOME DAYS AGO. IT IS WITH CONSIDERABLE DISAPPOINTMENT YOU CANNOT GIVE THE EXPLANATION OF THESE AIRCRAFT AS I FELT CERTAIN THEY BELONGED TO OUR GOVERNMENT.

THEY HAVE APPARENTLY MEANT NO HARM BUT USED AS AN INSTRUMENT OF DESTRUCTION IN COMBINATION WITH OUR ATOMIC BOMB THE EFFECTS COULD DESTROY LIFE ON OUR PLANET. CAPT.— CO-PILOT STEVENS OF UNITED AIR LINES AND MYSELF HAVE COMPARED OUR OBSERVATIONS IN AS MUCH DETAIL AS POSSIBLE AND AGREED WE HAD OBSERVED THE SAME TYPE OF AIRCRAFT AS TO SIZE SHAPE AND FORM. WE HAVE NOT TAKEN THIS LIGHTLY. IT IS TO US VERY SERIOUS CONCERN AS WE ARE AS INTERESTED IN THE WELFARE OF OUR COUNTRY AS YOU ARE.
KENNETH ARNOLD
BOISE IDAHO PILOTS LICENCE 24 333487.'

As we have seen, this report and that of the United Airlines pilots prompted the Air Force to send two officers to investigate. Given the additional sightings from around the country, the Air Force began to take a more serious interest and on September 23, 1947 General Nathan Twining, the head of the Air Materiel Command, sent a memo in response to a request from the Deputy Assistant Chief of Air Staff, Brigadier General Schulgen, about the state of the Air Force's current knowledge concerning the 'flying discs'. This secret report has since been declassified:

'September 23 1947
Subject: AMC Opinion concerning "Flying Discs"
To: Commanding General
Army Air Forces
Washington 25, D.C.
ATTENTION: Brig. General George Schulgen
AC/AS-2

'1. As requested by AC/AS-2 there is presented below the considered opinion of this command concerning the so-called "Flying Discs". This opinion is based on interrogation report data furnished by AC/AS-2 and preliminary studies by personnel of T-2 and Aircraft Laboratory, Engineering Division T-3. This opinion was arrived at in a conference between personnel from the Air Institute of Technology, Intelligence T-2, Office, Chief of Engineering Division, and the Aircraft, Power Plant and Propeller Laboratories of Engineering Division T-3.
2. It is the opinion that:

a. The phenomenon reported is something real and not visionary or fictitious.

b. There are objects probably approximating the shape of a disc, of such appreciable size as to appear to be as large as man-made aircraft.

c. There is a possibility that some of the incidents may be caused by natural phenomena, such as meteors.

d. The reported operating characteristics such as extreme rates of climb, maneuvrability (particularly in roll), and action which must be considered evasive when sighted or contacted by friendly aircraft and radar, lend belief to the possibility that some of the objects are controlled either manually, automatically or remotely.

e. The apparent common description of the objects is as follows:

(1) Metallic or light reflecting surface.

(2) Absence of trail, except in a few instances when the object apparently was operating under high performance conditions.

(3) Circular or elliptical in shape, flat on bottom and domed on top.

(4) Several reports of well kept formation flights varying from three to nine objects.

(5) Normally no associated sound, except in three instances a substantial rumbling sound was heard.

(6) Level flight speeds normally above 300 knots are estimated.

f. It is possible within the present U.S. knowledge – provided extensive detailed development is undertaken – to construct a piloted aircraft which has the general description of the object in sub-paragraph (e) above which would be capable of an approximate range of 7000 miles at subsonic speeds.

g. Any developments in this country along the lines indicated would be extremely expensive, time consuming and at the considerable expense of current projects and therefore, if directed, should be set up independently of existing projects.

h. Due consideration must be given the following:

(1) The possibility that these objects are of domestic origin – the product of some high security project not known to AC/AS-2 or this Command.

(2) The lack of physical evidence in the shape of crash recovered exhibits which would undeniably prove the existence of these objects.

(3) The possibility that some foreign nation has a form of propulsion possibly nuclear, which is outside of our domestic knowledge.

3. It is recommended that:

a. Headquarters, Army Air Forces issue a directive assigning a priority, security classification and Code Name for a detailed study of this matter to include the preparation of complete sets of all available and pertinent [*sic*] data which will then be made available to the Army, Navy, Atomic Energy Commission, JRDB, the Air Force Scientific Advisory Group, NACA, and the RAND and NEPA projects for comments and recommendations, with a preliminary report to be forwarded within 15 days of receipt of the data and a detailed report thereafter every 30 days as the investigation develops. A complete interchange of data should be effected.

4. Awaiting a specific directive AMC will continue the investigation within its current resources in order to more closely define the nature of the phenomenon. Detailed Essential Elements of Information will be formulated immediately for transmittal thru channels.

N.F. Twining.

Lieutenant General, U.S.A.

Commanding'

This document, known as the Twining memorandum, is highly significant, particularly in relation to Roswell. If a disc had crashed and been retrieved by the Army Air Force, as stated in its original press release of July 8, 1947, then there would undoubtedly have been some reference to it in this document. The only scenario that could explain its absence is if the recovery of the debris (and, allegedly, the bodies) had been classified at such a high level as to exclude Twining and his superior officer, General Schulgen, from the chain of command. This appears highly unlikely, although it is significant that Twining admits the possibility of some experimental operation that could have been going on without their knowledge – which would explain the sightings of the 'flying discs'. Conspiracy theorists can point to this with some justification to suggest that the memo does not wholly discount the Roswell Incident. However, it remains improbable that General Schulgen would have been unaware of what had been happening at Wright Field, which was the headquarters of Air Materiel Command, a division of the Army Air Force (and later the Air Force when the two commands were separated in 1947), and the organization most likely to have been involved in the investigation of any crashed UFO. (Supporters of MJ-12, of which Twining was a member, suggest that the memorandum is a smokescreen and that he was merely following orders about not making any reference to Roswell.)

Other secret documents reveal that the Air Force high command was genuinely concerned by the wave of sightings of 'flying discs' in 1947 and mystified as to their origin. Memos and reports from Army

Main Street, Roswell, in the 1940s.

The alien craft crashed in the heart of south-east New Mexico's ranching country.

The location in the New Mexico desert from which, according to Frank Kaufmann, a wrecked alien craft and five bodies were recovered.

An atomic bomb test in Nevada. The first atomic bomb was exploded in the New Mexico desert not far from Roswell two years before the 1947 incident.

Frank Joyce, a reporter for the local radio station, KGFI, announced the news of the Roswell crash and interviewed Mac Brazel, the ranch hand who had found some mysterious debris in the vicinity.

Senator Joseph Montoya, Governor of New Mexico at the time of the Roswell Incident, claimed to have seen two of the aliens at the local airbase.

Frank Kaufmann was a member of a security force attached to the USAAF 509th Squadron at Roswell Army Air Field. He claims that he helped to recover the dead alien occupants of a flying saucer that crash-landed at Roswell in July 1947, and that the bodies and the wrecked craft were kept in Hangar 84 at the local airbase for investigation.

Major Irving Newton, duty weather officer at Carswell Army Air Field, Texas, was ordered to Fort Worth by General Roger Ramey, Commander of the Eighth Air Force, to inspect some debris from the Roswell crash site. Newton is in no doubt that what he saw was part of a weather balloon.

Major Jesse Marcel with pieces of debris from the disputed craft. Marcel was the Intelligence Officer of the USAAF 509th Squadron, based at Roswell.

Jesse Marcel junior insists that the debris his intelligence officer father was asked to show at a press conference after the supposed alien landing was not part of what had crashed near Roswell. He remains convinced that the USAF's 'weather balloon' story was a cover-up.

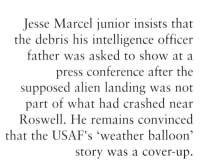

Rick Tungate says that in 1952, as a young USAF captain, he was sent to Roswell to sift through official documents, films and photographs relating to the Incident. His orders were to dispatch some items for storage elsewhere, while others were to be destroyed. Tungate also claims to have seen and communicated telepathically with an extraterrestrial survivor of the Roswell crash.

Professor Charles Moore was a member of the top-secret Project Mogul, based at Alamogordo, New Mexico, which was in progress at the time of the Roswell Incident. Moore and the USAF maintain that the balloon seen here was the 'alien' craft discovered at the isolated crash site.

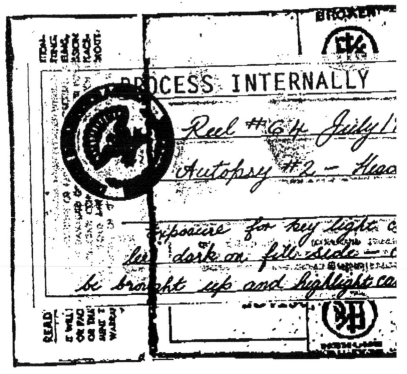

The labels that Ray Santilli, who owns the 'alien autopsy' footage, claims were on the film canisters when he acquired them.

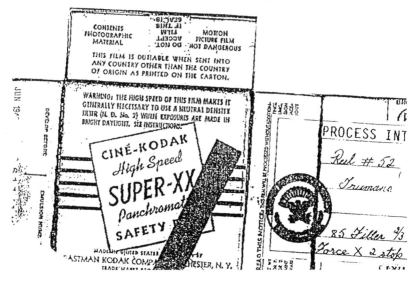

It was the perseverance of Congressman Steven Schiff, the representative for New Mexico, that led to a US government inquiry into the Roswell Incident. The official report was published in 1995, a year after the USAF published the results of its own investigation, likewise prompted by Schiff.

John Purdie with Frank Kaufmann. Purdie was the producer of the Channel Four television documentary *Incident at Roswell*, first shown in the UK in 1995.

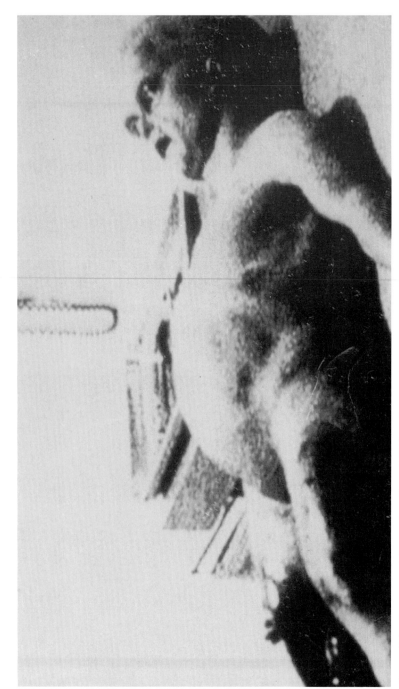

One of the 'creatures' from the alleged 'Alien Autopsy'.

Air Force headquarters in Washington reveal that the FBI had also been notified about the phenomenon and that its assistance was being actively sought. In a letter to the Director of the FBI, dated September 5, 1947, just under three weeks before the Twining memorandum, General Schulgen assured the FBI that there was no secret Air Force project which might explain away the various sightings. In a letter to the FBI's Liaison Section, Schulgen wrote:

'In answer to a verbal request of your Mr S.W. Reynolds, a complete survey of research activities discloses that the Army Air Forces has no project with the characteristics similar to those which have been associated with the Flying Discs.'

The background to this letter relates to what appears to have been a certain amount of bureaucratic infighting between the FBI and the Air Force over the phenomenon. An FBI departmental memo recorded that General Schulgen had requested FBI assistance in tracking down sightings of the 'discs' and an addendum noted:

'I would recommend that we advise the Army that the Bureau does not believe it should go into these investigations, it being noted that a great bulk of these alleged discs reported found have been pranks. It is not believed that the Bureau would accomplish anything by going into these investigations.'

Following this recommendation there is a handwritten note from Clyde Tolson, Hoover's deputy, saying, 'I think we should do this.' This in turn is followed by a handwritten note from J. Edgar Hoover, replying, 'I would do it but before agreeing we must insist upon full access to discs recovered. For instance in the [illegible] case the Army grabbed it and would not let us have it for cursory examination.'

Unfortunately, Hoover's handwriting is so bad that it is not clear which case he is referring to. The badly scrawled word appears to be 'La', which could mean Los Angeles or Louisiana or something completely different. (A later FBI document, dated July 24, refers to the Director's comments and reprints his note and the illegible word as 'La' without making it any clearer what it refers to.)

If it meant Louisiana then Hoover may have been referring to a case in Shreveport, which was a hoax involving a sixteen-inch aluminium disc and some radio parts that occurred on July 7, 1947. However, the Army Air Force did cooperate with the FBI on this case, so it is unlikely that Hoover would have cited it. There is an intriguing possibility that he is referring to Roswell, but given that the memo is dated July 15, 1947, in the midst of so many sightings, it is impossible to be sure.

Nine days later a memo to D.M. Ladd, the FBI agent handling the correspondence at its Washington headquarters, noted that the FBI had re-contacted General Schulgen and advised him of the Director's misgivings:

'General Schulgen indicated to [name of agent blacked out] that he desired to assure Mr. Hoover of complete co-operation in this matter and stated that he would issue instructions to the field directing that all co-operation be furnished to the FBI and that all discs recovered be made available for examination by the FBI agents. General Schulgen pointed out that he will from time to time make the results of the studies of his scientists available to the Bureau for the assistance of the FBI Field Offices. General Schulgen indicated that . . . there has been a decrease in the reported sightings of the discs which might be because of the fact that it has lost much of its publicity value. He indicated however that he believed it necessary to follow this matter through to determine as near as possible if discs were in fact seen and to determine their origin.'

Apart from interdepartmental rivalry, J. Edgar Hoover would undoubtedly have been interested in the 'flying disc' phenomenon as a result of the initial suspicions that it could have been some sort of Soviet secret weapon or even some fiendish communist plot to sow discord and panic among the American people – a notion that would be taken up by the CIA a few years later. The Air Force was also alive to the possibility of mischief-making.

The same memo reports that 'General Schulgen indicated that he believed that there was a possibility that this entire matter might have been started by subversive individuals for the purpose of creating mass hysteria. He suggested that the Bureau keep this in mind in any interviews conducted regarding reported sightings.'

The FBI seemed to have followed this advice and taken an active interest in both sightings and the sort of people who reported them. One FBI document which was filed on September 17, 1947 is of particular interest as it corroborates what has become the most famous sighting of all time and confirms the unusual UFO activity which preceded the Roswell Incident by just a few days. The document is a standard FBI Office Memorandum communiqué to Hoover at the Washington Headquarters and is worth quoting in full:

'To: Director, FBI
From: SAC Portland
Subject: REPORTS OF FLYING DISCS
SECURITY MATTER – X
Refer San Francisco letter dated September 4, 1947
[first part of sentence blacked out], Portland, reported without consulting any records that on June 24, 1947, while prospecting at a point in the Cascade Mountains approximately five thousand feet from sea level, during the afternoon he noticed a reflection, looked up, and saw a disc proceeding in a south-easterly direction. Immediately upon sighting this object he placed his telescope to his eye and observed the disc for approximately forty five to sixty seconds. He remarked that it is possible for him to pick up an object at a distance of ten miles with his telescope. At the time the disc was sighted by Mr. [name blacked out] it was banking in the sun, and he observed five or six similar objects but only concentrated on one. He related that they did not fly in any particular formation and that he would estimate their height to be about one thousand feet from where he was standing. He said the object was about thirty feet in diameter and appeared to have a tail. It made no noise.

'According to [name blacked out] he remained in the vicinity of the Cascades for several days and then returned to Portland and noted an article in the local paper which stated in effect that a man in Boise, Idaho, had sighted a similar object but that authorities had disclaimed any knowledge of such an object. He said he communicated with the Army for the sole purpose of attempting to add credence to the story furnished by the man in Boise.

'[name blanked out] also related that on the occasion of his sighting the objects on June 24, 1947 he had in his possession a combination compass and watch. He noted particularly that immediately before he sighted the disc the compass acted very peculiar, the hand waving from one side to the other, but that this condition corrected itself immediately after the discs had passed out of sight.

'Informant appeared to be a very reliable individual who advised that he had been a prospector in the states of Montana, Washington, and Oregon for the past forty years.'

This sighting corroborates Kenneth Arnold's legendary incident to such a close extent as to be almost uncanny. While there exists the possibility that the 'informant' was reporting this after having read of Arnold's encounter, it seems unlikely that at that time someone would have been motivated to make this up and then go to the trouble of notifying both the Army and the FBI. Given that the Special Agent in Charge of the Portland Office found him to be 'very reliable' and that the Bureau was already on the lookout for hoaxers and subversives, it is probable that the sighting is absolutely genuine and therefore historic confirmation of Arnold's extraordinary experience, which many regard as the first and most important encounter of modern times.

The Arnold case was also the catalyst for the Air Force to commence the first of its official and secret investigations into the UFO phenomenon: Project Sign. This was officially launched on December 30, 1947 by a letter from the Chief of Staff to the head of Air Materiel Command, which was soon to become known as Air Technical Intelligence Command (ATIC).

9

Project XS–304 was the suitably obscure file number attached to the classified Air Force study of 'flying discs'. On August 5, 1948 the Air Force presented General Hoyt Vandenberg, its Chief of Staff, with its 'Estimate of the Situation'. Although there was no mention of Roswell, General Vandenberg was so alarmed by its conclusions that he ordered all copies of the document to be burned. The situation report's crime had been to attach too much credence to the extraterrestrial hypothesis. According to Captain Edward Ruppelt, later to head the successor Air Force study of UFOs, 'Project Blue Book', the 'Estimate' had concluded that the UFOs were 'interplanetary in origin'.

General Vandenberg's rejection was supposedly based on his assessment that there was insufficient proof for the investigating group to have reached such a conclusion. Ufologists who subscribe to the conspiracy theory point to the fact that Vandenberg is named as one of the members of MJ-12 and was therefore merely maintaining the cover-up in the knowledge that aliens had really landed at Roswell. While this is plausible, there is no evidence other than suspicion.

Later Captain Ruppelt reported his understanding of General Vandenberg's justification for censoring the assessment of Project Sign: 'The General said it would cause a stampede. How could we convince the public the aliens weren't hostile when we didn't know it ourselves?'

On December 16, 1948 Project Sign underwent a further change of identity to become Project Grudge – which completed its evaluations in the summer of 1949, simultaneously downgrading and declassifying the mass of raw data which it had accumulated. The final report was based on an analysis of 243 domestic and 30 foreign incidents and included work subcontracted to the University of Ohio and specifically aimed at investigating the astro-physical dimension of the sightings (or, more prosaically, studying those cases where the incident could be safely blamed on Venus or some other celestial scapegoat). This section was being carried out under the auspices of Dr J. Allen Hynek, who had been the Air Force's consultant on astronomy. There was also a special study by the Rand Corporation to evaluate the 'remote possibility' that some of the observed objects may have been spaceships or satellite vehicles. Yet by the time Sign had metamorphosed into Grudge, the analysis was dismissive of the 'extraterrestrial' hypothesis: 'The possibility that some of the incidents may represent technical developments far in advance of knowledge available to engineers and scientists of this country has been considered. No facts are available to personnel at this Command that will permit an objective assessment of this possibility. All information so far presented on the possible existence of space ships from another planet or of aircraft propelled by an advanced type of atomic power plant have been largely conjecture.'

Naturally, one wishes to avoid the tempting trap of resorting to close textual analysis to revive any flagging conspiracy theories, yet it must be pointed out that the above statement is somewhat strange. The sentence 'No facts are available to personnel at this Command that will permit an objective assessment of this possibility' seems almost tailor-made to permit the report's creator a licence to be economical with the truth. And, while a long way from substantiating the Roswell story, the whole paragraph is not too many light-years away from the form of words that might have been chosen by someone possessed of superior knowledge and dark secrets yet bound by an oath of loyalty and the spiralling demands of secrecy not to reveal the truth. A truth that could all too easily stampede a gullible and impressionable public into a frenzy of hysteria, exactly as feared by General Vandenberg. Nor does the statement make any reference to the earlier conclusion of Project Sign – a curious omission, unless the report had been so successfully excised from the official memory that no one knew what its conclusions were.

Considering that the Air Force lost little opportunity to debunk the myth of 'flying saucers' and little green men, it is all the more strange that it should have been less than categorical in its denunciation in this report. One does not have to subscribe wholeheartedly to conspiracy theory to find something significant in phrases such as 'information so far . . .' and 'largely conjecture' used in reference to extraterrestrial explanations. Without reading too much into it, it is worth noting that the descriptions fall well short of the forthright denials that one has come to expect from officialdom. The paragraph ends lamely with a conclusion that is similarly lacking in the note of certainty that characterizes most official assessments touching on the interplanetary hypothesis. Here the report is discussing the probability of a hitherto incredible means of propulsion: 'based on experience with nuclear power plant research in this country, the existence on earth of such engines of small enough size and weight to have powered the objects described is *highly improbable*.' (author's italics)

Having waded through their 244 reports, the faceless officials behind Projects Sign and Grudge arrived at a point which was more or less identical to where they had started, for they concluded: 'Evaluations of UFOs to date demonstrate that these flying objects constitute no threat to the security of the United States . . . reports of UFOs were the result of misinterpretations of conventional objects, a mild form of mass hysteria or war nerves, and individuals who fabricate such reports to perpetrate a hoax or seek publicity.'

While the Air Force was seemingly preoccupied with playing down and dismissing the potential hazard of hostile flying saucers, mounting concern was beginning to be felt in other quarters of the American intelligence community. This dichotomy was to epitomize the divided mind of the Air Force and its paymasters over the following decades. During this period they professed with tedious frequency that there was nothing to the whole phenomenon other than a phenomenon that couldn't be explained, while all the time worrying about it in secret and attempting to find out what, if anything, lay behind it and whether it posed a threat to National Security.

On January 31, 1949, writing in a confidential memorandum to the Director of the FBI in Washington DC, the Special Agent in Charge of the San Antonio Office expressed concern about the protection of some of America's most vital secret installations in the face of the flying saucer menace, reporting that at a 'recent Weekly Intelligence Conference of G-2, OHI, OSI, and FBI, in the Fourth Army Area, officers of G-2, Fourth Army have discussed the matter of "Unidentified Aircraft" or "Unidentified Aerial Phenomena", otherwise known as "Flying Discs", "Flying Saucers", and "Balls of Fire". This matter is considered top secret by Intelligence Officers of both the Army and the Air Force.

'It is well known that there have been during the past two years reports from various parts of the country of the sighting of unidentified aerial objects which have been called in newspaper parlance "flying discs" and "flying saucers". The first such sightings were reported from Sweden, and it was thought that the objects, the nature of which was unknown, might have originated in Russia.

'In July 1948 an unidentified aircraft was "seen" by an Eastern Airlines pilot and co-pilot and one or more passengers of the Eastern Airlines plane over Montgomery, Alabama. This aircraft was reported to be of an unconventional type without wings and resembled generally a "rocket ship" of the type depicted in comic strips. It was reported to have had windows; to have been larger than the Eastern Airlines plane and to have been travelling at an estimated speed of 2700 miles an hour. It appeared out of a thunderhead ahead of the Eastern Airlines plane and immediately disappeared in another cloud narrowly missing a collision with the Eastern Airlines plane. No sound or air disturbance was noticed in connection with this appearance.

'During the past two months various sightings of unexplained phenomena have been reported in the vicinity of the A.E.C. Installation at Los Alamos, New Mexico, where these phenomena now appear to be concentrated. During December 1948, on the 5th, 6th, 7th, 8th, 11th, 13th, 14th, 20th and 28th sightings of unexplained phenomena were made near Los Alamos by Special Agents of the Office of Special Investigation; Airline Pilots; Military Pilots; Los Alamos Security Inspectors, and private citizens. On January 6, 1949, another similar object was sighted in the same area.

'[Name blacked out], a Meteorologist of some note, has been generally in charge of the observations near Los Alamos, attempting to learn characteristics of the unexplained phenomenon. Up to this time little concrete information has been obtained

'There have been day time sightings which are tentatively considered to possibly resemble the exhaust of some type of jet propelled object.

'Night-time sightings have taken the form of lights usually described as brilliant green, similar to a green traffic signal or green neon light. Some reports indicated that the light began and ended with a red or orange flash. Other reports have given the colour as red, white, blue-white, and yellowish green. Trailing lights sometimes observed are said to be red. The spectrum analysis of one light indicates that it may be a copper compound of the type known to be used in rocket experiments and which completely disintegrates upon explosion, leaving no debris. It is noted that no debris has ever been known to be located anywhere resulting from the unexplained phenomena.

'Recent observations have indicated that the unidentified phenomena travel at a rate of speed estimated at a minimum of three miles per second and a maximum of twelve miles per second, or a mean calculated speed of seven and one-half miles a second, or 27,000 miles an hour. Their reported course indicates that they travel on an East–West line with probability that they approach from the Northern quadrant, which would be the last stage of the great circle route if they originated in Russia. When observed they seem to be in level flight at a height of six to ten miles and thus travelling on a tangent to the earth's surface. They occasionally dip at the end of the path and on two occasions a definite change in path was indicated. These phenomena have not been known to have been sighted, however, at any intermediate point between Russia and Los Alamos, but only at the end of the flight toward the apparent "target", namely, Los Alamos.

'In every case but one the shape of the objects has been recorded as round in a point of light with a definite area to the light's source. One report gives a diamond shape; another indicates that trailing lights are elongated. The size is usually compared to one-fourth the diameter of the full moon, and they have also been compared in size to a basketball with trailing lights the size of a baseball.

'On no occasion has sound been associated directly with the phenomenon, but unexplained sounds have been reported from Los Alamos.

'On two occasions reports have been received of the sighting of multiple units. Some nine scientific reasons are stated to exist which indicated that the phenomena observed are not due to meteorites. The only conclusions reached thus far are that they are either hitherto unobserved natural phenomena or that they are man made. No scientific experiments are known to exist in this country which could give rise to such phenomena.'

As these sightings became more frequent, the defence establishment became increasingly concerned. Army and Air Force Intelligence and the CIA all investigated the sightings to no avail. In the New Year of 1949, Colonel Poland of US Army Intelligence (G-2), sent a memo on behalf of the Commanding General of the Fourth Army at Houston,

Texas to the Director of Army Intelligence at the Pentagon expressing their collective anxiety:

'Agencies in New Mexico are greatly concerned over these phenomena. They are of the opinion that some foreign power is making "sensing shots" with some super-stratosphere device designed to be self-disintegrating . . . Another theory advanced as possibly acceptable lies in the belief that the phenomena are the result of radiological warfare experiments by a foreign power, further, that the rays may be lethal or might be attributed to the cause of the plane crashes that have occurred recently.

'Still another belief . . . is that it is highly probable that the United States may be carrying on some top-secret experiments . . . It is felt that these incidents are of such great importance, especially as they are occurring in the vicinity of sensitive installations, that a scientific board be sent to this locality to study the situation with a view of arriving at a solution of this extraordinary phenomena with the least practicable delay.'

Moving with uncharacteristic speed, the military bureaucracy set up a secret conference on February 16, 1949 to discuss the UFO phenomena at Los Alamos. The distinguished company included Dr Edward Teller, the 'Father of the Atom Bomb', and Dr Lincoln La Paz, an eminent astronomer from the University of New Mexico. La Paz was absolutely convinced that the green fireballs were not conventional fireballs or meteorites. Along with several other scientists and military personnel, he had been astonished to witness one of the extraordinary sightings himself on December 12, 1948.

'This fireball appeared in full intensity instantly – there was no increase in light . . . Its colour, estimated to be somewhere around wave length 5200 angstroms, was a green hue, such as I had never observed in meteor falls before. The path was as nearly horizontal as one could determine by visual observation . . . Just before the end . . . the green fireball broke into fragments, still bright green.'

A special project was set up, Project Twinkle, to make a scientific study of the phenomena. But Dr La Paz and his team never arrived at a positive conclusion – or, if they did it was never published – and the sightings continued. Atomic research installations and other secret military sites would figure with mysterious frequency in UFO reports over the next thirty years. There are various theories as to why this should have occurred: from anomalous geological and weather conditions, creating strange special effects in the sky – the most likely of which is 'ball lightning' – to the fact that these installations have extremely tight security and as there is usually someone on guard duty twenty-four hours a day, it is likely that such a person will see more strange occurrences than would be witnessed in other locations.

The advantage of these occurrences at these sites was the fact that many of the witnesses were trained observers or scientists and therefore able to offer detailed descriptions of what they saw even if they couldn't explain it. Chet Lytle is just such a person. Today he is a tall, imposing, white-haired, elderly gentleman who is still active in electronics and manufacturing. In the 1940s he was a trained scientist who, early in the Second World War, designed radio transmitters and receivers for weather balloons and went on to found a small manufacturing company which carried out work for the Manhattan Project, producing components that were used in the design for the firing mechanism of the atomic bomb. A frequent visitor to the White Sands Missile Range, near Alamogordo, Lytle had his manufacturing operation at the Kirtland Air Force Base (White Sands and Kirtland are about two hundred miles apart). Lytle recalls one incident that occurred when an atomic bomb was being stored close to the runway at the airbase.

'We noted extraterrestrial vehicles who we thought were actually observing what we were doing. We were unable to nail these down except with theodolites that were available. The vehicles looked very much like the vehicle that we see [today]: a disc and a bump on top and moved very rapidly when they wanted to depart. It seemed like the actual observations occurred at unusual hours – many times in the early morning when we were there because we would do a lot of things on the base with the atomic weapons under the cover of darkness and it was in the early morning that we noticed these things and the observations seemed to be from vehicles that were concerned about what we were doing here at Kirtland Air Force Base.'

Lytle is convinced that the 'vehicles' soon realized when they were being investigated and would then move 'very rapidly out of sight at high speeds'. He estimates that they were capable of moving at anywhere between 5000 and 10,000mph.

On a separate occasion at Wright Field, Lytle received further confirmation of the UFO mystery and identical evasive tactics when he was invited to view a film taken in flight by Air Force pilots. 'I observed a monitor screen of the vehicles that came in there when they sent a jet up and the jets were attempting to catch up with the

UFOs and they were unable to keep up with them and as soon as they were observed the vehicles moved very rapidly out of sight.'

Although unable to remember the exact date, Lytle places it in the late 1940s or early '50s. This would make sense as it was the time when saucermania was at its highest and the period of sightings at secret defence installations which had led to heightened concern within the Air Force. Lytle's experience is one that was shared by many scientists and high-ranking officers who worked at the various top-secret military installations that are clustered around the New Mexico desert. Even arch-sceptic Charles Moore, engaged on Project Mogul and other balloon launches at Alamogordo in 1947, filed an official report of his own 'close encounter'.

'I've seen a lot of UFOs,' Moore admitted when I met him in New Mexico in 1995 to hear his account of Project Mogul and his conviction that it was one of their balloons that was picked up on the Foster ranch and lay behind the mystery of the Roswell episode. 'Some of them were our balloons or other people's balloons. I've seen one object which was when I was preparing to fly a large balloon for the Navy. I was making a wind measurement and saw an object that resembled a balloon but moving much more rapidly and I tracked it with my theodolite and it went against the wind, which I determined later, and took about sixty-five seconds to go across the sky down into the north-east and then increased in elevation angle by getting small quite rapidly and we reported it.'

The Army Air Force, to whom Moore was under contract, was also unable to explain it and it joined the growing list of unexplained sightings that made up part of the case log for Project Blue Book.

Although today the USAF dismisses out of hand any notion that any unidentified flying objects or 'unidentified aerial phenomena' (UAP) could have an extraterrestrial explanation, in the wake of the vast number of sightings in America and their own research projects in the late 1940s, as we have seen in the censored 'Estimate' report, they were prepared to keep a much more open mind. Despite General Vandenberg's order to destroy all copies of the report, he was unable to completely remove the notion of the 'ETH' from official thinking. In one of the Appendices to Project Sign, there were various references to the 'Extraterrestrial hypothesis'. In 'Appendix "C" "Some Considerations Affecting the Interpretation of Reports of Unidentified Flying Objects"', compiled by G.E. Valley, a member of the Scientific Advisory Board from the Office of the Chief of Staff,

United States Air Force, in a section headed 'Space Ships', it was noted that:

'The following considerations pertain:

a. If there is an extraterrestrial civilization which can make such objects as are reported then it is most probable that its development is far in advance of ours. This argument can be supported on probability arguments alone without recourse to astronomical hypotheses.

b. Such a civilization might observe that on Earth we now have atomic bombs and are fast developing rockets. In view of the past history of mankind, they should be alarmed. We should, therefore, expect at this time above all to behold such visitations.

'Since the acts of mankind most easily observed from a distance are A-bomb explosions we should expect some relation to obtain between the time of A-bomb explosions, the time at which the space ships are seen, and the time required for such ships to arrive from and return to home base.'

The concept of 'flying saucers' being space vehicles from another planet was further explored by J.E. Lipp of the Missiles Division of the Rand Corporation. In a letter to the head of research and development at the Air Force, he outlined some of the possibilities of life beyond earth while another research report investigated the design and performance characteristics that might be associated with spaceships. In a fascinating insight into how far scientific knowledge has progressed in a relatively short space of time, Lipp considered the possibility of life forms on both Mars and Venus. Lipp wrote: 'Astronomers are largely in agreement that only one member of the Solar system (besides Earth) can support higher forms of life. It is the planet Mars. Even Mars appears quite desolate and inhospitable so that a race would be more occupied with survival than we are on Earth.'

Then Lipp quotes *Earth, Moon and Planets*, by F.L. Whipple: 'If we have correctly reconstructed the history of Mars, there is little reason to believe that the life processes may not have followed a course similar to terrestrial evolution. With this assumption, three general possibilities emerge. Intelligent beings may have protected themselves against the excessively slow loss of atmosphere, oxygen and water, by constructing homes and cities with the physical conditions scientifically controlled. As a second possibility, evolution may have developed a being who can withstand the rigors of the Martian climate. Or the race may have perished.'

Lipp extrapolates from the Martian hypothesis to speculate: 'It is not too unreasonable to go a step further and consider Venus as a possible home for intelligent life. The atmosphere, to be sure, apparently consists mostly of carbon dioxide with deep clouds of formaldehyde droplets and there seems to be little or no water.

'Yet living organisms might develop in chemical environments that are strange to us: the vegetable kingdom, for example, operates on a fundamentally different energy cycle from man. Various people have suggested that an advanced race may have been visiting Earth from Mars or Venus at intervals from decades to aeons. Reports of objects in the sky seem to have been handed down through the generations. If this were true, a race of such knowledge and power would have established some form of direct contact. They could see that Earth's inhabitants would be helpless to do interplanetary harm. If afraid of carrying diseases home, they would at least try to communicate. It is hard to believe that any technically accomplished race would come here, flaunt its ability in mysterious ways and then simply go away . . . a race which had enough initiative to explore among the planets would hardly be too timid to follow through when the job was accomplished.

'One other hypothesis needs to be discussed. It is that the Martians have kept a long-term routine watch on Earth and have been alarmed by the sight of our A-bomb shots as evidence that we are warlike and on the threshold of space travel . . . The first flying objects were sighted in the spring of 1947, after a total of 5 atomic bomb explosions, i.e Alamogordo, Hiroshima, Nagasaki, Crossroads A and Crossroads B. Of these, the first two were in positions to be seen from Mars, the third was very doubtful (at the edge of Earth's disc in daylight) and the last two were on the wrong side of Earth. It is likely that Martian astronomers, with their thin atmosphere, could build telescopes big enough to see A-bomb explosions on Earth, even though we were 165 and 153 million miles away, respectively, on the Alamogordo and Hiroshima dates. The weakest point in the hypothesis is that a continual, defensive watch of Earth for long periods of time (perhaps thousands of years) would be dull sport, and no race that even remotely resembled man would undertake it. We haven't even considered the idea for Venus or Mars, for example.'

*   *   *

The notion that UFOs might be evidence of some benign interest from our extraterrestrial neighbours soon became popular currency and a host of increasingly incredible accounts of visitations by handsome visitors from out of this world began to appear in the popular press and in magazines and books. An author named Dr Daniel Fry (the doctorate seemed as fanciful as the story he had to tell) wrote a book with the topical title of *White Sands Incident*. He claimed that, while working at the White Sands Proving Ground, the New Mexico base for America's early rocket tests and development of missile technology, he had seen a flying saucer land. Curious, he approached and was about to reach out a hand to make contact when a voice was heard saying, 'Better not touch the hull, pal, it's still hot!'

Once things had cooled down, Fry made contact with a being answering to the strangely terrestrial name of 'A-lan', which was conveniently abbreviated to 'Alan' for the sake of interstellar communication. The 'Alan' being invited Fry aboard and kindly flew him to New York City and back, the round trip taking less than thirty minutes. During the flight Alan asked Fry to author a book about his extraordinary experiences so that the world wouldn't fall into the 'terrible abyss' of a nuclear holocaust. Alan patiently explained to the earthling writer that he and his people were unable to make such an appeal in person because they knew that the appearance of space people would upset the delicate 'ego-balance' of Earth's entire civilization. Additional and timely advice came in the message that universal 'Understanding' among the people of Earth would solve most of our social and political ills. The advice was apparently heeded in part, as so far we have succeeded in not blowing ourselves up.

Other contemporary accounts of close encounters included that of a self-employed sign painter from New Jersey, Howard Menger, who had been introduced to a flying saucer and its occupants as early as 1932 in a small forest. In sharp contrast to the small and vicious creatures of today, who seem determined to carry out fiendish and uncomfortable medical experiments on their abductees in the privacy of their airborne operating theatres, the earlier aliens of the 1950s were considerably nicer. Menger's New Jersey specimen was a beautiful long-haired blonde, reclining on a rock beside a crystal-clear brook. Instead of witnessing the emaciated arms and larger than human head with almond-shaped eyes, Menger was confronted by a creature clad in a translucent 'ski-suit' underneath which our lucky 'contactee' could make out 'the curves of her lovely body'. Not surprisingly, this encounter in the wilds of New Jersey produced a 'tremendous surge of warmth, love and physical attraction'. This vision of extraterrestrial heaven explained to the young boy that she 'had come a long way' and promptly disappeared. His next encounter occurred while on leave from the Army in Juárez, Mexico, just across the border from El Paso, Texas. A young man with long, blond hair invited the young soldier to join him in the back of a taxi, and although Menger turned him down, he discovered later that the young man was another emissary from outer space. He was also informed that the Mexicans were one of the privileged races, having been contacted 'long before the . . . Conquistadores made contact with the Aztecs'. The fair-haired extraterrestrials had shared many of their secrets with the older civilizations of earth only to see all their knowledge and superior technology lost through invasion and conquest by more aggressive races.

During a subsequent posting to Hawaii, Menger drove off the beaten track to some picturesque caves where he was fortunate enough to experience another encounter. This time the vision was of a dusky beauty contained within a pink, translucent tunic and trousers. She transmitted the same powerful expression of spiritual well-being combined with 'a strong physical attraction one finds impossible to allay when in the presence of these women'.

Menger survived these intergalactic stirrings and the war to write a book in 1959 titled *From Outer Space to You*, a chronicle of his numerous encounters as an intermediary for the aliens, in which capacity he was obliged to supply them with various artefacts from earth. These included a collection of brassières for a flying saucer full of girls whose ungrateful response on receiving them was to throw them back at him, remarking that where they came from they didn't wear such things! The aliens appeared rather more friendly when in return for his assistance they reciprocated by revealing to him the secrets of a 'free energy motor'. No doubt to the consternation of Ford and General Motors, the author was able to illustrate the device with the aid of a photograph of himself holding a small device consisting of ball-bearings attached to a spring via a central mechanism.

Menger was also able to console himself with the knowledge that he was not alone in his experience of a close encounter with a female of the extraterrestrial species. Truman Bethurum published his diary of adventures in outer space in 1954, *Aboard a Flying Saucer*. The author was a former road builder from California and his encounter was initially with the more familiar 'small sized men . . . about five feet tall'. Speaking perfect English, the all-male delegation invited him on board to meet their female captain, Aura Rhanes, described by the author as being 'tops in shapeliness and beauty'. Aura hailed from the planet Clarion, which was perpetually hidden behind our moon, a place devoid of politics and taxes where creatures like her could pass themselves off as human when they came to earth. The author was provided with evidence of this when he met Aura in a restaurant drinking orange juice and she ignored him.

Perhaps the most celebrated of all the contactees of this period was George Adamski, a Polish immigrant born in 1891 who went on to become one of the most celebrated and later infamous of all ufologists. He co-authored *Flying Saucers Have Landed* with British writer Desmond Leslie in 1953 and it became a best-seller. There followed a book based on his extraordinary interstellar travels, *Inside the Space Ships*, which related his numerous encounters with alien beings, all of whom were uncannily similar to us in appearance apart from the fact that they were uncommonly beautiful. His new travelling companions came from Jupiter, Venus and Saturn, to name but a few. He also published several photographs, now widely dismissed as fakes, and claimed that the leader of the 'Space People' was known as 'The Master'. Adamski was fortunate enough to spend many hours in philosophical discourse with 'The Master' as they sped together across the universe, enjoying an in-flight service of drinks and hospitality from a succession of beautiful alien girls. Despite the blatant improbability of his adventures, Adamski was hailed as a star performer on the American lecture circuit as well as on radio and television talk shows. He has certainly earned the distinction of being the first successful money-spinning author to create a whole body of pictures and writing based on nothing more tangible than the public's willingness to believe a good story in preference to the truth!

Adamski's aliens had the interests of the human race at heart, patiently explaining to their captive audience that their mission was to warn the earthlings of the danger that they ran in experimenting with their new atomic weapons which threatened to destroy the planet. The author's mission was to pass on the message, a mission he accomplished with both material success and an ability to perpetuate the hoax over many years before his death in 1965.

It is significant that many of the elements of Adamski's adventures as a contactee would be faithfully reproduced in later accounts, not only the ones mentioned, penned by his contemporaries, but also those that have emanated more recently from the word-processors of writers such as the best-selling Whitley Strieber, whose book *Communion* is an account of how he has been abducted by aliens since his childhood. That the author was already a successful writer of science fiction and novels does not seem to have dampened the public's appetite for swallowing such tall stories. Perversely, people seem more inclined to believe them the more transparent the motive of those who are trying to sell them!

10

A number of social and technological factors came together in the years just after the Second World War to stimulate the public appetite for outlandish tales and science fiction. Most importantly, the end of the war had liberated the American people from the anxieties of the 1940s and, around this time, there were a number of scientific developments which appeared to fulfil the unwitting prophecies of an earlier generation of science-fiction writers. When the 'flying saucer' sightings of 1947 reached epidemic proportions, this almost hysterical interest was eagerly seized upon by the growing number of publishers, writers, journalists and film-makers who were riding and creating the bandwagon that was the driving force behind the demand for tales of the fantastic from demons in the sky to monsters of the deep, from the hard-back books of Jules Verne to the comic magazine exploits of Dan Dare, Buck Rogers and Superman.

One key figure in this expanding universe was Ray Palmer, who was the Editor-in-Chief of *Amazing Stories*, a monthly magazine in America dedicated to 'true' stories that contained an element of the unbelievable and the fantastic. A favourite theme of the series was contained in several stories written by Richard Sharpe Shaver, a self-proclaimed explorer who wrote accounts of his journeys to a mysterious subterranean kingdom deep inside the earth which was inhabited by two warring tribes: the Deros and the Teros. Among the claims that Shaver made was the proposition that it was possible to see the craft of these subterranean races flying through the heavens above their underground kingdom as well as spaceships from other planets colonized by the descendants of the people of Atlantis who had apparently emigrated into space at the time of the destruction of Atlantis some 12,000 years before. Shaver's stories became enormously popular, with some editions of the magazine achieving sales of 250,000 copies.

The June 1947 issue was wholly devoted to Shaver's underground kingdom and the October issue was quick to capitalize on the 'saucer' craze of that summer. 'A part of the now world-famous Shaver Mystery has now been proved! On 25 June (and subsequent confirmation included earlier dates), mysterious supersonic vessels, either space ships or ships from the caves, were sighted in this country! A summation of facts proves that these ships were not, nor can be, attributed to any civilization now on the face of the Earth.'

Another magazine, which was more of a newsletter than a publication, was *Doubt*, which had been started by members of the Fortean Society, a group dedicated to the memory of Charles Fort, the founding father of writings about strange phenomena, the unexplained, the paranormal and celestial happenings. The 1947 autumn edition contained extensive coverage of the 'flying discs' phenomenon. Ray Palmer was also quick off the mark to follow up on the famous Kenneth Arnold case. He wrote to him on July 15, asking if he would be prepared to put his experience in writing for the magazine and would be willing to investigate another sighting which had occurred nearby at the port of Tacoma. There, two witnesses had observed a flying saucer which they reported had blown up, showering them with fragments, some of which they had managed to keep. Arnold was intrigued by Palmer's assignment and although he had turned down several other offers to capitalize on his adventure, he agreed on this occasion and enlisted his friend and fellow eyewitness, the United Airlines pilot, Captain E.J. Smith. Arnold even contacted his two Air Force investigators, Brown and Davidson, who agreed to come and interview the new witnesses. However, after the debris was denounced by Arnold as a piece of lava the rest of the case quickly fell apart. It was one of the increasing number of hoaxes which, unfortunately, would in succeeding years become the staple diet of the supermarket tabloids, where they were invariably presented as true. However, it is to the credit of the editor of *Amazing Stories* that he went to the trouble of investigating such a case when it would have been all too easy just to publish the story. Today's American supermarket tabloids, such as the *National Enquirer* and *World News*, have yet to discover 'investigative journalism' or, some might add with justification, 'journalism' of any sort.

Palmer capitalized on the success he had enjoyed with *Amazing Stories* and started up his own magazine, *Fate*, the following year. His first edition, in 1948, contained a detailed account of Arnold's Cascade Mountains sighting.

A major reason for the fast-growing public interest in the subjects covered by magazines like *Amazing Stories* and *Fate* was the development of technologies that until recently most people had deemed to be rooted in the imagination of science-fiction writers. First and foremost was the development of rockets. Unlike Britons, who had become frighteningly familiar with the sound and shape of the V-1 and the V-2, most Americans had barely heard of, let alone seen, any rockets or jets by the end of the war. When the inventor of Hitler's terrifying secret weapons was spirited out of occupied Germany by American intelligence at the end of the war, America's space programme was born. What had hitherto been confined to the pages of science-fiction books and comics could now be seen for real in the deserts of New Mexico and in the upbeat weekly newsreel reports at the cinema.

Wernher von Braun was born in Wirsitz (now Wyrzysk, Poland). He received a PhD from the University of Berlin in 1934 and began experimenting with rockets in his youth. From 1937 to 1945 he was director of the German Rocket Research Centre at Peenemünde on the Baltic Sea, in charge of developing the V-2 long-range liquid-fuel rocket, used to bombard England during the final stages of the Second World War. In 1945 he was captured by American intelligence and in exchange for his freedom agreed to go to the USA as a technical adviser to the US rocket programme at the White Sands Proving Ground in New Mexico. In effect he was in charge of the facility and along with the captured bounty of several German V-2 rockets, Von Braun presided over a series of launches and attempts to develop a new range of rockets. In 1950 he was transferred to Huntsville, Alabama, where for ten years he headed the Redstone missile programme. Von Braun was naturalized a US citizen in 1955 and in 1960 became director of development operations at the George C. Marshall Space Flight Center (NASA) in Huntsville. He played a pivotal part in the development of the USA's space programme and was a significant factor in assisting the Americans in their race to beat the Russians in the new frontiers of space exploration. He was also responsible for the development of the Saturn V launch vehicle that was used, with the Apollo spacecraft, in the manned lunar landing programme.

In the summer of 1947 Von Braun and many other captured German scientists, along with their American counterparts, were experimenting in New Mexico with captured V-2 rockets and working on a programme that included the designs for a new generation of rockets and missiles. Although it is generally recognized that this was the beginning of the Space Programme, the primary aim of Von Braun's flight experiments at White Sands was to provide a more accurate and powerful version of his V-2: to fly higher, travel further and carry more explosives.

'The V-2 programme started here around 1946,' recalls Don Montoya, the public information officer at White Sands, a keen historian of the missile range. 'That's the time that Wernher von Braun and a lot of his scientists who were under him in Germany but who had been obtained by the Americans under a programme called "Operation Paperclip" came to this area. First of all they were stationed at Fort Bliss, Texas, and they made their journey every single day up to White Sands Proving Ground starting around early January 1946 . . . the number of German scientists who came up here reached [its] height in about March 1946 and then the first successful launch of a V-2 – which was reassembled from parts that had been captured and reconfigured – took place in May of 1946 and achieved an altitude of about seventy kilometres above the earth's surface.' In the early days when up to one hundred former Nazi scientists were engaged on Project Hermes, the code-name for America's first rocket development programme, they would attempt to rebuild usable rockets from V-2 pods and launch them as high and as far as they could. General Electric, the giant defence and consumer electronics company, was an eager participant, hoping to discover the secrets of the technology now being practised by the Germans.

'The V-2s were primarily used for scientific purposes more than any kind of military purpose, scientific payloads such as photography, X-ray and cosmic experiments were taken a lot in the nose cones of the V-2s that were launched from White Sands,' Montoya explains. 'These included anything from amoebas and mice to one series which was known as Project Albert, which launched a small monkey in one of the nose cones; needless to say, the monkey didn't survive due to some technical difficulties with the nose cone re-entering the earth's atmosphere.'

At Holloman Air Force Base, which was adjacent to White Sands, the Aero-Medical division was also conducting experiments. The purpose of its programme was to detect the effects of high-altitude space flight on living organisms. Declassified film footage from this period shows that a veritable menagerie of animals were press ganged into service for the greater glory of Uncle Sam. One film shows a row of four white-coated collar-and-tied scientists solemnly throwing a succession of large domestic cats into the air while they were in a plane which was flying to simulate weightlessness.

Back on the ground at the base, a lengthy rail track was constructed to take a rocket-propelled sledge into which the scientists could strap various animals such as dogs and chimpanzees. The purpose was to measure the effects of sudden acceleration and deceleration on the body and there is a series of gruesome pictures on the film depicting some hapless chimpanzee being strapped into an elaborate harness while wired up to an array of instruments designed to monitor its vital functions. Several animals were sacrificed in the name of science as the American researchers carried out trials to measure the effects of space flight on the body.

Although many would find it inconceivable that experiments of this kind should be carried out now, in 1947 no such scruples existed. According to an official record of the flight test programme, 'five biological flights were conducted at White Sands Proving Ground by the Aero-Medical division of Wright Patterson Air Force Base. Live animals were sent into space to investigate the possible danger and limiting factors of space flight.' David G. Simon, then a USAF captain and project engineer until after the second flight, stated, 'But what are the problems of space flight in a rocket? By theorizing, the various possible dangers and limiting factors can be appraised and appropriate means of protection against each surmised. However, only by actually performing the experiment can one prove or disprove the validity of the hypothesis, learn better ways of protection against known hazards and realize for the first time the existence of unsuspected dangers. Only the recovery of a live animal showing no demonstrable ill-effects will permit the claim that no major difficulty has been overlooked.'

It seems likely that there may have been even more horrific experiments with animals which have perhaps never seen the light of day. Conjecture about this gives rise to the possibility that some animals may have been put into the warhead of a specially modified rocket which then crashed near Roswell, thus explaining the accounts of bodies and possibly explaining the request to the local undertaker's apprentice, Glenn Dennis, for child-size coffins. Is it conceivable that Von Braun and his team were presented with the opportunity for a flight experiment involving humans? Perhaps dwarves or children from an orphanage were persuaded to take part in some terrible experiment which went hideously wrong and was then covered up. It is a terrifying act to contemplate, and it should be added that there is no evidence that the US government was engaged in such inhuman tests but, unfortunately, it is not beyond the bounds of possibility.

After all, Wernher von Braun was judged by many to be a war criminal who had escaped justice. The underground complex at Peenemünde, where he constructed his early weapons of terror, was staffed by slave labourers who lived and worked in inhuman conditions under the control of the Nazis. Disease and brutality were rife and thousands died to realize his dream of a secret weapon which would tilt the balance in Hitler's favour in the last months of the war.

It is almost inconceivable that such an experiment could have occurred in America in 1947 – but not inconceivable. It might have been presented as a unique opportunity in which there was a good chance of survival for the occupants, in which case it cannot be ruled out that the Americans would have gone along with it. Given that accounts have now surfaced of terrifying experiments conducted by the US government on live humans with radiation tests and mind-altering drug tests, also on live subjects, which were kept secret until they were discovered, it is not wholly fanciful to speculate that the Roswell crash could have been the result of some inhuman experiment. It has always been officially denied that there were any secret experiments that might explain the eyewitness accounts from Roswell which speak of alien bodies. And while the lack of evidence makes it reasonable to give the military the benefit of the doubt, such experiments remain a possibility that should be considered, if only to be dismissed. Moreover, they would suggest a motive for the destruction of records and the concoction of an elaborate cover story in order to protect those who sanctioned such experimentation. The involvement of the former Nazi Von Braun would add to the embarrassment of later officials who might feel duty bound to maintain an official silence even fifty years after the event.

The notion of some secret experiment that might have given rise to strange dead bodies such as those referred to by several eyewitnesses in Roswell was given further substance when I interviewed Charles Moore and asked him his reaction to the fact that many people had reported accounts of 'dead aliens'. 'True – people reported . . . but that I think is another story and something there may be more on later but it has nothing to do with what we were flying,' he replied the first time I interviewed him. When I telephoned him from the UK some weeks later and asked whether he could give me any further information on what he meant by that somewhat cryptic remark, he responded by saying that he had been in touch with the Pentagon and that we should expect in 1995 or 1996 another announcement from the Air Force which would contain more details, possibly in the form of an entirely new report. This would finally explain the accounts of strange bodies at Roswell. As I continued to press him, Moore became increasingly agitated, saying that he had already said more than he should, and he ended the conversation rather abruptly. When I telephoned him again, he was even more curt and seemed distinctly worried that he had mentioned as much as he had.

Needless to say, no report has emerged, but I would place an enormous amount of confidence in Charles Moore telling the truth about a new version of the events surrounding Roswell. He was unwilling to give any details but was adamant that there would be an explanation about the bodies. In the absence of firm evidence, it is legitimate to speculate that some other experimental flight could be responsible.

Considering the flight tests launched at White Sands were within some two hundred miles of Roswell, irrespective of the remote possibility that there were live creatures on board, the suspicion has inevitably arisen that the craft which crashed may have been a stray V-2 or some other experimental vehicle. Although the rocket tests were under the nominal control of the Army, the Air Force was involved at a number of stages in the development of various programmes. Although, at the time of the Roswell 'crash', the space experiments were cloaked in secrecy, most of the information has now been declassified and the official response from White Sands has been to deny any involvement in Roswell – either in investigating any craft which may have crashed there or being itself responsible for a rocket or any other craft that may have gone astray.

Today, the White Sands range is still used for missile tests and its vast expanse, which stretches as far as the eye can see, is the ideal location for experiments that need to be conducted well away from the public, both for their safety and to preserve the highest levels of secrecy. Some of the old buildings from the Von Braun era still survive and an impressive bright red rocket from the early days of the programme is permanently fixed to one of the launching pads as a reminder of the base's early history.

As for the possibility of a rocket landing as far away as the crash site, whether it is the one identified by Frank Kaufmann or the one on the ranch where Mac Brazel discovered the debris, Don Montoya is sure that none of the V-2s could have had the range to fly that far. 'All V-2s landed basically anywhere from about ten to twenty miles, maybe even as many as forty miles up range due north. The only V-2, and it wasn't really a V-2, although it did use V-2 parts, was a Hermes 2 missile which had the configuration of a V-2 but it had some dummy fins at the top and instead of going north, accidentally the giro had been set to go south and the safety people, who were looking at it, assumed that since it had such a steep climb it would land safely within the White Sands boundaries. Unfortunately, after forty-seven seconds, it made its way towards due south and landed just outside of Juárez [Mexico], and almost caused an international incident. No one got hurt in the episode and that occurred back on May 29, 1947. But that's the only missile or rocket that went astray at White Sands Missile Range.'

Because of official interest from both Congress and the General Accounting Office, Don Montoya, as public information officer for White Sands, has been involved in subjecting its records to careful scrutiny. Here, as with other government agencies requested to conduct a search, a blank was drawn.

'It's nice to think that something from White Sands could have done that,' admits Montoya, who, unlike most government officials, seems genuinely intrigued by the case and probably would have liked nothing better than to have been able to solve it. 'Unfortunately, we have researched our records extensively and on that specific date and time, and even that month, we had nothing that could conceivably have been within that area. We had been launching some balloons but nothing in that particular month when the crash at Roswell occurred and all our rockets that we did launch could be accounted for during that time period and there was nothing that White Sands had available at that time that could reach that far over to Roswell. We have maintained a very strict sense of safety, both for the personnel here working on the ground, as well as any kind of rocket or missile debris going off the White Sands boundaries in either direction either east or west, north or south.

'So we searched our records and we've been in contact with the

National Archives and other Congressional Agencies who have asked us within the past year about this incident and we have checked our records over and over again and even given some of the records to show no records or missiles or tests that we know of did occur that could be confused or associated with the Roswell Incident.'

Unless one concludes that the records have been deliberately concealed or destroyed, it seems likely that White Sands is innocent when it comes to any alternative explanations for the Roswell Incident. However, significantly (and perhaps inadvertently), Montoya was not wholly convinced by the balloon explanation – whether a weather balloon or Project Mogul – for he added: 'There had been some balloon tests that did come out of Alamogordo but once again we did have the records for 1947 and they showed no incidents of any kind of balloons straying off towards that area. As far as White Sands is concerned we're pretty clean on this incident.'

Interestingly, Montoya also knows of eminent scientists who, like Chet Lytle, have also worked at the base and witnessed strange lights in the sky which they have been unable to explain. As far as he is concerned, 'The Roswell crash is a complete mystery. We have had people here who believe in UFOs and probably have their own stories. People, who I don't wish to name at this point in time, but who have believed in UFOs and have seen them in the outlying areas such as El Paso and Las Cruces and, of course, there has always been those rumours about UFOs being captured by Holloman Air Force Base back in the late 1950s . . . Personally I'd love to see a UFO. Unfortunately, I haven't been fortunate enough to have an experience!'

11

Although there is no substantial evidence to explain away the Roswell Incident as the result of a super-secret experiment, this is by no means impossible. Official documents dating from the late 1940s, from both the FBI and the Air Force, raised the possibility of some secret operation being conducted by their own government of which even they might be unaware. General Twining's famous memorandum about the phenomenon being 'real' also raises the possibility, as does an intriguing memo from the FBI. Dated August 19, 1947 and addressed to D.M. Ladd, the senior FBI agent who had been the recipient of the previous memos, it deals with 'flying discs'. The sender's name has been deleted.

The memo begins with the extraordinary statement that 'Special Agent [name blacked out] of the Liaison Section, while discussing the above captioned phenomena with Lieutenant Colonel [name blacked out] of the Air Forces Intelligence, expressed the possibility that flying discs were, in fact, a very highly classified experiment of the Army or Navy. Mr. [name blacked out] was very much surprised when Colonel [name blacked out] not only agreed that this was a possibility, but confidentially stated it was his personal opinion that such was a probability. Colonel [name blacked out] indicated confidentially that a Mr. [name blacked out], who is a scientist attached to the Air Forces Intelligence, was of the same opinion.'

Even though the names have been obliterated, the proposition that UFOs are some secret experiment is seriously raised by not just one person but a lieutenant colonel, a colonel and a scientist.

The document continues by offering some of the reasons underlying the claim: 'Colonel [name blacked out] stated that he based his assumption on the following: He pointed out that when flying objects were reported seen over Sweden, the "high brass" of the War Department exerted tremendous pressure on the Air Force's Intelligence to conduct research and collect information in an effort to identify these sightings. Colonel [name blacked out] stated that, in contrast to this, we have reported sightings of unknown objects over the United States, and the "high brass" appeared to be totally unconcerned. He indicated this led him to believe that they knew enough about these objects in question to express no concern. Colonel [name blacked out] pointed out further that the objects in question have been seen by many individuals who are what he terms "trained observers," such as airplane pilots. He indicated also that several of the individuals are reliable members of the community. He stated it is his conclusion that these individuals saw something. He stated the above has led him to come to the conclusion that there were objects seen which the Government knows all about.'

The point is then raised that if the 'flying discs' are US government experiments it would not be reasonable to expect the FBI to conduct investigations into the phenomenon. The unnamed colonel agrees, saying it would be 'extremely embarrassing' to the Air Forces Intelligence if it was learned that the discs were 'ours'. Although the memo does not reach any conclusions, it states that Generals Chamberlin and Todd had both given assurances that the Army was not involved. Despite previous assurances from the Air Force, the unnamed Air Force colonel had contacted General Schulgen and mentioned 'the possibility of an embarrassing situation arising between the Air Forces Intelligence and the FBI. General Schulgen agreed with Colonel [name blacked out] that a memorandum would be prepared for the signature of General McDonald, A2, to General LeMay, who is in charge of Research and Development in the Air Corps. Colonel [name blacked out] indicated that this memorandum will set forth the characteristics of the objects seen by various reliable individuals. The memorandum will then request General LeMay to indicate whether or not any experiments are being undertaken by the Air Forces which could possibly be connected with any of the observed phenomena. Colonel [name blacked out] stated that when a reply is received from General LeMay, a communication will be addressed to the Bureau.'

Whether this memo was forthcoming or not is not known, but even if it was, the suspicion that seeps through from this memorandum about the Air Force, within the Air Force, and from the FBI, speaks volumes. It also addresses a point often raised by the sceptics: namely, if the UFO phenomenon is true and the government knows about it, how has it managed to keep it secret for so long? Here we have the FBI and the Air Force admitting that secret experiments could be occurring which they have no knowledge of – if *they* did not know then it is likely that such secrets could be kept from the public. This applies whether the UFOs are some secret government experiment or whether the government had actually captured a crashed saucer – as alleged in the MJ-12 documents. The proposition that a high-level secret programme could be in operation without the knowledge of the FBI and many in the Air Force and other branches of government is also circumstantial evidence in favour of the idea that, if the Roswell Incident had in fact occurred and a saucer had been retrieved, then it might indeed have been possible to keep the secret not just from the public but also from members of the respective services.

This astonishing possibility, which has implications for both the possible retrieval of saucers and the development of 'flying discs' as part of some super-secret experiment, is given further support in another declassified memorandum, from the Special Agent in Charge of the Knoxville Office to the Director of the FBI in Washington, J. Edgar Hoover, dated January 10, 1949. The subject heading is '"Flying Saucers" observed over Oak Ridge area "INTERNAL SECURITY-X"'.

The document begins: 'There are being submitted herewith two photographs of reputedly "flying saucers" which were seen at Oak Ridge, Tennessee, sometime during July of 1947. All of the information contained in this letter was received from [several words blacked out], Atomic Energy Commission, and Army, who is the principal army technician at the Nuclear Energy for the Propulsion of Aircraft Research Center at Oak Ridge, Tennessee.'

The photographs in question were taken in July 1947 by, presumably, the aforementioned but anonymous technician or an employee at the Oak Ridge nuclear facility. Whoever it was, the man was taking pictures of his family in front of his house in the late afternoon of a July day (the exact period of the wave of saucer sightings and the month of the alleged Roswell crash), when he noticed a vapour trail, which he managed to photograph. He took another picture, the last on the roll, and succeeded in getting another image of the object in the sky. The pictures were given to the local newspaper, the *Knoxville*

News Sentinel, which duly published them. The photographer also made copies and distributed them among his colleagues at the Oak Ridge facility. Apparently someone became alarmed at the prospect of these photographs achieving a wider circulation (the newspaper print had not been very clear and the accompanying text was apparently vague), and ordered that all copies should be recovered and those who had seen them should be warned not to say anything about them. The pictures were to be sent to Air Force Intelligence and the memo reported that a study of the negatives (by whom is not clear) revealed that the pictures were genuine and not a hoax, stating that 'both the vapour trail and the corona of fire are dark on the negative, indicating that it was an actual exposure. It was the opinion of [name blacked out] that the photographs were, without doubt, authentic.' So far, relatively interesting not least because there are few photographs which have been given a clean bill of health by official sources. The memorandum then reports an interview with either the person who took the photographs or a source from Oak Ridge who had studied them – almost certainly a scientist. Predictably, that person's name was blacked out, so we don't know who it was.

The interviewee readily admitted that he knew nothing of an official nature about the 'flying saucers' or 'mystery missiles' except that Air Force Intelligence officials believed them to be 'man-made'. The memo says: 'It was his further belief that a great deal of information had been compiled concerning these missiles by air force intelligence, and that research on the matter was being extensively done at Wright Field, Dayton, Ohio. He also expressed the opinion that information at the disposal of United States Army Air Force Intelligence had, in all probability, been made available to the Bureau at Washington, DC.'

Then the interviewee outlined his own theories about the 'saucers': 'According to him, flying discs have long been a theoretical possibility and, in fact, a possibility which would indicate one of the best means by which to break through the barriers of the supersonic area. Scientists have, for many years, been attempting to develop this type of aircraft. Some experimentation has been done even in the United States, but insofar as is known in the United States at the present time, there have never been any practical developments. As a second factor of consideration, [name blacked out] stated that insofar as is known to US scientists at this time, there is no known chemical fuel which would make possible [the] tremendous range of flight such as is ascribed to the reported "flying saucers." There is only one possible fuel which could be utilized which is in accord with present theory, and that is the utilization of atomic energy. As further evidence of this possible means of propulsion, [name blacked out] called attention to the vapor trail and gaseous corona described as a ball of fire, which he states might give some evidence to the fact that a radio-active field is present. The interviewee, who is clearly a scientist with fairly high security clearance, continues by deducing that the vapor trail represents some sort of atmospheric change along the "path of the missile" thus ruling out any conventional aircraft.

'He continued that information furnished by him should be treated with the utmost confidence, in that he was not speaking officially, but as a personal matter of cooperation. He stated that the matter was being given absolutely no dissemination by the air force or other military personnel, and that they had not deemed it advisable to advise him of all information pertaining to the missile. He continued, however, that in his conversation with representatives at Wright Field and in reading reports returned to this country by foreign agents, he had gathered together certain information which might be of assistance in determining whether or not these so-called missiles were authentic, usable and of danger to the United States. First, he pointed out that knowledge of such a possible aircraft is not by any means new, it having been known as early as four years ago that some type of flying disc was being experimented with by the Russians. In addition, thereto, he stated that more recent reports have been received from representatives of the Central Intelligence Agency in Southern Europe and Southern Asia to the effect that the Russians were experimenting with some type of radical aircraft or guided missile which could be dispatched for great distances out over the sea, made to turn in flight and return to the base from which it was launched. This fact was extremely worthy of notice as experiments in this country have so far only developed to the point where we are concerned with delivering a missile to the required point of impact, and no consideration has been given to imparting to that missile the ability to return. Secondly, he stated that it is a known fact that the Russians are attempting to develop some type of nuclear energy, that they received a wealth of information concerning nuclear energy at the time of their occupation in Germany, and that they too have at their disposal the limited supply of the necessary fissionable materials.'

The FBI's high-level source goes on to say that while he has no proof of the Russians being in possession of this technology, he points out that they have some very advanced scientists in the nuclear field as well as 'some of the most advanced and capable scientists of the German Nation'. (He omitted to point out that his own country had the rest.)

The source stated that as far as he knew, no 'saucer' had ever been recovered and that the only evidence that existed were telephoto photographs that were in the possession of engineers at Wright Field, Dayton. While this witness makes no reference to the Roswell Incident, it is likely that if it did occur he would not have known anyway. However, he does report another incident around the same time which has some similarities: 'one report has been received concerning a collision of these missiles with another type of aircraft. This report according to him, took place a short time prior to the report of numerous discs over the United States, and the report emanated from Czechoslovakia. This report was that a Czechoslovakian transport had collided with some unidentified missile while in mid-air over the ocean, and that said missile and said transport had been completely disintegrated without recovery of parts or survivors from either. It was the belief of [name blacked out] that this undescribed missile was perhaps the same type of thing as the flying saucer. Another factor of notice, according to [name blacked out], and as is portrayed by the photographs, it would appear that the missiles can be maintained at a certain altitude above the contour of the ground. This could be done by means of some type of radio altimeter or radio control . . . He stated that he himself observed on one occasion, a single vapor trail coming from some type of aircraft at unbelievably high altitudes, which vapor trail extended from horizon to horizon in a perfectly straight line. He observed the vapor trail while it was in the process of formation and states that it was completely unlike any vapour trail he had ever observed before in all of his experience with the air force.'

The anonymous witness is convinced that the objects which he continually refers to as 'missiles' are controlled in their movement and therefore not a natural phenomenon. He adds: 'this matter . . . is nevertheless a source of great concern to the military establishment of this country. Great efforts have been expended by the service to determine just what the nature of these missiles might be and, upon so determining, decide whether or not an adequate defence can be established. He also stated that it has given impetus to the research being done by the air force in their own program of nuclear energy for the propulsion of aircraft to develop guided missiles.' Finally, the source states that he did not believe there was any particular connection between the sightings and the location of Oak Ridge, a top-secret nuclear research facility: 'they were seen in this area merely as they were seen in forty-six of the forty-eight states of the United States during the month of July when so many reports were being received'.

Apart from the revelation of two highly credible sightings, one of which is described as an actual crash, these do not appear to have been included in the Air Force's Project Blue Book listing of sightings. This memorandum is also a remarkable insight into the way that an American citizen is virtually acting as an espionage agent for another intelligence agency. Clearly, the FBI was suspicious of the Air Force, Hoover was complaining that the Air Force had not allowed his agency access to a disc that had been recovered (a strange comment if he was referring to one of the many hoaxes or practical jokes as it is fairly unlikely that the FBI would have bothered with a fake) and there were suspicions that some secret experiments were going on linked to the saucers that were being kept from various agencies who had a legitimate claim to know about them.

All this raises the question not only of whether Roswell could have perhaps been an incident where a saucer actually crashed but also whether the redoubtable J. Edgar Hoover would have been able to find out about that incident if it was real. Despite his formidable reputation for ferreting out secrets, an ability which made him a feared opponent of several elected presidents up to and including Nixon, the internal suspicions raised by the FBI itself suggest that such a secret might have been withheld from him. Of course, it is possible that Hoover was informed later on and sworn to secrecy. However, what does seem likely is that if the Roswell Incident did occur Hoover would have eventually found out about it, either through his own efforts or by being briefed by the guardians of the secret.

Although secret experiments cannot be absolutely ruled out as an explanation for Roswell, alternative scenarios, such as balloons or rocket tests, seem to offer equally unsatisfactory explanations. If the witness statements are taken into account then there is just as much, if not more, circumstantial evidence for an extraterrestrial hypothesis than there is for any of the other possible solutions.

It is hardly surprising that people have turned to the flimsiest of evidence in the search for answers to the mystery. This has had the unfortunate effect of leaving the whole field wide open, potentially vulnerable to hoaxes and forgeries. Several witnesses have been discredited long after the event, although none of those so far quoted in this book, however unlikely their story, has been definitively proved to have lied.

Indeed, the lack of tangible information has proved to be to the advantage of those who have either fabricated testimony or forged documents. The problem is that, as with some of the witnesses' accounts, it is surprisingly difficult to disprove some of the information that has materialized.

12

If the MJ-12 documents represented a reasonably sophisticated attempt at forgery by forces unknown, the next tantalizing piece of 'evidence' to emerge was even more extraordinary in what it purported to portray.

In 1994, Ray Santilli, a hitherto obscure businessman who ran a video distribution company announced to the world that he had come into possession of an extraordinary piece of black and white footage which appeared to be the autopsy of humanoid creatures retrieved from a spaceship which had crash-landed in New Mexico in 1947. The film depicted two people covered from head to toe in what are now known as NBC suits, basically a one-piece white garment with a hood and plastic visor, which are used by soldiers and scientists when they have to take precautions against nuclear, biological and chemical hazards. The footage lasts approximately fifteen minutes and for such a short piece offilm it has achieved a notoriety and infamy, not to say celebrity, probably unparalleled in the history of cinema! The two figures are shown approaching a corpse resting on a gurney, inspecting the body and then selecting a scalpel and other instruments from a tray to carry out a dissection. The proceedings are photographed by one camera and therefore one cameraman. The film is not particularly well photographed and the details of the inside of the creature are not very clear. This, either deliberate or the result of poor-quality camerawork, is one of many frustrations produced by the film segment.

The creature appears to be smaller than a normal human, with a larger than normal head and two almond-shaped eyes. Its head is completely bald and appears to be naturally hairless rather than shaved. In human terms, the relationship between the limbs and the body is fairly normal, although the arms appear to be slightly longer than a human's. There are six fingers and six toes, their size and shape likewise human in appearance.

The post-mortem begins with a Y-shaped incision from the top of the neck around the front shoulder-blades. Suspiciously, the actual cutting and peeling back of the skin is not recorded in real-time. The viewer witnesses strange-looking dark matter being removed from the inner cavity of the chest and stomach area of the corpse. These 'organs' are placed in a standard hospital steel tray and carried off to one side. When this film was shown to a professional forensic pathologist, Dr Ian West, a renowned expert who has worked for Scotland Yard as a medical adviser in some of the most celebrated murder mysteries of recent times, he declared himself satisfied with the medical technique of the two 'doctors'. As far as he could observe, there was nothing intrinsically fake or acted in their manoeuvres or methods. Called upon to deliver his verdict as to what he honestly thought he saw being depicted, Dr West was almost wholly convinced that the film was a hoax, but he was sufficiently intrigued and fascinated to state that while he was 'ninety-five per cent' certain that it was a fake, he admitted to a slight degree of doubt, saying, 'It could be real'. It is interesting that such an eminent expert was willing to entertain such a doubt, albeit small.

Other experts to whom John Purdie and I exposed the documentary extract were usually more emphatic in their opinion about the authenticity of the footage. 'Fake' was the unequivocal verdict of a movie special effects expert, although he added that it was a very good example of special effects and that it would have been extremely expensive to have deliberately created the creature and the post-mortem. The budget, he estimated, was anything up to $200,000, which is a considerable amount of money for such a short piece of film, although it is probably an overestimate. But whatever the budget, if it was a hoax there would be no guarantee for whoever financed it that he would recoup and make a profit on the initial investment since there would always be the risk of the hoax being exposed. Certainly, a person who is willing to take a gamble has many easier ways of making money.

As it turns out, the film has been a financial success. The figure of $100,000 has been bandied about as being the sum Santilli actually paid for the footage; his revenue from the sale of stills to various newspapers and magazines plus the actual footage to various TV stations will certainly have recouped any investment several times over. The sale to Fox Television alone is thought to have netted $200,000, and video sales of the full-length unexpurgated autopsy even more. However, this was against the odds. Most pieces of film which achieve a high financial value are rare or exclusive because they portray a particular news event to the exclusion of any others or they represent a unique opportunity – such as the tape of a recent BBC interview with Diana, Princess of Wales.

If we assume for a moment that the film is a hoax, then, given the financial risk that its maker faced, we must consider two possibilities. The first is that whoever perpetrated the hoax was a supremely confident gambler. Alternatively, the film was made by someone whose initial outlay was so minimal as to make the risk worthwhile – perhaps a small film studio with time on its hands.

However, the businessman who brought the film into the daylight of publicity and notoriety vehemently denies that the film is a fabrication. That man is Ray Santilli, whose company, Merlin, specializes in assembling archive footage of musical performers and re-selling it to the mass market. He claims that he came across the 'autopsy footage' by pure chance, at a music convention in the USA where he contacted an elderly cameraman with a view to buying footage of Elvis in concert. In the course of their negotiations, Santilli says, the old man offered him something with a potential far beyond anything featuring the singing GI. The man told Santilli that he had been employed by the military in 1947, and had been an official cameraman, based in Washington DC and assigned to photograph various experimental tests, including the first atomic bomb test. In the summer of 1947, he claimed, he was sent to New Mexico to film a crashed craft. He showed Santilli the result, projected on to the walls of his living room in Florida. It turned out to be the 'alien autopsy'. According to the cameraman, he had managed to keep some of the cans of film. These particular pieces of film were all ones which had needed special developing because of various lighting considerations. Somehow these had become separated from the others and had never been collected from him. One of the reasons for this was that the film developing process coincided with the separation of the Army and the Air Force, a major undertaking beset by administrative chaos. As a result of this oversight the cameraman held on to the film for the next forty years.

Although he has been frequently asked about the identity of the cameraman, Ray Santilli has consistently refused to divulge his name. In the several weeks that we spent negotiating with him to broadcast the footage in Channel Four's *Secret History: The Roswell Incident*, he steadfastly and infuriatingly refused to reveal who he was. Under a great deal of pressure to at least provide us with some evidence that the man actually existed, Santilli reluctantly agreed to let John Purdie accompany him to Miami to try to meet the elusive cameraman. According to Purdie, when they were in Miami Santilli made many genuine attempts to contact the man. Purdie witnessed several telephone conversations, one of which he videotaped. This showed Santilli attempting to persuade the cameraman to come to a meeting at the hotel, and it seemed as if the man had agreed, but he failed to turn up. After a frustrating forty-eight hours in Miami, confined to his hotel room waiting for telephone calls, Purdie called it a day and flew on to Washington with the promise that the cameraman would contact him by telephone. After he had sat in his hotel room for another frustrating day and a half, the telephone finally rang. The voice at the other end of the line was gruff and unfriendly. Whoever it was speaking, claimed that he was the cameraman and said that he was fed up with all the pressure in general and Santilli in particular for landing him in such a predicament. He said he was telephoning at Santilli's request to show that he did indeed exist but would not be drawn into any further conversation. And that was that.

The episode went some way to allaying our suspicions that the whole thing was a scam set up by Santilli. In both Miami and, before that, London, he had appeared to be genuinely trying to set up a meeting with the cameraman and was profusely apologetic when the promised meeting failed to materialize. He claimed that his relationship with the cameraman over a two-year period had deteriorated to such an extent that he was barely able to speak to him. It seemed that the man was furious that his identity had been compromised and that he had been dragged into a controversy that was attracting such widespread media attention. He had always insisted on his total anonymity and now felt that Santilli had betrayed him by thrusting him into the limelight. According to Santilli, the elderly cameraman had viewed the whole transaction as a purely commercial deal, the terms of which guaranteed his anonymity. He was concerned for his privacy for a number of reasons, not least that he was aware that he was probably not entitled to have held on to the original footage. Also, he wanted to make some money to finance his daughter's wedding and wished to protect himself from the prying eyes of the Internal Revenue Service. Anything Santilli did to publicize the film was then interpreted by the cameraman as something which would endanger his private negotiations and it was this concern which apparently contributed to the rapid deterioration of relations between the two men. Santilli says that he did at least succeed in getting the cameraman to produce a statement providing some background to the filming of the autopsy.

This is the statement of what he referred to as 'Operation Anvil': 'I joined the forces in March of 1942 and left in 1952. The ten years I spent serving my country were some of the best years of my life. My father was in the movie business, which meant that he had a good knowledge about the workings of cameras and photography. For this reason I believe I passed a medical that would not normally allow me in, due to polio as a child.

'After enrolment and training, I was able to use my camera skills and became one of the few dedicated cameramen in the forces. I was sent to many places, and as it was war time, I fast learned the ability of filming under difficult circumstances.

'I will not give more detail on my background, only to say that in the fall of 1944, I was assigned to Intelligence, reporting to the Assistant Chief of Air Staff. I was moved around, depending on the assignment. During my time, I filmed a great deal including the tests at White Sands (Manhattan Project/Trinity).

'I remember very clearly receiving the call to go to White Sands . . . Roswell. I had not long returned from St Louis, Missouri, where I had filmed the new Ramjet. It was June 1 when McDonald asked me to report to General McMullan for a special assignment. I had had no experience of working with McMullan but after talking to him for a few minutes, I knew that I would never wish to be his enemy. McMullan was straight to the point, no messing. I was ordered to a crash site just south-west of Socorro. It was urgent and my brief was to film everything in sight, not to leave the debris until it had been removed, and I was to have access to all areas of the site. If the commander in charge had a problem with that, I was told to get them to call McMullan. A few minutes after my orders from McMullan, I received the same instructions from Tooey, saying it was the crash of a Russian spy plane. Two generals in one day, this job was important.

'I flew out from Andrews with sixteen other officers and personnel, mostly medical. We arrived at Wright Patterson and collected more men and equipment. From there we flew to Roswell on a C-54. When we got to Roswell, we were transported by road to the site. When we arrived, the site had already been cordoned off. From the start it was plain to see this was no Russian spy plane. It was a large disc, "flying saucer", on its back, with heat still radiating from the ground around it.

'The commander on site handed over to the SAC medical team who were still waiting for Kenney to arrive. However, nothing had been done as everyone was just waiting for orders.

'It was decided to wait until the heat subsided before moving in as fire was a significant risk. This was made all the worse by the screams of the freak creatures that were lying by the vehicle.

'What in God's name they were, no one could tell, but one thing's for sure, they were circus freaks, creatures with no business here. Each had hold of a box which they kept hold of in both arms close to their chests. They just lay there crying, holding those boxes. Once my tent had been set up, I started filming immediately, first the vehicle, then the site and debris. At around 0600, it was deemed safe to move in. Again, the freaks were still crying and when approached, they screamed even louder. They were protective of their boxes, but we managed to get one loose with a firm strike at the head of a freak with the butt of a rifle.

'The three freaks were dragged away and secured with rope and tape. The other one was already dead. The medical team were reluctant at first to go near these freaks, but as some were injured, they had no choice. Once the creatures were collected, the priority was to collect all debris that could be removed easily as there was still a risk of fire. This debris seemed to come from exterior struts that were supporting a very small disc on the underside of the craft which must have snapped off when the disc flipped over. The debris was taken to tent stations for logging, then loaded onto trucks. After three days, a full team from Washington came down and the decision was taken to move the craft. Inside it, the atmosphere was very heavy. It was impossible to stay in it longer than a few seconds without feeling very sick. Therefore, it was decided to analyse it back at base, so it was loaded onto a flattop and taken to Wright Patterson, which is where I joined it.

'I stayed at Wright Patterson for a further three weeks, working on the debris. I was then told to report to Fort Worth [Dallas, Texas] for the filming of an autopsy. Normally, I would not have a problem with this, but it was discovered that the freaks may be a medical threat, therefore I was required to wear the same protective suits as the doctors. It was impossible to handle the camera properly, loading and focusing was very difficult. In fact, against orders, I removed my suit during the filming. The first two autopsies took place in July 1947.

'After filming, I had several hundred reels (each film canister was only three minutes in length). I separated problem reels which required special attention in processing (these I would do later). The first batch was sent through to Washington and I processed the remainder a few days later. Once the remaining reels had been processed, I contacted Washington to arrange collection of the final batch. Incredibly they never came to collect or arrange transportations for them. I called many times and then just gave up. The footage has remained with me ever since. In May of 1949 I was asked to film the third autopsy.'

True or false, this statement is undoubtedly intriguing. And, despite an overwhelming instinct to doubt everything that it records, this author feels that it may contain a vestige of truth. Admittedly, this feeling is based on nothing more than the study of hundreds of statements and documents relating to the Roswell Incident in general and the UFO phenomenon in particular, but I do believe that there is something here that is not simply a hoax. It is difficult to advance any hard evidence to support such a conclusion, but it seems to me that the cameraman's statement – taken together with all the witness accounts and Frank Kaufmann's categorical assertion that there was a crash with all the associated debris and the bodies – has something of a ring of truth to it. Also, while I don't think that Santilli has told us the full story about the cameraman and the extraordinary footage that he has released to the world, I am prepared to give him the benefit of the doubt. In short, I don't believe that he has faked this scenario or that he is behind a deliberate deception as far as the footage is concerned. And although I am not prepared to give the film the seal of approval, there is at the time of writing no definitive evidence to show that it is a hoax. Santilli has a responsibility to provide more details so that his footage can be put under further scrutiny. Equally, those who have denounced it as bogus have a responsibility to provide some evidence to justify their assertion. So far neither side has done either. My own position is that the film should be granted a very small measure of credence until the elusive conclusive evidence appears.

One fascinating aspect of the film is the degree of secrecy that has been maintained about it. Pre-production and post-production requirements for the 'autopsy scene' would involve a team of people which would range in number from a minimum of six to a maximum of twenty. Therefore it is mystifying that not one single person has come forward to reveal that the film was a hoax. If anyone was to set out to deliberately fake this material, then they would need a team of co-conspirators in order to pull it off. At the very least, they would need a special effects designer and someone with the necessary skills to create the 'aliens' themselves. They would also require a set designer for the room in which the post-mortem took place, as well as a costume designer to advise on the special suits worn by the 'doctors'. Then there would have been a technician to provide the lighting and a camera operator. A laboratory would have developed the footage and an editor/projectionist would have screened the film. Inevitably, several scenes not shown in the final footage would have ended up on some cutting-room floor – and perhaps in the memory of a hired film editor somewhere in the world. Then there would be the need to pay all the people involved and collect the revenues due from the sale of the film and the still photographs derived from it. It is by no means impossible that all this could have been done by the company responsible for disseminating the final product to the rest of the world – in this case Santilli's company. It is possible that there was complete loyalty to the project's secrecy among all those working for the company and even those, such as the cameraman and the special effects designer, who would almost certainly have come from outside it. But it is extraordinarily difficult to believe that no one involved with the filming – not the cameraman, the special effects designer, the accountant, the secretary, those who moulded the parts needed for the corpse, the actors who played the doctors – that none of these people would come forward at some point and reveal the truth. They each had the power to show that the film was nothing more than a highly sophisticated deception produced in a studio and designed to deceive an unsuspecting public. It would be human nature for any one of them to let slip to a friend or relative that they were involved in that 'notorious film of an alien autopsy'. And one would also have to accept too that this person could resist the temptation to make a large sum of money by selling their story to a media organization. If Rupert Murdoch's Fox Television was prepared to pay $250,000 for the exclusive rights to the footage, what price might a rival broadcaster pay for the true story behind what could then be revealed as one of the greatest film hoaxes ever perpetrated? The answer is a considerable amount.

It is worth remembering that most fakes and hoaxes, certainly those that have been perpetrated in recent times, have tended to unravel extremely quickly – the greater the publicity the faster they fall apart. For example, the 'Hitler Diaries' were exposed in a matter of days; after all, it is no longer so much a question of whether the hoax is good enough to withstand the scrutiny of experts as of whether those involved in the deception can be relied upon to maintain their collective cloak of secrecy. In this case there would have to be some incentive: either a sense of overwhelming loyalty to those seeking to make millions from the deception, or a share of the profits from the sales and exploitation of the product. Again, this seems unlikely, for while a fairly substantial outlay would be needed to produce the film in the first place, the risk of exposure would militate against any guarantee of a return.

Like the special effects designer cited earlier, other specialists in the same field who have viewed it have been unanimous in their judgement that it is a hoax and a good one. Even if it was real, it is unlikely that a special effects designer would say that it was; ironically, confronted with a picture of a genuine alien, no one would know whether it was real or not because there is no frame of reference. Given that Hollywood special effects designers can re-create almost anything and, more importantly, can create anything, they are in a sense the least qualified to judge whether something is fake or real. Their whole craft is dedicated to making the unreal realistic – so the inevitable question is, how would they know? What they would be expected to know is whether any member of their profession had been involved in constructing such a creature, which would most likely be a costly undertaking. Within the relatively small and closeted world of film effects there would surely be some hint of gossip, some passing on of inside knowledge, by a workshop assistant or a laboratory worker who had been involved in the hoax.

To return to the credibility of the footage itself, special effects artists including Trey Stokes, whose credits include *The Abyss*, *The Blob*, *Batman Returns*, and *Robocop II*, pointed out that the posture and weighting of the corpse on the table in the film is inconsistent for a body in the supine position and that it was therefore apparently made from a body cast taken in the upright position. While this could be true, supporters of the film's authenticity might counter the argument by saying that we do not know how an alien body is constructed. Therefore, when in the equivalent of rigor mortis, it might display different characteristics from those which we would expect to see in a human corpse.

In view of what is known about the film and its background the proposition that the film is not a hoax is not as far-fetched as would appear on the surface. Of course, there is the possibility that the film is genuine but does not depict the autopsy of an alien – it could be some strange medical experiment or a military exercise of some sort. Although rather unlikely, such explanations cannot be ruled out.

Interesting doubts about the authenticity of the footage have been raised by medical scientists who have either viewed the film or seen still pictures of the aliens in the press. For example, Dr Paul O'Higgins, an anatomist from University College, London, declared: 'I would think the chances that an alien which evolved on another world would look so like us would be astronomically remote!'

When I accused Santilli of being behind the hoax himself, he promised that he had not 'faked it' and also pointed out that if he had why would he use as a model a creature that was so humanoid? He claimed that if he wanted to really fake an alien autopsy he would ensure the creature was more alien in its appearance.

As well as suggesting that the film-maker had fallen into the trap of anthropomorphism, O'Higgins was critical of the procedures used in the post-mortem. 'To judge from the film, the autopsy was carried out in a couple of hours. Yet these were alien creatures. They represented an unparalleled opportunity to science. We are expected to believe we casually cut them up in an afternoon? I would have taken weeks to do such an autopsy.'

Another pathologist, Ed Uthman of Chicago University, was less than convinced by the appearance of the alien's internal organs. 'The most implausible thing of all is that the "alien" just had amorphous lumps of tissue in her body cavities. I cannot fathom that an alien who had external organs so much like ours could not have some sort of definitive structural organs internally.

'Particular aspects of the alleged alien's external body shape such as the protrusions of certain underlying muscles and bones, like the clavicle, imply a corresponding human internal structure. Yet what was removed from the body cavity looks entirely non-human. This incongruity in itself is a serious flaw; in effect what we have is a hybrid that is basically human on the outside and non-human on the inside. An entity that is half-human, half something else. While such creatures exist in mythology – minotaurs, centaurs, mermaids werewolves etc – they do not exist in reality. The resemblance of the "dead alien" to a human body suggests that it is either a specially created creature born and manufactured from the imagination of a special effects film designer or that it is a weird deformation of an original human being.' (Nevertheless, doctors, including the forensic pathologist Ian West, have stated that the deformities do not bear any resemblance to those that are known to medicine. There have even been suggestions that the corpse could be a surgically altered human body.)

As for Santilli himself, every statement and every word that he has uttered in connection with the film has been seized upon and analysed by the ufologists. He has certainly been guilty of a number of inconsistencies but he has also been fairly plausible in explaining them away. While there are a host of discrepancies in his various pronouncements on the background to the film, there seems to be nothing so devastating as to discredit him totally. One anomaly was the fact that originally Santilli apparently claimed that President Truman could be seen in the autopsy coverage. Allegedly, he said that Truman could be observed standing with other individuals behind a glass window where he was so visible that it would be possible to read his lips and interpret his words. In another statement UFO researcher Kent Jeffery describes a conversation that Santilli had had with a film producer who had in turn spoken to Jeffery. Santilli had apparently offered a detailed description of the debris site, describing the terrain as somewhat hilly and that the craft was visible, not in one piece, but in a number of large pieces, necessitating the use of a large crane, and that numerous soldiers in uniform were in the scene, photographed sufficiently clearly for their faces to be recognized. (When we were talking to Santilli about using the footage in our documentary for Channel Four, he also intimated that there was footage of the recovery site with vehicles etc.) Given that such scenes, particularly the supposed presence of President Truman, offered the possibility of definitive proof of the authenticity of the footage, they were obviously a vital key to solving the mystery of the film's pedigree. But they never materialized.

Kent Jeffery also refers to Santilli having originally claimed that the film was derived from fifteen '10 minute' film reels but that this was later changed to twenty-two '3 minute' reels. There have also been all sorts of claims and counter-claims about Kodak, and authentication of the film via the ageing of the film stock. Here again, Santilli is rumoured to have stated that the footage was shot on 1947 nitrate film, whereas Kodak has never produced 16mm nitrate stock. Again – and here the author adds his voice of doubt to those of others – there have been frequent promises to supply sections of the original 16mm print so that it could be tested. Obviously this would have to be film where an image from the autopsy scene would be visible, but no such strip of film has ever been produced. When we were engaged in producing the Channel Four documentary in the summer of 1995, we constantly requested it and were constantly promised that it was on its way.

In a recorded television interview I asked Santilli, 'Are you going to provide a proper film extract which can be properly tested by Kodak which has proper images on it?'

Santilli replied, 'I'll provide you with what I can, which will be a film with image, and the only way that I can do that is by securing some film from the collector that bought the first autopsy which is currently *en route* to us.'

A couple of months later, in a live interview on the Seattle television programme *Town Meeting*, broadcast on November 10, 1995, Santilli sought to convey the impression that original film with suitable images from the alien autopsy footage had been submitted worldwide. 'Film with image and not leader tape has been given and that film has been given to the English broadcasters and the French broadcasters,' he declared, and when asked specifically about Kodak he said that 'it has been submitted to Kodak by the broadcasters'.

In reality no one has received a single frame of any film footage which resembles the actual footage broadcast and the only medium in which the footage has been viewed has been on videotape. No outsider has apparently seen it in its original form on 16mm stock, either in a can or projected. When I asked Santilli about the logistics of transferring the material from its original 16mm form to video he claimed that the original film was in such poor condition that it required special care and attention by a specialized film laboratory to recover and retrieve the film, which in itself was a slow, expensive and painstaking process. When I asked him to tell me the name of the film laboratory that had been engaged in this delicate task, he replied that they were keen to maintain a low profile but that he would try to get their name to me. Needless to say, this never happened. Kodak, who have been besieged by endless telephone calls from UFO fanatics seeking information about the film, after a press release was issued stating that Kodak had authenticated the footage, remained willing to test whatever film clip might come their way. Tony Amato, who is a product specialist in the Kodak Motion Picture Division, has been standing by for months, awaiting the arrival of a clip to test. Through an intermediary of Santilli, Kodak was given to understand that a suitable film extract was on its way and that its arrival was imminent. It never turned up.

An earlier piece of film, which was examined in Los Angeles and did turn out to be of the correct vintage, was nothing more than a piece of film leader which could have come from any number of film collections and was therefore completely valueless in relation to authenticating the 'alien autopsy' sequence. According to Amato, Kodak would be willing to work with just a couple of frames of the original print and subject them to a test where the damage would be only slight, the equivalent of a punch-hole in one frame – fairly minor when it is considered what the enhanced value of the footage could be from any test that managed to authenticate it. (In 16mm film one frame represents 1/24 second – less than 1/25,000 of the eighteen-minute duration of the footage.)

Kodak has also pointed out that since the chemical composition of Kodak film has changed over the years, the approximate date of manufacture of a given piece of film can be determined by analysing its exact chemical formula and matching it with records of the chemical compositions for the company's films from different years. Because Kodak never releases the formula for any of its film processing methods, authentication of the film's date of manufacture by any other laboratory would be of questionable value. Any film received by Kodak for testing would be returned intact (apart from the small punch-hole in one frame) within two weeks.

Despite Kodak's patience and willingness to play ball, no film strip has emerged – and, it has to be said, even if it did and the test proved that it was from 1947, it would still not add up to definitive proof that it was the film record of a genuine alien autopsy. There would be two possible explanations: one, that the film stock was genuine 1947 vintage but the recording could have been taken much later by using the carefully preserved film stock; and secondly, that the film stock was genuine and recorded at the right time for Roswell but the event depicted was not the post-mortem of a dead alien but the film of some special effect, as suspected by the many special effects designers who have seen the footage. Although it is unlikely that designers then had the necessary expertise to create such a creature, it is not impossible. Then again, the number of people required at that time would have been commensurately larger, making it even more likely for word to have slipped out as to what they were doing.

We were finally presented with a strip of film which was of the correct vintage but bore no relation to any of the pictures seen in the film itself. The image was of a military or naval officer wearing a peaked cap. When confronted with this, Santilli merely replied that he had been let down by the 'private German collector', a wealthy man who now held all the original film material. The collector was apparently becoming sick and tired of all the requests for bits of 'his film' but had finally relented and sent the strip in question which, as it turned out, was completely useless for any form of authentication. Santilli's description of the collector conjured up a strange vision of an individual jealously hoarding for his own private enjoyment a piece of film for which he had allegedly paid a serious sum of money. It was rather an unlikely scenario and indeed it turned out that the collector was a rather unlikely individual who, curiously, was not remotely interested in flying saucers. If he was a collector then his collection consisted of something other than rare, expensive and dubious films of dead aliens.

His name was Volker Spielberg, a sometime business partner of Santilli and someone who was involved in the music and video distribution business in Germany. Spielberg lives in Austria but has a small office in Hamburg. During a live television interview for the French network TF1 broadcast on October 23, 1995, Santilli was asked again about the original footage and again made the excuse that the matter was out of his hands. TF1 had meanwhile carried out a thorough investigation into the 'private collector' and a pre-recorded film showed Spielberg's small office in Hamburg and his apartment in Austria, where his name could be seen on the front door bell.

The TF1 narrator then announced that Spielberg was not in fact a film collector – at which point Ray Santilli became annoyed and accused TF1 of violating its agreement to keep certain aspects of the film confidential. Jacques Pradel, the presenter, then responded by pointing out that Santilli had failed to live up to certain promises that he had made – not least providing some clips of the original film. The programme also played an excerpt from the recording of a September 28, 1995 telephone conversation between TF1 researcher Nicolas

Maillard and the elusive Spielberg. Maillard pointed out the potential significance of the original film footage that Spielberg possessed and asked for his co-operation in submitting a piece of it for verification. The following is a transcript of part of Spielberg's response: 'I want to be left alone. I'm a collector. I want to be out, and I want to have no contact with nobody regarding this matter because this is my personal thing . . . Simply I'm not interested. You see the whole matter is of no interest to me, I have made up my mind. I have my belief and that's it. And I got what I want. I'm happy and that's it. What have I to do with this? As to my knowledge, I'll keep all the cans, yes, as to my knowledge, that's all I can tell you. Well, as to my knowledge, I um, uh, possess all the film reels. Whether this is true or not that's not up to me to judge, but that is my belief, yes. I don't want to support any fucking TV or radio station in this particular matter, no . . . ! Come on, I've done my job, and all I can tell you is I'm happy! I got what I want and that's it! I haven't bartered for any broadcast of public, and for any fucking papers and all that's going on worldwide. I'm not happy about it anyway, but that's a different story, I have to accept that and I have to admit it's much too late to stop it, but no, I just want to be, if I may say so to you, left alone, OK . . . ?'

Spielberg's Garbo-like desire for privacy was expressed in a tone that was a shade distant from the polite request that had once been expressed by the famously reclusive idol of stage and screen. When the French television presenter suggested that more information could benefit society at large, as well as the viewer watching the programme, Spielberg's response was less than generous. 'No! No! I don't think so. I have a totally different opinion. Fuck the world! I mean, the world is full of egoism and so am I . . .'

Although Santilli has been less than forthcoming about Spielberg's exact role in this drama, he has never denied that they had a business relationship revolving around the music industry. Its mysterious metamorphosis into a committed and obsessive connection, because of an unauthenticated piece of black and white footage of limited financial value but potentially inestimable worth should it prove genuine, was a subject that Santilli managed to avoid. Inevitably, this has caused suspicion that there is something highly suspicious about the partnership between the two in relation to the footage.

Another section of the 'Santilli footage' consists of a scene which reveals some of the artefacts recovered from the alleged craft. It takes place in the interior of a tent where pieces of what look like cast-metal mouldings are laid out on a trestle-table. A figure in military uniform whose face is never glimpsed is seen collecting different objects tagged with labels attached by string, and these are then held up to the camera before being laid out on the table. Among the visible pieces is a panel (one of two) consisting of a sort of metallic-looking tray with the indented mould of a pair of hands with six digits. A separate shot shows the soldier's hands picking up what looks like an iron girder – what the Americans call an 'I-beam' on account of the horizontal edge at the top and bottom of the object. The camera pans across the object to reveal lettering which does not correspond to our alphabet but which resembles a series of letters in the Greek alphabet and corresponds with an uncanny similarity to the words 'Video TV'.

The final section of the film shows a different and smaller tent, inside which two figures dressed in white doctors' coats are apparently tending to one of the alien figures and carrying out what might be emergency medical procedures. The lighting within comes from a flame lantern, making it difficult to distinguish any details, in addition to which the medical figures are wearing white coats and are masked, so that it is virtually impossible to make out their facial features. The alien creature appears different from its counterparts in its size and dimensions, being slightly thinner and taller. This scene relates to what the cameraman has allegedly described as an emergency attempt at medical resuscitation, following the discovery of some signs of life in the creature. Another oddity of this section was pointed out in a *Sunday Times* article of July 30, 1995 headlined 'Film that proves aliens visited earth is a hoax', written by veteran investigative journalist Maurice Chittenden. (The article was, in fact, inaccurate on several points and failed to prove that the film was a hoax.) The report stated that some unusual security marking had appeared on the right-hand side of the screen throughout the film only to disappear later when their authenticity was challenged and discredited. The marking in question was:

'RESTRICTED ACCESS a101 Classification SUBJECT 1 of 2 JULY 30th 1947.'————————————————

The *Sunday Times* article pointed out that 'restricted access' is not a recognized US military code and that the 'a101' classification had been dismissed as pure 'Hollywood'. In addition, the date format did not correspond to the standard military procedure which is day–month–year and should have translated into '30 July 1947'. Maurice Chittenden revealed that the marking had later disappeared when the film was shown to a small audience. Gary Shoefield, who works with Santilli, denied that footage marked 'Restricted Access' had ever been released but Santilli disingenuously admitted including that as part of the film and then later removing it – the justification was that he had come across the wording on the labels of the film canisters.

In the Fox Television special broadcast in America, the tabloid TV show excitedly hailed the two panels as possible alien 'control panels'. Kent Jeffery remarked that they 'looked more like pieces from the pavement in front of Mann's Chinese Theater in Hollywood'. As for the I-beam, it looks exactly like the sort of girder used in a building site for the inner structure of a building or, as Jeffery remarked, a 'prop fashioned in a sheet-metal shop'. It is a strange thing to have produced because, unlike the so-called panels, which hint at a sensibility which might be that of an alien culture, or could at least derive from the imagination of a special effects designer attempting to create something which would not be out of place in a 1950s 'B' movie about an alien invasion of earth, the I-beam could not look more terrestrial. If it was inspired by a reading of Jesse Marcel's description of the debris that his father brought home and showed him, then what he said has been curiously misread. Those I-beams were thin and delicate, unlike the one photographed, which has the proportions of a small girder from a building site. Marcel junior had also described strange writing along the side of the beam which may also be the basis for the lettering that resembles 'Video TV'.

One of the most damning features about the film is the fact that it is photographed in a way that immediately arouses suspicion rather than allaying it. For example, whenever there is a human featured, the face is never identified. Similarly, when organs are removed from the alien corpse the camera is never focused sharply enough to allow careful analysis of what the organic matter actually is – all that is seen is an unusual 'splodge' bearing little resemblance to anything organic. Of course, it could be argued that as we have no conception of what an alien's internal organs look like, strictly speaking we can neither authenticate nor dismiss the film on the grounds of their appearance.

Indeed, the whole film can never be proved either real or fake by simply studying what is on the screen. The only way to find evidence is to take a close look at those who brought it into the public arena.

13

To date, the best research into the background of the film and its cameraman, and therefore the alien autopsy itself, has been conducted with a commendable thoroughness by an experienced researcher in the UFO field: Kent Jeffery. Jeffery is the son of a distinguished Air Force officer and the founder of the Roswell Initiative, which is a grass-roots movement seeking to persuade the US government to release any information it might hold on the incident and to gather supporters to act as a pressure group.

The most tantalizing clue to the film's provenance lies in the identity of the cameraman whom Santilli claimed he first met while negotiating over a music video. Assuming that this person does actually exist, then the question of the film's authenticity could be cleared up fairly rapidly. Indeed, it could be argued that if Santilli was convinced of his background and thus the genuine nature of the film, it would be foolhardy of him not to have checked it out thoroughly as any evidence which favours the film's authenticity would send its value skyrocketing. Instead, his attitude has been extremely cautious and highly protective, the result, he claims, of prior agreements resulting from fraught negotiations over successive months with the 'cameraman', who was extremely difficult to deal with and obsessive about protecting his identity and shielding himself from the publicity and attention.

All of this ignores the fact that if the film was genuinely a record of some secret operation, particularly the retrieval of an alien craft by the US military, then the government would know in the shake of a dice who the cameraman was, where he lived, his telephone number and probably a great deal more. If he does exist and was really concerned to protect his identity – and it is understandable that he would be if the film he had managed to hold on to did contain visual evidence of the greatest secret ever – why didn't he concoct a cover story to the effect that he had somehow come across the film, instead of opening himself up to identification by the government?

Then there are discrepancies in some of the details that have been attributed to the cameraman in the statement released by Santilli, which purports to be an account of the unidentified man's military service. Kent Jeffery has focused on these to make some revealing comparisons between the cameraman's assertions and the authentic military procedures that were in place at the time.

In the autobiographical statement that he allowed Santilli to give out, the cameraman tells of being stationed in Washington and then being ordered to fly to Roswell by way of Wright Field to film 'some Russian plane crash'. The distance involved is approximately 1600 miles – in 1947 a journey of ten to twelve hours, giving an arrival time at the scene several hours after the craft crashed. Yet the cameraman's statement describes filming the initial approach of the soldiers to the stricken craft and the: 'screams of the freak creatures that were lying by the vehicle', screams that got even louder as the cameraman approached. It is difficult to believe that the military waited more than twelve hours before approaching the craft and the freak creatures – in short, until the cameraman arrived.

If the presence of a cameraman was so vital, then why not fly someone in from Roswell, Alamogordo, White Sands or Los Alamos? It is likely that one or more of these installations would have had military cameramen with the right equipment and security clearance.

The cameraman also revealed that he had filmed the Trinity test, the first atomic bomb explosion in New Mexico in 1945 and that shortly before the Roswell film he had been shooting the test flight of McDonnell Aircraft Company's new XH-20 Ramjet helicopter, nicknamed 'Little Henry', in St Louis, Missouri. This potential clue was cleverly seized upon by the French station TF1 and on October 16, 1995, Nicolas Maillard received a faxed letter from the public relations department at McDonnell Douglas (the successor to McDonnell Aircraft, which became part of Boeing in December 1996), stating that McDonnell used its own employees, not military cameramen, to film all their flight tests, including those of the XH-20 Ramjet helicopter. The letter even supplied the names of the two McDonnell employees who had actually shot the Ramjet tests, Chester

Turk, who was using a movie camera, and Bill Schmitt, who was using a stills camera.

Santilli has hinted that the name of the cameraman is Jack Barnett, encouraging a flurry of speculation and widespread harassment of several wholly innocent Jack Barnetts across America. In June 1995, Philip Mantle, the former Director of Research for the British UFO group BUFORA, who was researching many aspects of the story at Santilli's behest, got the chance to talk by telephone to a man who, he was told, was Jack Barnett. TF1, as we had done before them, had also made several requests for an interview with the cameraman, and as with us, they were promised that contact would be made eventually – but none was ever made. Santilli did however agree to relay a list of questions to the cameraman. On September 14, 1995 a reply was faxed to TF1 – two of the answers were of particular relevance.

First, TF1 asked: 'What tests of the Ramjet "Little Henry" did you film in St Louis in May 1947?'

'Initial experimental tests . . .' was the vague response.

The second question by the French programme makers concerned the incident itself: 'Why didn't the Army use colour film for such an event?'

The reply came back: 'I was given instructions to leave immediately to film an aviation crash of a Russian spy plane. I did not have time to order either colour film stock or special camera equipment. I used standard-issue film stock and a standard-issue Bell and Howell.' This answer might explain why the recovery footage is seen in black and white but it hardly holds good as an explanation for the filming of the autopsy, which was apparently shot much later at Fort Worth airbase in Texas.

The other oft-repeated clue to the cameraman's identity was the story that Santilli had frequently repeated by way of explaining how he had first made contact with the cameraman during a trip to America in search of rare footage of Elvis Presley. TF1's reporter Nicolas Maillard succeeded in tracking down the man who was the source for that footage. His name was not Jack Barnett; it was Bill Randle.

Randle was a Cleveland, Ohio disc jockey and he had supplied Santilli with the Presley footage in 1993 – the same footage which Santilli had claimed he had acquired from the cameraman. In fact, the purchase was concluded in Randle's office on July 4, 1992, in the presence of Gary Shoefield, who at that time was working for Polygram, but was later to join Santilli's company and became involved in the marketing and distribution of the autopsy footage. The actual film to which Santilli and thence Polygram were acquiring the rights was the first known film of Elvis Presley live on stage and was part of a larger documentary that was a joint effort between Randle and Universal Pictures in 1955. The footage sold to Santilli is relatively short and includes segments from two concerts: an afternoon performance at a Cleveland high school and an evening show at a local auditorium. Both performances took place on Thursday July 20, 1955 and featured the Four Lads, Bill Haley and the Comets, Pat Boone and the then unknown Elvis Presley. Both performances were filmed by a freelance cameraman hired by Randle.

The name of this photographer was Jack Barnett. This at least provided the background for the name that Santilli had thought appropriate to give his 'cameraman'. Barnett, the son of Russian immigrants to the USA, was born on January 1, 1906 and died in 1967. He was a newsreel cameraman on the Italian front during the Second World War, but was not a military cameraman and had not served in the US Army. Possessing what they justifiably thought was devastating evidence to knock serious holes in Santilli's entire story, the programme makers at TF1 planned to unleash this new information in Santilli's presence during the course of a live interview on October 23, 1995 with their star presenter Jacques Pradel. Yet, as on other occasions when the truth has appeared to be at a slight variance with the version of events offered by Santilli, when footage of Bill Randle was played on the screen Santilli appeared relatively unfazed. He immediately launched into what appeared to be a new cover story or a new real story. He remarked that he was very pleased that they had been able to find Bill Randle and then went on to say that the person from whom he had purchased the footage was not the cameraman but that he had met the real cameraman afterwards – following the sale of the Presley footage in the summer of 1992 (although previously, as confirmed by Randle, Santilli had given the year as 1993). Unfortunately the show began to run out of time and in its closing minutes they ran the tape of the shifty Volker Spielberg – at which point Santilli became noticeably uncomfortable.

If the Presley story was untrue, Santilli would undoubtedly have had no compunction about using it, with the justification that he was merely attempting to protect his source, as he had given him his assurance that he would protect his identity. (This was an integral part of the whole deal and the essential element which enabled Santilli to 'buy' the cameraman's trust and hence persuade him to part with the footage – a task which was eased by the hand-over of a substantial amount of dollars.) It is worth pointing out that in the many conversations I have had with Santilli, he comes across as being one of the most plausible people I have ever met. He always has highly convincing explanations for any discrepancy that crops up. Indeed, it is very difficult to pin down anything he says as a deliberate lie rather than a half-truth or a slight inaccuracy inspired by such high motives as not to appear in any way intentionally misleading. In fact, when he felt that I was becoming increasingly sceptical about the entire nature of the 'alien' footage he expressed hurt and dismay that I should not believe him, and seemed genuinely taken aback.

If there was any truth in the cameraman's alleged background, then one group of men who would have known were his contemporary professional photographers in the Army Air Force. In 1996 three surviving military cameramen were traced and contacted by Kent Jeffery in the course of his research into the 'Santilli footage'.

Joe Longo is the President of the International Combat Camera Association, an organization consisting of several hundred former combat cameramen throughout the world. He served as a combat cameraman for the Air Force in the Pacific Theatre during the Second World War and then again during the Korean conflict in the 1950s. When he left the military, he went to work as a cameraman at the Lookout Mountain Air Force Station in Southern California. Among his duties there were assignments on classified research projects with the Atomic Energy Commission, as well as the X-15 project. In the early 1960s he filmed the celebrated scene of test pilot Scott Crossfield's X-15 falling away from under the wing of a B-52 bomber, firing its rocket engine and heading for outer space – fifty miles above the earth's surface.

Bill Gibson has the unusual background of having served as a combat cameraman in all three branches of the armed services. In April 1942 he filmed the launching of sixteen B-25s on their way to the famous 'Doolittle raid' over Tokyo. The scene of the heavily laden bombers taking off from the deck of the aircraft carrier the USS *Hornet*, and barely becoming airborne, is one of the most famous of the Second World War. Many years later he would cover another historically famous launch: that of Apollo 11, on its way to the moon.

Shortly after the Doolittle raid, the *Hornet* was torpedoed and sunk and Gibson, along with the other survivors, was rescued by the USS *Hughes*.

After the war Gibson photographed the early American V-2 launches at White Sands, as well as the balloon launches and recovery operations of Project Mogul. In the late 1940s he worked on two classified UFO-related studies for the Air Force: Projects Grudge and Twinkle. As a consultant to NASA in the late 1960s, he designed the camera that brought us man's first steps on the moon.

As if all this was not already a highly distinguished career, Gibson was then assigned for eight months to the White House, where his subject was President Truman. No stranger to world figures, Gibson also included among his assignments Franklin Roosevelt, Ronald Reagan and George Bush, as well as Winston Churchill, Albert Schweitzer and Wernher von Braun, becoming close personal friends with the last named.

The third member of this distinguished triumvirate was Lieutenant Colonel Daniel A. McGovern, who served during the Second World War with the Eighth Air Force in the European theatre as a combat cameraman on B-17 bombers flying highly dangerous missions over Germany. He was responsible for much of the footage used in the famous wartime documentary *Memphis Belle*. On one mission, flak from anti-aircraft guns blew a hole in the B-17 at his station only moments after he had stepped away. On another occasion he survived a crash landing in southern England after his aircraft was badly damaged by German gunners.

After the Japanese surrender of August 1945, McGovern was the first American military cameraman to photograph the awesome devastation on the ground at Hiroshima and Nagasaki. Just four weeks after the bomb had been dropped, he was there with his camera where he shot several thousands of feet of 16mm colour film in both cities. The film was classified shortly after it was shot and even today much of it has still not been released.

Like Bill Gibson in the late 1940s, McGovern also worked on Projects Grudge and Twinkle, for which operations he was the project officer. For some six months in 1947, UFOs were spotted with alarming frequency and by reputable observers, often pilots and military personnel, in the close vicinity of some of the country's most sensitive and secret installations, including Kirtland Air Force Base and White Sands. So concerned were the authorities that it was decided to institute a special programme, supervised by the Air Force, to capture on film the UFOs that appeared to be 'spying' on top-secret military sites. Special cameras were set up, both on the ground and aboard jet fighters, which were scrambled a number of times when the objects showed up on radar. Although no official records exist of any film of the mysterious objects, there were several sightings that were later released under the Freedom of Information Act. Among the credible observers of the UFOs was McGovern himself. According to his written statement, he noticed 'the objects came from below the horizon, at high speed, at an angle of some 45 degrees and at an altitude of some 70,000 or 80,000 feet, changed their direction from a vertical climb to horizontal, then the brilliant white light emitted from the UFOs disappeared in the skies'.

McGovern remained in 'specialized photography' throughout his twenty-year military career. At the time of his retirement in 1961 he was stationed at Vandenberg Air Force Base, California, where he was commander of the Photographic Squadron. After retiring he became the civilian chief of the photographic division for the Air Force Flight Test Center at Edwards Air Force Base in California.

As they were all members of the same part of the military service responsible for photographic operations, Longo, Gibson and McGovern were all understandably intrigued by the emergence of both the 'alien autopsy' footage and the claim that it was made by a man who, if he is to be believed, would not only have been one of their contemporaries but also would most likely have been known to one or all of them, if not personally then certainly by reputation, and in all likelihood would have accompanied at least one of them on assignment. Certainly, all three were highly familiar with the military training and the bureaucratic procedures necessary for the filming of any classified event. With the Cold War beginning, virtually anything that was photographed was deemed to be classified or secret in some way; in fact, almost everything was regarded by the military as something that someone else would like to spy upon and so anything written or recorded, filmed or photographed was automatically subject to secrecy.

The three veterans agreed to assess what evidence there was surrounding the claims of Santilli's 'cameraman'. They studied the footage of the autopsy and examined the photocopies of the labels from the film canisters that Santilli had obtained and had in turn provided to the French TV programme on TF1. The three were unanimous in pointing out discrepancies in both the story and the labels.

As far as the appropriate military procedures of the time were concerned, the usual rules and regulations would have been applicable for all their assignments, and therefore would have automatically been part of the operating procedure for the 'alien autopsy' cameraman. According to their expert assessment, his scenario does not add up.

Regarding the claim that he was stationed in Washington DC and flew on June 1, 1947 to Roswell, New Mexico, they point out that there were indeed qualified cameramen with the requisite 'Top Secret' security clearances stationed at military installations all over the country, including New Mexico. Cameramen, both movie and stills, could have been dispatched immediately to the scene from a local military installation such as Alamogordo or Roswell, rather than from Washington. As this was potentially one of the most serious incursions into American airspace ever to have occurred, it must follow that speed was of the essence and the high command would surely have wanted to get cameramen to the scene as quickly as possible.

Santilli's cameraman claims that he processed the film himself and that the authorities in Washington did not bother to collect all the reels. The military veterans dismiss this scenario as complete nonsense. On top-secret projects, a cameraman never, under any circumstances, processed the film himself. Furthermore, military regulations required that all film, whether processed or not, had to be accounted for, and not just every reel, but every frame of every reel. To ensure compliance, either the length of the film on a reel was physically measured (e.g. 99 feet, 10 frames) or a machine called a frame counter was used.

In addition, Santilli's man is quoted as saying that there were three autopsies. The footage he allegedly retained covered a major part of one of these autopsies. On that basis alone, it is inconceivable that the authorities overseeing the operation would have overlooked so much missing film.

Three basic types of film stock were in use by the military in 1947: 16mm colour, 35mm black and white and 16mm black and white. For very special or important projects – under which category the autopsy and the scene at the craft would have been classified – 16mm colour film would have been used. Santilli's cameraman used 16 mm black and white film.

Furthermore, according to McGovern, who had himself filmed a number of autopsies during his military service, all medical procedures were automatically recorded on colour stock. He has also pointed out that for important medical procedures, two cameras were used, both in fixed positions. The first camera would be mounted on a tripod sitting on a riser (to give the cameraman extra elevation) adjacent to the operating table, while the second camera would be overhead, mounted on the ceiling to provide a 'top shot'. Santilli's footage was shot on one camera.

All three experts also pointed out that a motion-picture cameraman would almost always be accompanied by a stills photographer and that the two would work together as a team. During an autopsy every step of the procedure would be carefully photographed by the stills photographer, who would invariably figure in the frame of the motion-picture cameraman. (Medical personnel have also remarked that still pictures would definitely have been taken.) In the Santilli autopsy film there is no evidence either of a stills photographer or of any actual photos. But if, as the cameraman states, there were three separate autopsies, a stills photographer would certainly have been present. Even if there was acute concern about security, a stills camera could have been used by one of those present – the cameraman himself or even one of the doctors. Given the unique and extraordinary nature of the event, and the priceless opportunity it would have afforded to medical science and biology, it is unthinkable that such a procedure could have been carried out without there being an attempt to obtain the most comprehensive and accurate photographic record of everything that was discovered by the post-mortem(s).

Even the technique of Santilli's cameraman, according to the veterans, was inconsistent with the highly standardized procedures and methods that were prescribed by the military at the time. Longo, Gibson and McGovern are in a position to know: all three trained other military cameramen during that period. They agree that the camerawork in the autopsy film is so atrocious that it would have fallen a long way short of fulfilling even the most basic quality-control standards laid down by the military. As Longo quipped, 'If anybody in my unit shot film in that manner, he'd be back scrubbing pots in the kitchen!'

According to the box label submitted by Santilli, the film stock used was Kodak High Speed Super XX Panchromatic Safety Film. The three cameramen agree that a Bell and Howell Model 70, the camera claimed to have been used to cover the autopsy, should, with this type of film, have given very sharp detail. Even with the mediocre lighting conditions surrounding the subject, the picture quality should have been way above what was achieved in the actual film – in fact, their verdict was that it should have been 'excellent'. They calculated that with that combination of stock and camera, with the focus set at twenty-five feet and the aperture at f8, and under normal indoor lighting, everything between about eighteen inches from the camera and infinity would be in focus. This was not so with the autopsy film. McGovern concluded that it had been 'deliberately blurred so that no subject is visible in detail'.

The three cameramen were also quick to point to problems with the labelling of the film canisters. For example, the seal that showed an eagle logo, obviously used to confer an official appearance, was one that none of them had ever seen. In their experience, of the thousands of boxes of film ordered by the military from Kodak, none was stamped with a seal. One of the Santilli labels reads: 'Reel #52; Truman; 85 Filter 2/3 Stop; Force X 2 stop-Possible'. The official verdict was that an '85 filter' was used only with colour film. The '2/3 stop' indicates the amount of light that would be blocked by the filter and 'Force X 2 stop' indicates the amount of additional exposure time required to compensate for the additional loss of light. In effect, it is a prescription for underexposing the film and then compensating by overdeveloping it in the processing laboratory – a procedure that would unnecessarily increase the graininess and lower the 'sharpness' of the picture.

Given all of the above, in addition to the frankly incredible nature of the film's subject matter, all three former cameramen are convinced that the film is a fraud. In fact, McGovern is willing to keep an open mind and if Santilli will offer more information he, in turn, will help to authenticate the cameraman.

If the man's full name and serial number were provided, it would be possible to verify his service record with the Air Force Records Center in St Louis, Missouri. McGovern, who has held top-secret security clearance, has even offered to keep all this information absolutely confidential – revealing only his conclusion as to whether the cameraman is genuine or not in his claim of military service. Aside from his name and serial number, McGovern's only other stipulation is that the cameraman should make a fifteen-minute telephone call so that he can evaluate his claims and, using his considerable knowledge of service personnel and postings, ensure that he is not an impostor. The two men may have certain things in common, for in June 1947 Lieutenant Colonel Dan McGovern was also stationed in Washington DC, the same location as the cameraman who was ordered to undertake the mysterious assignment that took him to the deserts of New Mexico.

Having had several encounters with Santilli, I can almost hear the answers to the questions raised by the valid points made by the forum of ex-military cameramen. The problems with the labels would be parried by some suggestion such as the fact that this was how they were handed over to Santilli: if the labels or some detail on the canisters is wrong, it may be down to the person who handed them over, but there is no attempt on Santilli's part to deceive anyone.

As for the quality of the film, Santilli has already defended this by claiming that the cameraman was forced to wear a protective suit. Not only was it extremely hot and uncomfortable, but the small plastic visor through which he had to look and use the camera's viewfinder was inadequate and it kept steaming up. The lack of a stills photographer could be explained away by stating that the autopsy was deliberately kept to a small number of witnesses to preserve secrecy or that still photographs were taken but this was done separately and they have never been released, along with the rest of the film. No doubt the cameraman might claim that he was used for some of the most highly secret assignments at the time and thus had a false name and identity even within the Air Force. He might further argue that the reason he was sent to Roswell, despite the journey taking longer than one from a nearer base, was that he was the only cameraman that General McMullen and his superiors could have trusted with absolute discretion on a mission that threatened to become one of the most secret in the world.

The more one thinks about it, the easier it becomes to concoct a whole series of answers which, while they may be nothing more than a tissue of lies, are inherently difficult to disprove. To a large extent, both the autopsy footage and the MJ-12 documents currently inhabit a grey no man's land, stranded somewhere between truth, fiction, wishful thinking and sophisticated hoax.

14

If any agency knows the truth about Roswell, it is likely to be the Central Intelligence Agency. Although it currently maintains that it does not take any interest in the subject, in common with other military and intelligence branches of the government, it was actively involved in considering and investigating the phenomenon from the late 1940s onwards. In *Above Top Secret* Timothy Good provides a comprehensive and exhaustive summary of the involvement of the different agencies, and the book is highly recommended to anyone interested in the subject. Although Good's later books display a rather more credulous approach, subscribing to the extreme conspiracy theories which maintain that there is a secret agreement between the aliens and the US government, *Above Top Secret* is for the most part a sober and extremely well researched work of non-fiction.

The book correctly identifies the Office of Scientific Intelligence, OSI, as being the division of the CIA most concerned with UFOs. This division had originally expressed concern about the 'green fireballs' sighted over various military installations in New Mexico which had led to the inconclusive Project Twinkle.

The incident that set the alarm bells ringing inside America's recently formed secret intelligence agency was the invasion of Washington by a fleet of flying saucers in 1952.

The sightings began with a Pan American Airways flight, piloted by First Officer William Nash and Second Officer W.H. Fortenberry, who were flying a DC-4 from New York to San Juan on July 14. At 9.12 p.m. six glowing discs approached at a fantastic speed a mile below the airliner in the vicinity of Langley Air Force Base in Virginia. The objects were described as being approximately one hundred feet in diameter and were flying in formation.

The leading disc, apparently having sighted the DC-4, slowed down abruptly, then the next two discs 'wobbled' momentarily, after which all six UFOs 'flipped up on edge', enabling the pilots to estimate their thickness at about fifteen feet.

The objects then accelerated away, but once again lined up in their original position in formation, and a strange glow around them increased as they performed this manoeuvre. Two other discs then appeared under the DC-4, glowing brightly as they joined the six ahead; all the discs suddenly darkened, but glowed again when eight objects appeared in line. Finally, the discs climbed to high altitude and disappeared, at a speed computed by the pilots to be 200 miles per minute – i.e. 12,000mph. When they landed at Miami, the crew were debriefed by the Air Force Office of Special Investigations.

Five days later entire fleets of flying saucers were spotted over the Washington DC area by several pilots of both commercial and military aircraft. The objects were also tracked on radar at Andrews Air Force Base as well as the Air Traffic Control Center at Washington's National Airport just a few miles from the White House. The objects were observed to hover, fly at relatively slow speeds, estimated at 100–130mph, and also accelerate to fantastic speeds.

One week later, on the night of July 26, there was another 'invasion' over Washington. UFOs were again tracked by radar at National Airport and Andrews Air Force Base. The radar returns were described by the Civil Aviation Authority personnel as 'generally solid', and a CAA flight inspector reported '5 objects giving off a light glow ranging from orange to white at an altitude of 2200 feet'. Some commercial pilots reported visuals from 'cigarette glow' (red-yellow) to a 'light'. F-94 jet fighters were scrambled to intercept the UFOs, without much success. One pilot flew through the radar returns, another pilot mentioned seeing four lights and then one light but being unable to 'close upon it'. An Air Force lieutenant reported 'seven good solid targets' and, after checking with the airport's weather station, discovered that there was a slight temperature inversion but not sufficient to create the illusions and the radar returns. An official Air Force report noted that 'most returns were "solid" . . . but never before had they appeared in such quantities over such a prolonged period and with such definition as was experienced on the night of 26/27 July 52'.

The extraordinary event made headline news around the world, comparable to the initial excitement of the Roswell Incident, except that this lasted longer.

The Air Force hurriedly held a chaotic press conference to denounce the entire thing as 'temperature inversion', a climatic phenomenon which can give rise to false radar returns but is highly unlikely to have explained all the strange sightings of the two nights. Meanwhile there was serious consternation behind the scenes, with Air Force intelligence analysts definitely not subscribing to the official explanation.

An FBI memorandum written a few days later quoted a briefing from Commander Boyd of the Current Intelligence Branch, Estimates Division, Air Intelligence, who 'advised that the objects sighted may possibly be from another planet . . . but that at the present time there is nothing to substantiate this theory but the possibility is not being overlooked'.

Which it certainly would have been had the Air Force believed its own explanation of the 'temperature inversion' theory. The widespread hysteria bordering on panic which greeted the 1952 Washington sightings prompted the CIA to launch its own investigation. Three months after the Washington scare the Assistant Director of the CIA's Scientific Intelligence Division, Marshall Chadwell, sent a four-page memorandum to the Director of the CIA. He expressed concern that the Air Force was the only 'unit of government' investigating the mystery of the UFOs and, quoting their statistics, stated: 'Since 1947, ATIC [Air Technical Intelligence Command] has received approximately 1500 official reports of sightings . . . During 1952 alone, official reports totalled 250. Of the 1500 reports, Air Force carries 20 percent as unexplained and of those received from January through July 1952 it carries 28 percent unexplained . . . public concern with the phenomena . . . indicates that a fair proportion of our population is mentally conditioned to the acceptance of the incredible. In this fact lies the potential for the touching off of mass hysteria and panic . . . In order to minimize risk of panic, a national policy should be established as to what should be told the public regarding the phenomena . . . I consider the problem to be of such importance that it should be brought to the attention of the National Security Council in order that a community-wide coordinated effort towards its solution may be initiated.'

Other documents show that the CIA was also worried that if evidence of its interest became public then it would only serve to encourage people to believe that the government was holding something back, thus 'making the problem even more serious in the public mind than it already was'. The CIA, like its counterparts in the FBI and Air Force Intelligence before it, also considered whether the 'flying saucers' could be some secret US government weapons project, but concluded that this was impossible: 'This has been denied officially at the highest level of government and to make certain we queried Dr Whitman, Chairman of the Research and Development Board. On a Top Secret basis, he too, denies it.'

The CIA also ruled out the possibility that the UFOs were some secret Soviet weapon, although it was alarmed at the implications for defence against a possible Soviet attack and the vulnerability to exploitation of the phenomena for the purposes of psychological warfare. Noting that there were influential civic groups taking an active interest in 'flying saucers', the CIA noted that 'we, from an intelligence point of view, should watch for any indication of Russian efforts to capitalize upon this present American credulity.

'Of even greater moment is the second danger. Our air warning system will undoubtedly always depend upon a combination of radar scanning and visual observation. We give Russia the capability of delivering an air attack against us, yet any given moment now, there may be current a dozen official unidentified sightings plus many unofficial. At the moment of attack, how will we, on an instant basis, distinguish hardware from phantom? The answer of course is that until far greater knowledge is achieved of the causes back of the sightings – the little understood phenomena [deleted] has described – we will run the increasing risk of false alerts and the even greater danger of tabbing the real as false.'

Thus there was a very real and secretly recognized danger of UFOs triggering a nuclear strike. On December 2, Chadwell sent another memo to the CIA's Director, following a further briefing from the Air Force stating that 'the reports of incidents convince us that there is something going on that must have immediate attention . . . Sightings of unexplained objects at great altitudes and travelling at high speeds in the vicinity of major US. defense installations are of such nature that they are not attributable to natural phenomena or known types of aerial vehicle.'

At the end of 1952 the CIA convened a panel of scientists known as the Robertson Panel, which met for three days in secret at the

Pentagon from January 14 to 17, 1953. The report was not declassified until 1975 and there is a suspicion that the full report has never been released. The Chairman of the Scientific Advisory Panel from whom it acquired its name was Dr H.P. Robertson, who was a specialist in physics and advanced weapons systems. Frederick C. Durant, an expert in missiles and rocketry, was an associate member, and at the time of writing was still alive. I met him in Washington to hear his recollections of CIA involvement in the study of UFOs and to see if he could shed any light on the Roswell Incident.

'I was active as an engineer with the American Rocket Society. I'd been very interested in the potential of rockets for potential satellite flight,' recalled Durant, a thin and ascetic-looking man, who was both active and lively for his advancing years. 'I was invited to act as a consultant to the Central Intelligence Agency for a study they were making on UFOs. At that time, this was in 1952, there were many sightings that could not be explained by the Air Technical Intelligence Command, ATIC, which headed up the Blue Book investigation.' Durant remembers that the Robertson Panel was a very interesting project, involving as it did some of the finest scientific minds in the United States, bringing expertise on nuclear research, radar development and astronomy together with Durant's own expertise of rocket science. Durant was keen to emphasize the political conditions that prevailed in the early 1950s. 'The Cold War with the Soviet Union was very frigid,' he recalled. 'Most of the concern within the Central Intelligence Agency was in the military aspect of UFOs.'

If it was not possible for the North American Defense Commands to be able to identify lights in the sky and be able to distinguish them from radar echoes of incoming bombers from the Soviet Union over the North Pole, then there was a very serious danger of an attack not being recognized in time or, even worse, a false alarm. In addition, 'the psychological warfare aspects of this was one of the considerations and finally there was a very definite concern about the clogging of telephone communications. In the so called UFO flap of 1952, the telephone lines in Washington here were totally clogged. Everybody was getting busy signals and this again from a national security standpoint was a considerable concern.'

These were some of the problems that it was hoped that the CIA's Robertson Panel could resolve. 'The first meeting was held in January,' said Durant, surrounded by walls lined with scientific books and a large collection of Arthur C. Clarke's works. 'It was only four days long, intensive studies, the panel met at the Agency and I'm not quite sure why, but I was a junior on the list, I was asked to be Secretary and I ended up writing the Robertson Panel Report. The report itself is about forty pages long and it lists all of the best reports of sightings that Captain Edward Ruppelt who headed up the Blue Book at the Air Force Technical Intelligence Command could put together and those seventy-five reports were winnowed down to about, oh, a couple of dozen, that were intensely studied by the Committee. The first reaction I can recall distinctly: Dr Alvarez [the Panel's Radar expert] said, "But there's no data here. There's no scientific data. There's nothing that can be measured; these are all personal impressions and we have no base from which to work." It's interesting that there were two known good films at that time that had been shot in 16mm. One of them was the Tree Martin, Utah, sighting and the other was Great Falls, Montana. These films were shown several times and surprisingly the Utah sighting turned out to be high-flying birds and this was unacceptable at first thought, but then they were able to come up with actual photographs of seagulls in bright sunlight at a certain angle and you got nothing but white blobs in the sky and that has generally been accepted for that particular sighting. The other, the Great Falls, Montana, showed two lights moving together, which, as a former flyer, you know, they looked to me like two aircraft coming down and there were later determined to have been two aircraft in the area.'

Critics of the Robertson Panel have claimed that its members set out to debunk the reality of the flying saucers and did not begin to address the many unexplained incidents, the 'incredible sightings by credible witnesses'. Although the Robertson Panel may have legitimately been lacking any scientific evidence, it would be fair to say that those present were fairly sceptical and that the subject had already begun to be dismissed by the more hard-headed among the military and scientific establishment. In addition, it could be argued that the CIA and the military had a genuine motive for discouraging the growth of the phenomenon. (Many ufologists go further and state that it was a deliberate CIA exercise to debunk the flying saucer phenomenon because they knew it was real.) As Durant admits, there was considerable disquiet about the panic created by the mass sightings over Washington and the implications for communications and national security.

It became one of the major concerns for the Robertson Panel, recalls Durant: 'high signal to noise ratio as Lloyd Berkner referred to it . . . the fact that this might seriously affect the Air Defense Intelligence Systems and if the UFOs became discredited by the general public they expected that there'd be ways to keep false or poorly documented reports out of these channels.'

Durant recalled that they had also considered the sightings over the atomic and secret defence installations which had been investigated earlier by the FBI and the Air Force, but they had tended to ignore them on the grounds that people were more likely to be watchful in such areas. Durant, along with his fellow scientists on the CIA panel, was sceptical about the whole phenomenon. Today, he is still a non-believer.

'To my mind,' he says, 'even after what has been some forty years, I have no reason to change my views that any of these lights in the sky are not mistaken identification of known phenomena and much as I'd like to believe that we have been visited by small extraterrestrials, there has never been any artefacts recovered. No extraterrestrial artefact that the Academy of Sciences will examine and state is an extraterrestrial object built by intelligence. The only extraterrestrial evidence we have are of course meteorites and fireballs and astronomical phenomena. But as far as aliens, I do not accept that we have been visited by aliens. I would say this at the same time: I do believe there is life in outer space, intelligent life, much more intelligent than we are on this planet and that at some time, past or future, we shall be visited and we'd expect to be but there's not the slightest evidence that this has been so in my view. I speak as a pragmatist, as an engineer, and I like facts and there's no factual evidence of actual visitors and certainly no recovered little space men.'

Durant's response is not to be dismissed, particularly as he admits to the real possibility of life beyond earth. I was intrigued to see what his reasoning was for this belief, and he explained: 'I used to tell my students at the Smithsonian: "You go out at night and look up at a dark sky and see all those stars of which there are billions and billions of galaxies of our size and the planets that will be expected to be formed around many of these stars or suns and if they're a proper distance, not too cold, not too hot, from a sun, I would expect life to evolve in the same way that it has on this planet." Now, I cannot accept that we are alone in the Universe. We're undoubtedly alone in our particular configuration, but life of some sort I would expect, and at some time we may expect those visits. It's a long time before we can visit at stellar distances but I believe in SETI, being the Search for Extra-Terrestrial Intelligence.'

Durant is also dismissive of General Twining's admission in his 1947 memorandum to the head of the Air Force that the phenomenon is 'something real'. 'There are a lot of people confused and a lot of people were led down the garden path in the decades that are past,' laughs the CIA's former 'flying saucer' expert. 'I should mention the aspect of a conspiracy within the government not to release documents. "We do have knowledge and we do have it in Dayton, Ohio or somewhere . . ." It's so laughable! Anyone who has worked in government, as I have, knows you cannot keep a secret for two weeks or two months! The leaks! It's just not possible.'

I pointed out to Durant that some things had been kept secret, such as radiation experiments on human beings which have only recently come to light. Although he acknowledges the point, he maintains that a conspiracy to cover up the existence of UFOs would be impossible to perpetuate. Whether a secret of such cosmic significance could genuinely be kept under wraps is an issue worthy of consideration. There are powerful arguments on both sides which, to my mind, eventually cancel each other out. That deep and dark secrets have been kept in the past is self-evident, and that there are many secret experiments and intelligence operations being conducted in our name every day of the week about which we know nothing, is also true. But could a world-shattering event from fifty years ago have been kept a secret all this time? The answer is: with difficulty.

Let us imagine that the Roswell Incident occurred and that it was covered up and the truth was finally revealed years later. At that point one side could claim, yes, the secret was kept and the other, no, the secret was revealed by the researchers and the UFO investigators and, whether genuine or not, by documents such as MJ-12. The natural propensity of people not to believe the government and to support conspiracy theories allows them to have it both ways. As far as the Robertson Panel was concerned, Durant states that they did not even consider the Roswell Incident. Again, he is convinced that the whole thing was blown out of all proportion and that it was a mistake, from the initial press release to the newspaper stories that followed. As for those who have sworn that it did happen, the distinguished scientist just laughs. 'I'm sorry,' he smiled. 'They are either wrong, or have been lied to, or they are lying. That's all I can say.'

There remains the possibility that if the Roswell Incident did occur, then it was kept secret from the Robertson Panel. Durant dismisses the suggestion. 'This is five years later and the incidence of these sightings had increased greatly and the steps taken by the intelligence community and military intelligence and the defence community were to acquire the best information possible. I truly believe we had the best intelligence available in the intelligence community, including the White House and the National Security Council. Believe me, you would not have been able to keep secret the existence of these bodies. Do they still exist? Are they still squirrelled away? Do you think they've been burned, or buried? What happened to them? Where are they? Nobody told you that? That's a secret! No, I'm sorry, I can't accept it. They say I'm stubborn but in some forty years since these investigations, I've kept up generally, I held a symposium at the Smithsonian in 1980 which was about thirty years after the first sightings and Allan Hynek and a chap named Hendry of the UFO types and Captain Oberg, who was ex-intelligence Air Force, and Philip Klass [the noted sceptic and writer for *Aviation Week*] we had a full-day symposium and it was very interesting. At the tail end I acted as moderator and I asked each of the panellists, I said: "Let me ask you, all six of you, 'Do you believe there are recovered aliens from Roswell or any other incident that are being kept secret from the public?'"

'And not one of them said, "I believe that." I asked, "Do you believe that such stories of aliens and their existence is a conspiracy of some element of the government? Do any of you believe there is such a conspiracy?" And they all said, "No!" And when the chips are down that's my view too!'

The answer might have been different nearly twenty years later, now that a substantial number of American citizens not only believe in the reality of UFOs but a statistically significant section of the population actually believe that they have been abducted by aliens on board spaceships and then returned to their homes in the country, the suburbs and even in the great cities of the metropolis. Not just abducted but subjected to a series of horrendous experiments which, according to the accounts of several women, involve some form of hybrid breeding programme which is vital to the aliens', and possibly our, survival. Much has been written elsewhere on this phenomenon and it represents a relatively new dimension of the UFO mystery, but it is relevant here in that it is an indication of what people are prepared to believe – and there can be no doubt about the sincerity of the many abductees. While there will always be fakers and hoaxers, the majority of the victims are genuinely traumatized by what they claim has happened to them and in many cases they are embarrassed to come forward with tales of their abductions.

Durant rightly or wrongly dismisses these reports, at least insofar as they might be evidence of extraterrestrial visitations. As for Roswell, he believes that the Project Mogul balloon is the best explanation and dismisses it as a UFO event on the grounds that it was not even considered as such by the Blue Book Project, the Air Force list of all the most convincing cases.

Durant, who worked with and knew Wernher von Braun, and has written his biography for the *Encyclopaedia Britannica* and Microsoft's *Encarta* CD-Rom, is also adamant that it could not have been a V-2 or some strange experiment involving manned flight. As far as he is concerned, 'The Robertson Panel reported in 1953 and concluded for the Central Intelligence Agency that the phenomenon of UFOs was not real. In other words, they could all be explained.'

15

Despite the apparent certainties of the Robertson Panel on UFOs, all of America's intelligence agencies and the Air Force continued not only to take an active interest in the subject but also went to some lengths to keep their interest secret.

Clearly, there was still a national security dimension to any unidentified flying object that might be sighted, but within the Air Force there were those who were convinced that there was no 'direct threat' to the United States. While most sightings were regarded as having an innocent explanation, the Air Force calculated in 1952 that 20.1 per cent of reported sightings were unknown in origin, and could not be attributed to balloons, aircraft, birds or any of the other standard explanations. It was for this reason that the Air Force decided to continue their study, stating: 'There are reports we cannot explain. We believe we can explain all but about 20 percent, but if you noted the breakdown of conclusions, we only can positively identify about 7 percent. With the world situation what it is and with the present advances in science, it behooves [sic] the Air Force to have systems whereby they can receive reports of, evaluate and determine the identity of objects reportedly flying over the United States.' The briefing paper added that there was also no guarantee that some other power 'could not develop some object that by present day standards is unconventional in appearance or performance' and that while there was no evidence of any threat to the public at that time, this did not guarantee that there might never be. 'The project will be continued. Even if a system for the foolproof explanation of every sighting is developed it will continue because you never know what may happen in the future.' The author of this report was at pains to stress that reporting procedures had to be improved and also announced that cameras were being installed at various locations to improve the quality of evidence.

While the CIA were busy setting about trying to play down the risk and reality of the UFO phenomenon, the Air Force, at least towards the end of 1952, was still openly considering the possibility of extraterrestrial explanations. Project Sign had led to Project Grudge, which in turn gave way to Project Blue Book. According to the official statement now released by the USAF (Fact Sheet 95-03): 'From 1947 to 1969, the Air Force investigated Unidentified Flying Objects under Project Blue Book. The project, headquartered at Wright Patterson Air Force base, Ohio, was terminated Dec. 17, 1969. Of a total of 12,618 sightings reported to Project Blue Book, 701 remained "unidentified".'

The decision to discontinue UFO investigations was based on an evaluation of a 1969 report prepared by the University of Colorado entitled 'Scientific Study of Unidentified Flying Objects'; a review of this report by the National Academy of Sciences; and previous UFO studies and Air Force experience investigating UFO reports during the 1940s, '50s and '60s. 'As a result of these investigations, studies and experience gained from investigating UFO reports since 1948, the conclusions of Project Blue Book were: (1) no UFO reported, investigated and evaluated by the Air Force was ever an indication of threat to our national security; (2) there was no evidence submitted to or discovered by the Air Force that sightings categorized as "unidentified" represented technological developments or principles beyond the range of modern scientific knowledge; and (3) there was no evidence indicating that sightings categorized as "unidentified" were extraterrestrial vehicles.

'Since the termination of Project Blue Book, nothing has occurred that would support a resumption of UFO investigations by the Air Force. Given the current environment of steadily decreasing defense budgets, it is unlikely the Air Force would become involved in such a costly project in the foreseeable future.'

In March 1952, a few months before the near panic that resulted from the wave of sightings over the nation's capital, Project Grudge had metamorphosed into Project Blue Book, the longest-running and perhaps most thorough of the USAF's successive investigations into unidentified flying objects. Two years later on May 15, 1954, General Nathan Twining, by this time the Air Force Chief of Staff, reported in a speech to an audience at Amarillo, Texas that the 'best brains in the Air Force' were still trying to solve the problem of the flying saucers. The project had so far not dismissed the interplanetary hypothesis. 'If they come from Mars,' Twining continued, 'they are so far ahead of us we have nothing to be afraid of!'

It was a disingenuous remark, which apart from flatly contradicting the conclusions of the CIA's Robertson Panel, also conflicted with earlier Air Force assurances to the public that the phenomenon posed no threat to the security of the most powerful and scientifically advanced nation in the world. By now, various interested private citizens and organizations devoted to the study of the phenomenon were deeply suspicious of the attitude of the USAF and the information that was being made available to the general public. Their suspicions were confirmed when the Air Force issued a directive on August 12, 1954, AR 200-2, which stated that it had an obligation to report all UFOs as a 'possible threat to the security of the United States and its forces, and secondly, to determine technical aspects involved'.

The directive was a highly detailed blueprint designed to extract the maximum detail for intelligence purposes relating to any UFO sighting. It essentially formalized what had become custom and practice within the military establishment by setting out numbered paragraphs with exact instructions to be followed by pilots and observers who might witness a UFO. For example, it advised that reports should include the following elements:

'(1) Description of the object[s]:
(a) Shape
(b) Size compared to a known object (use one of the following terms: Head of a pin, pea, dime, nickel, quarter, half dollar, silver dollar, baseball, grapefruit, or basketball) held in the hand at about arm's length.
(c) Color
(d) Number
(e) Formation, if more than one
(f) Any discernible features or details
(g) Tail, trail, or exhaust, including size of same compared to size of object(s)
(h) Sound. If heard, describe sound.
(i) Other pertinent or unusual features.'

The final paragraph was the one that rang alarm bells with those who were convinced that the Air Force was deliberately concealing vital facts from the public:

'9. Release of Facts. Headquarters USAF will release summaries of evaluated data which will inform the public on this subject. In response to local inquiries, it is permissible to inform news media representatives on UFOB's when the object is positively identified as a familiar object (see paragraph 2b), except that the following type of data warrants protection and should not be revealed: names of principles, intercept and investigation procedures, and classified radar data. For these objects which are not explainable, only the fact that ATIC will analyse the data is worthy of release, due to the many unknowns involved.
N.F. TWINING
Chief of Staff, United States Air Force.'

The various studies by the Air Force inevitably unearthed a wealth of fascinating information and, by its own admission, a large number of unexplained cases which provided irrefutable proof of the phenomenon and tantalizing evidence for the possibility of interplanetary craft. Nevertheless, there was also an increasing tendency, which seems to have evolved over time, for the Air Force to become more sceptical and to deliberately play down the significance of the entire UFO mystery. This has been interpreted by some as evidence of the fact that the Air Force's study of the phenomenon has always been dictated by a higher interest – one which had been conceived to protect the public from the truth and deliberately to understate the significance of any sighting.

As we have seen, there is evidence of this tendency, certainly in terms of national security considerations and the concern over false alarms and public hysteria, but there is a theory that the public dissemination of information was guided by an additional hidden agenda which was utilized to conceal the truth, or at least protect the extent of secret government knowledge about UFOs. This policy of secrecy has given rise to the myriad of conspiracy theories which have coalesced to create a fog of confusion surrounding Roswell and many other celebrated UFO encounters.

Where legitimate desire for official secrecy, caution and dis-information begins and where the 'cosmic cover-up' ends is impossible to delineate. Certainly, if there is no more to the UFO phenomenon than the most sceptical of sceptics have consistently claimed, then responsibility for perpetuating the belief that the public have been kept in the dark and fuelling suspicion, paranoia and delusions of government conspiracies can to a large extent be laid at the door of various government agencies, including the Air Force, for being less than frank with the public on a number of occasions in the past. Indeed, there are solid grounds upon which such paranoia and mistrust can be founded because, curiously, it was not solely the suspicions of cranky, obsessive citizens' groups, weaned on a diet of science fiction, that pioneered the mistrust in which the USAF and other government agencies came to be held in the 1960s and beyond. Some of those most vociferous in their suspicion and scepticism towards the official line were former high-ranking government officials and scientists whom one would have expected to have held precisely the opposite point of view.

One of the most famous converts was Allen J. Hynek, the former official astronomer to the USAF, who had been involved in the study of UFO reports for the Air Force since the early days of Project Sign. Hynek went on to found one of the most respected of today's many UFO study organizations, the Centre for UFO Studies (CUFOS), which is based in Chicago. Displaying a courageously unorthodox approach, Hynek, who was highly regarded as an astronomer, lamented the fact that he found it virtually impossible to launch a serious discussion of the UFO phenomenon with his fellow scientists, whether fellow astronomers or experts from another field.

In one outspoken public statement, he complained: 'There were personnel in high places who really wondered and appeared troubled by what was going on, but they couldn't admit it. Not publicly!

'The procedure was just about always the same – they [the serious investigators] were usually transferred to another line of work . . . I saw this happen time after time . . . Orders were passed down from the top office in the Pentagon – the Secretary of the Air Force. On several occasions, I was called in to see Secretary Harold Brown. Never once was I asked my opinion as an astronomer. I was always told, "That was a balloon," or "That was a flock of geese!" It was clear that Project Blue Book was a finger exercise.'

Hynek's lack of faith seemed to be vindicated by the decision of the Air Force to transfer the responsibility for Project Blue Book to the University of Colorado in 1966 under the auspices of a committee headed by Dr Edward Condon. This led to the publication in 1969 of the report 'Scientific Study of Unidentified Flying Objects'.

Condon was a distinguished scientist who had worked on the development of the atomic bomb and radar and had been part of an official study into the status of the Atomic Energy Commission in the 1950s. In 1958 he had accused the American government of deliberately underestimating the effects of nuclear fallout, incurring the wrath of Richard Nixon and the House Un-American Activities Committee but establishing Condon's credentials as an outspoken scientist who would not be cowed by the official version of the truth. Condon also possessed a noted sense of humour and found hugely amusing the accounts of preposterous interstellar journeys peddled by the likes of George Adamski. But he was a confirmed sceptic, perhaps too confirmed to have headed an open scientific enquiry. This was certainly the view of the prestigious civilian study group, the National Institute and Committee on Aerial Phenomena (NICAP), whose members included several high-ranking former intelligence officers and military and Air Force personnel. Under the guidance of Donald Keyhoe, the famous author of some of the first UFO books to present the notion of a government cover-up and the 'extraterrestrial hypothesis', NICAP attempted to channel information and case studies to the Condon committee, some of whose members were openly sympathetic to NICAP's hypothesis. Condon, however, made no secret of his disdain for such scientifically unproven theories and Keyhoe decided to withdraw cooperation from the project. The study was then beset by internal dissent and was fatally compromised by the discovery of a leaked memo from the assistant dean of the University of Colorado, Robert Low, who had unwisely written: 'In order to undertake such a project one has to approach it objectively. That is, one has to admit the possibility that such things as UFOs exist. It is not respectable to give serious consideration to such a possibility. Believers, in other words, remain outcasts. The simple act of admitting these possibilities just as possibilities puts us beyond the pale, and we would lose more in prestige in the scientific community than we could possibly gain . . .'

Set against the terms of reference for the original study, which was a formal contract with the USAF for an impartial study of the subject 'conducted under conditions of strictest objectivity by investigators, who as far as can be determined have no predilections or preconceived positions on the UFO question', Low's admission and fear of ridicule fatally compromised external confidence in the Condon Report. UFO researchers have long maintained that it was at best a biased study and at worst a 'disinformation' exercise controlled by the CIA, and it has to be said that this is a criticism which has some justification. Condon dismissed two members of the committee who were favourably disposed to the reality of UFOs and the possibility of the extraterrestrial hypothesis – ostensibly for leaking the memo which Low had authored. And in his final report Condon concluded with an air of finality which in itself has invited scepticism: 'Our general conclusion is that nothing has come from the study of UFOs in the past 21 years that has added to scientific knowledge. Careful consideration of the record as it is available to us leads us to conclude that further extensive study of UFOs probably cannot be justified in the expectation that science will be advanced thereby.'

In common with all its predecessors, the Condon Report provided no solutions other than to dismiss the UFO phenomenon as unworthy of further consideration. Such a sweeping dismissal did little to inspire faith that unbiased minds were at work; indeed, it inevitably handed the gauntlet for future research to some of the even less scientifically minded UFO research groups. The more respectable of these have, in fact, developed some impressive case studies and introduced a professional rigour to both their 'field studies' and their analysis of individual sightings which would put the Condon Committee and some of its predecessors to shame. Their eyewitness sightings often include assessments of those who are actually reporting them. However, they are confronted with the same dilemma that was observed by both the Robertson Panel and the Condon Committee: namely, that there is no direct scientific evidence upon which to base any scientific conclusions.

It is true that until some physical artefact or incontrovertible proof emerges, the UFO phenomenon will remain at best an intriguing mystery and at worst an irrelevant distraction.

16

Where UFOs are concerned, the absence of evidence is not necessarily the evidence of absence! The conundrum is, how do you prove something does not exist when there is no proof of its existence in the first place? Similar doubts afflict the sceptic when confronted by all mysteries which attract widespread belief in the face of a rational tendency to dismiss the phenomenon, from faith healing and ghosts, to many religions and, of course, flying saucers. Where there is evidence of doubt there is doubt about the evidence. This leaves neither side capable of proving its case to the other while at the same time it entrenches each side deeper in the conviction that it is right. When believers are faced by non-believers, each side, reacting to the other's opposition, reaffirms and deepens its own prejudice. Characteristically, this prejudice masquerades as a certainty derived from 'evidence' which is usually flimsy and based on nothing more substantial than a collective account of similar experiences. Such experiences possess sufficient individual variation to provide the illusion of a unique experience nevertheless shared by a variety of people in their own way, as distinct from the sort of common delusion to which like-minded people frequently fall prey.

Out of this collective experience of individual sightings, abductions and genuine observations of lights in the sky has grown an entire phenomenon of the modern psyche. From this thoughtful material it is all too easy to create mythical characters such as the cameraman who filmed the alien autopsy but whose existence can never be proven and a group of secret scientists and government officials who are privy to the deepest secrets of alien life.

Perhaps the only certainty about flying saucers and the Roswell mystery is that neither will go away. The whole subject has now become one of mainstream fascination, permeating the public consciousness in popular television drama and high-budget feature films. Part of the reason for this massive growth is the renewed scientific speculation about the possibility of life on other planets. With the discovery of the meteor from Mars which may contain evidence of life beyond earth, the notion of the extraterrestrials has been given a new lease of life. While the sceptics dismiss the finding as a publicity stunt by NASA and a crude attempt to garner a greater budget from the federal government, there is a rapidly growing army of UFO believers and American citizens who are convinced by their own personal experience of abduction that not only are the 'saucers' real but also their inhabitants. This other-worldly race, commonly described as being small in stature with large black almond-shaped eyes, oversized heads and spindly limbs, are commonly known as 'The Greys', because of their greyish colour, although accounts vary as to whether this grey appearance is due to a close-fitting overall uniform or their natural skin colour.

Fascinating though the abduction phenomenon is, there is, in fact, even less evidence for its reality than there is for the existence of UFOs. However, because claims of alien abduction are so widespread, it has become another factor in fuelling a public fascination with both UFOs and the arguments about the possibility of life on other planets. It is worth considering whether some of the current arguments could in theory support an extraterrestrial explanation for the Roswell Incident.

Scientists have inevitably looked into the distant past of our planet to try to determine what might lie in the future in relation to any contact with extraterrestrials. The critical argument is that, however improbable, the various forces of nature have combined to create the building blocks of life on earth which, over the millions of years of our early history, have led to the creation of *homo sapiens*.

In the certain knowledge that there are an infinite number of planets and stars, some scientists suggest that there must be other civilizations in some far-flung corner of the galaxy – or perhaps much closer. There is a counter argument which simply states that the evolution of life on this planet came about through a convergence of circumstances of such infinitesimal probability that the chances of the same process being replicated anywhere else are so unimaginably minute as to be impossible. This theory, which is still very much favoured by neo-Darwinists such as Richard Dawkins, was partially undermined by a successful experiment conducted in 1953 by Stanley Miller and Harold Urey at the University of Chicago. They were attempting to simulate the conditions that might have existed on earth four billion years ago. The 'primordial soup' was reconstructed by pouring methane, water and ammonia into a glass vessel and then passing an electric current through it for several days. The 'soup' changed colour, becoming reddish brown, and after analysis the liquid was found to contain amino acids – the organic molecules common to all living organisms.

The problem remained that even if there were alternative life forms elsewhere in the universe we have no means to reach them. While it is recognized that other, more advanced civilizations may have solved the problem of interstellar travel, such a breakthrough appears to be way beyond our current levels of scientific knowledge. Scientists have considered the difficulties of such travel and how these might be solved. According to NASA: 'Chemically powered rockets fall orders of magnitude short of being able to provide practical interstellar space flight . . . One could . . . use Jupiter in a swingby gravity assist manoeuvre to escape the solar system . . . Since however the nearest star, Alpha Centauri, is four light years away, the rendezvous, if all went well, would take place in 40,000 years. Clearly we must have at least a thousandfold increase in speed to consider such a trip and this means some radically new form of propulsion.'

It is estimated that even with a nuclear-powered spaceship the round trip to the nearest star would still take eighty years. The journey would be fraught with problems. The NASA publication quoted above says: 'Let us ignore all limitations of present day technology and consider the performance of the best rocket that can be built according to known physical law. This is the photon rocket, which annihilates matter and anti-matter converting the energy into pure retro-directed radiation. . . . It is hard to imagine a vehicle weighing much less than 1000 tons that would provide the drive, control, power, communications and life support systems adequate for a crew of 12 for a decade.'

Apart from the immense technical difficulties inherent in each of the various types of space craft that the NASA experts consider, there is also the problem that, to discover life in other parts of the universe, we might have to make many thousands of fantastically expensive sorties into space. 'A sober appraisal of all the methods so far proposed forces one to the conclusion that manned interstellar flight is out of the question not only for the present but for an indefinitely long time in the future. It is not a physical impossibility but it is an economic impossibility at the present time. Some unforeseeable breakthroughs must occur before man can physically travel to the stars.'

It was for this reason that the Search for Extra Terrestrial Intelligence, SETI, adopted the idea of attempting to scan the universe for radio signals that would allow us to make contact with other life forms. The above quotations about the feasibility of interstellar travel were published in a NASA booklet examining the feasibility of SETI. A pioneer of the SETI programme is Frank Drake, who designed the famous equation named after him, which uses a mathematical formula to calculate the number of technological civilizations that might exist in our galaxy.

In the late 1970s a NASA workshop set out the logic for SETI: 'It is certainly out of the question, at our present level of technology or, indeed, at any level we can foresee, to mount an interstellar search by spaceship. On the other hand, we believe it is feasible to begin a search for signals radiated by other civilizations having technologies at least as advanced as ours. We can expect, with considerable confidence, that such signals will consist of electromagnetic waves; no other known particle approaches the photon in ease of generation, direction and detection. None flies faster, none has less energy and is therefore cheaper than the radio frequency photon. It has long been argued that signals of extraterrestrial origin will be most apt to be detected in the so-called microwave window: wavelengths from about 0.5 to 30cm. Natural noise sources rise to great height on either side of this window, making it the quietest part of the spectrum for everyone on the Galaxy . . . Existing radio telescopes are capable of receiving signals from our interstellar neighbours, if of high power or if beamed at us by similar telescopes used as transmitters. The large antenna at Arecibo could detect its counterpart thousands of light years away. Indeed, it could detect transmissions from nearby stars less powerful but similar to our own television and radars.

'Terrestrial UHF and microwave emulations now fill a sphere some twenty light years in radius. The unintended announcement of our technological prowess is growing stronger each year and is expanding into space at the speed of light. The same phenomenon may well denote the presence of any technological society. In fact our own radar leakage may have already been detected by a nearby civilization. In addition, advanced societies may radiate beacons for a variety of reasons, possibly merely to bring emerging societies into contact with a long established intelligent community of advanced societies throughout the galaxy. A search begun today could detect signals of either type.

'We propose a search for signals in the microwave part of the radio spectrum, but not at this time the sending of signals. Even though we expect our society to continue to radiate TV and radar signals we do not propose to increase our detectability by, say, intentionally beaming signals at likely stars. There is an immediate payoff if we receive a signal; transmission requires that we wait out the round trip light time before we can hope for any results. Transmission should be considered only in response to a received signal or after a prolonged listening program has failed to detect any signals.'

(In fact a message was beamed at star cluster M13, in the constellation of Hercules some 25,000 light years away, by the Arecibo radio telescope on November 16, 1974. The signal transmitted at 2.380GHz delivered an effective power of three trillion watts, the strongest man-made signal ever transmitted.)

'Not only is the technology for detecting ETI already at hand, but every passing year will see the radio frequency interference (RFI) problem grow worse while only modest improvements in technology can occur. Perfect receivers would not double the sensitivity of search system over that which we can already achieve. Given optimum data processing, large increases in sensitivity are to be had only by increasing collecting area. It is true that data processing technology is improving rapidly, but presently achievable data processing technology is adequate and inexpensive. Further the techniques need to be developed in association with existing facilities and comprehensive searches made before it becomes evident that a more sensitive system is needed. Great discoveries are often the result more of courage and determination than the ultimate in equipment.'

Although the SETI programme has been fraught with budget and finance problems it is still underway, receiving private donations from, among others, Steven Spielberg, and although some signals which have been detected were originally thought to be promising, nothing definitive has so far emerged.

The programme also raises the question as to where 'flying saucers' might fit in if they are found to exist as the mode of travel of a more advanced civilization. As far as we know, no radio signals have been detected emanating from any UFOs and yet, if they exist, they must have some form of communication system. Is it conceivable that they communicate by some means which we are unable to detect? Even if UFOs are some form of intelligent machine, manned by robots or a species designed for interstellar flight, they would still need some form of communication with whoever sent them, otherwise there would be no point to their existence!

If SETI is successful, it may not solve the UFO phenomenon but it would certainly help. One of the first questions that could be asked of our new extraterrestrial neighbours could be: 'Did they come down to visit earth in the summer of 1947 and land at Roswell, New Mexico?'

Until then it is unlikely that the Roswell mystery will ever be resolved to the satisfaction of those who continue to believe in the government cover-up. As we approach the millennium, it is perhaps no coincidence that there has been a quantum leap in the acceptance by people all over the world of the possibility of life beyond our planet. This new awareness may simply represent a fundamental shift in the old certainties of religion and social patterns, but it may also be an awakening to an imminent discovery for which, as a race, we are subconsciously preparing ourselves.

While UFOs and the Roswell Incident may not have been proved real, they have achieved sufficient reality to be considered worthy of abundant scientific and journalistic consideration. It is that shift, whereby phenomena which were previously judged to be inconceivable have now moved into the mainstream, which offers the best hope to science and the other disciplines attempting to discover definitive answers.

Office Memorandum • UNITED STATES GOVERNMENT

TO : D. M. LADD

DATE: 7/24/47

FROM : E. G. Fitch

SUBJECT: FLYING DISCS

Reference is made to my memorandum to you in the above captioned matter dated July 10, 1947, indicating that Brigadier General George F. Schulgen of the Army Air Corps Intelligence had requested that the Bureau cooperate with the Army Air Corps Intelligence in connection with the above captioned matter. The Director noted on the referenced memorandum, "I would do it but before agreeing to it we must insist upon full access to discs recovered. For instance in the La. case the Army grabbed it and would not let us have it for cursory examination."

This is to advise that Special Agent ███████ has recontacted General Schulgen and advised him in connection with the Director's notation. General Schulgen indicated to ███████████ that he desired to assure Mr. Hoover of complete cooperation in this matter and stated that he would issue instructions to the field directing that all cooperation be furnished to the FBI and that all discs recovered be made available for the examination by the FBI Agents. General Schulgen pointed out to ███████████ that he will *b7c* from time to time make the results of the studies of his scientists available to the Bureau for the assistance of the FBI Field Offices. General Schulgen indicated to ███████████ that there has been a decrease in the reported sightings of the discs which might be because of the fact that it has lost much of its publicity value. He indicated, however, that he believed it necessary to follow this matter through to determine as near as possible if discs were in fact seen and to determine their origin.

General Schulgen inquired of ███████████ the method by which the Bureau would make the information obtained from the Bureau's inquiries, known to the Air Corps, in the Field as well as at the War Department level. Mr. ███████ pointed out to General Schulgen that the best procedure appeared to be through the regular established channels. It was pointed out to General *b7e* Schulgen that the Bureau Field Offices maintain close liaison with the Intelligence Divisions of the various Armies as well as close liaison with the Intelligence Division of the War Department. General Schulgen indicated that he would be satisfied to receive information through this means. RECORDED 62-83894-36

General Schulgen indicated to ███████████ that he believed that there was a possibility that this entire matter might have been started by subversive individuals for the purpose of creating a mass hysteria. He suggested that the *b7c* Bureau keep this in mind in any interviews conducted regarding reported sightings. General Schulgen stated to ███████████ that he would make available to the Bureau all information in the possession of the Air Corps regarding the sightings which were first reported so that the Bureau could conduct some investigation regarding these individuals to ascertain their motives for reporting that they had observed flying discs. When General Schulgen makes the information available regarding these individuals, it will be promptly brought to your attention.

SEP 30 1947

COPIES DESTROYED
270 NOV 18 1964

Declassified FBI document revealing liaison between the FBI and the USAAF on the investigation of 'flying discs'.

STANDARD FORM NO. 64

Office Memorandum • UNITED STATES GOVERNMENT

TO : Director, FBI   DATE: 9-17-47

FROM : SAC, Portland

SUBJECT: REPORTS OF FLYING DISCS
SECURITY MATTER - X

Refer San Francisco letter dated September 4, 1947.

███, Portland, reported without consulting any records that on June 24, 1947, while prospecting at a point in the Cascade Mountains approximately five thousand feet from sea level, during the afternoon he noticed a reflection, looked up, and saw a disc proceeding in a southeasterly direction. Immediately upon sighting this object he placed his telescope to his eye and observed the disc for approximately forty-five to sixty seconds. He remarked that it is possible for him to pick up an object at a distance of ten miles with his telescope. At the time the disc was sighted by Mr. ████████ it was banking in the sun, and he observed five or six similar objects but only concentrated on one. He related that they did not fly in any particular formation and that he would estimate their height to be about one thousand feet from where he was standing. He said the object was about thirty feet in diameter.and appeared to have a tail. It made no noise.

According to ████████ he remained in the vicinity of the Cascades for several days and then returned to Portland and noted an article in the local paper which stated in effect that a man in Boise, Idaho, had sighted a similar object but that authorities had disclaimed any knowledge of such an object. He said he communicated with the Army for the sole purpose of attempting to add credence to the story furnished by the man in Boise.

████████ also related that on the occasion of his sighting the objects on June 24, 1947 he had in his possession a combination compass and watch. He noted particularly that immediately before he sighted the disc the compass acted very peculiar, the hand waving from one side to the other, but that this condition corrected itself immediately after the discs had passed out of sight.

Informant appeared to be a very reliable individual who advised that he had been a prospector in the states of Montana, Washington, and Oregon for the past forty years.

FJS:KAM
62-1531
2 cc: San Francisco (62-2938)

RECORDED
INDEXED

55 SEP 30 1947

Declassified FBI document providing crucial corroboration of the historic
Kenneth Arnold sighting of 24 June 1947.

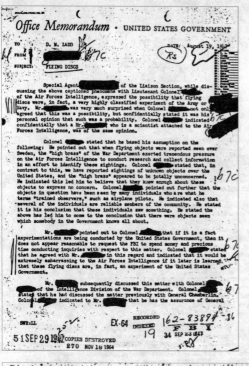

Office Memorandum · UNITED STATES GOVERNMENT

TO : D. M. LADD

FROM :

SUBJECT: FLYING DISCS

DATE: August 19, 19___

Special Agent _____ of the Liaison Section, while discussing the above captioned phenomena with Lieutenant Colonel _____ of the Air Forces Intelligence, expressed the possibility that flying discs were, in fact, a very highly classified experiment of the Army or the Navy. Mr. _____ was very much surprised when Colonel _____ not only agreed that this was a possibility, but confidentially stated it was his personal opinion that such was a probability. Colonel _____ indicated confidentially that a Mr. _____ who is a scientist attached to the Air Forces Intelligence, was of the same opinion.

Colonel _____ stated that he based his assumption on the following: He pointed out that when flying objects were reported seen over Sweden, the "high brass" of the War Department exerted tremendous pressure on the Air Forces Intelligence to conduct research and collect information in an effort to identify these sightings. Colonel _____ stated that, in contrast to this, we have reported sightings of unknown objects over the United States, and the "high brass" appeared to be totally unconcerned. He indicated this led him to believe that they knew enough about these objects to express no concern. Colonel _____ pointed out further that the objects in question have been seen by many individuals who are what he terms "trained observers," such as airplane pilots. He indicated also that several of the individuals are reliable members of the community. He stated it is his conclusion that these individuals saw something. He stated the above has led his to come to the conclusion that there were objects seen which somebody in the Government knows all about.

Mr. _____ pointed out to Colonel _____ that if it is a fact experimentations are being conducted by the United States Government, then it does not appear reasonable to request the FBI to spend money and precious time conducting inquiries with respect to this matter. Colonel _____ stated that he agreed with Mr. _____ in this regard and indicated that it would be extremely embarrassing to the Air Forces Intelligence if it later is learned that these flying discs are, in fact, an experiment of the United States Government.

Mr. _____ subsequently discussed this matter with Colonel _____ of the Intelligence Division of the War Department. Colonel _____ stated that he had discussed the matter previously with General Chamberlin. Colonel _____ indicated to Mr. _____ that he has the assurance of General

SWR:LL   EX-64

51 SEP 29 1947

RECORDED
INDEXED
19

162-83894 - 56
F B I
34 SEP 23 1947

270 NOV 18 1964   COPIES DESTROYED

Declassified FBI document which suggests that 'flying discs' could be part of a top US military programme.

MEMORANDUM FOR MR. LADD

Chamberlin and General Todd that the Army is conducting no experimentations with anything which could possibly be mistaken for a flying disc.

Colonel _____ of the Air Forces Intelligence subsequently contacted Mr. _____ and indicated that he had discussed this matter with General Schulgen of the Army Air Forces. General Schulgen had previously assured both Mr. _____ that to the best of his knowledge and information no experiments were being undertaken by the Government which could be mistaken for flying discs. Colonel _____ indicated to Mr. _____ that he had pointed out his beliefs to General Schulgen and had mentioned the possibility of an embarrassing situation arising between the Air Forces Intelligence and the FBI. General Schulgen agreed with Colonel _____ that a memorandum would be prepared for the signature of General McDonald, A2, to General LeMay, who is in charge of Research and Development in the Air Corps. Colonel _____ indicated that this memorandum will set forth the characteristics of the objects seen by various reliable individuals. The memorandum will then request General LeMay to indicate whether or not any experiments are being undertaken by the Air Forces which could possibly be connected with any of the observed phenomena. Colonel _____ stated that when a reply is received from General LeMay, a communication will be addressed to the Bureau.

Mr. _____ will follow this matter closely with Colonel _____ and General Schulgen so that the Bureau will be promptly advised of all information regarding the flying discs, especially any information indicating that they are, in fact, an experiment of some Governmental agency.

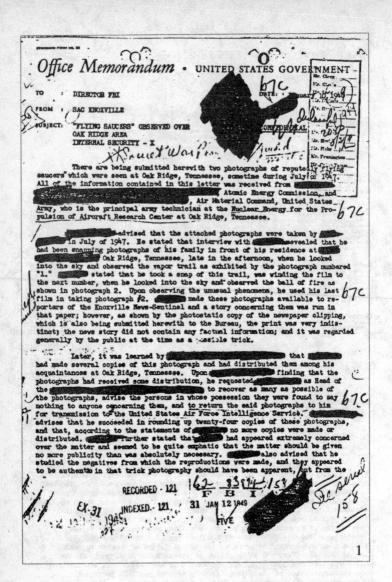

Office Memorandum • UNITED STATES GOVERNMENT

TO : DIRECTOR FBI   DATE: ~~January 31, 1949~~

FROM : SAC KNOXVILLE

SUBJECT: "FLYING SAUCERS" OBSERVED OVER
OAK RIDGE AREA
INTERNAL SECURITY - X

CONFIDENTIAL

There are being submitted herewith two photographs of reputedly flying saucers which were seen at Oak Ridge, Tennessee, sometime during July of 1947. All of the information contained in this letter was received from ████████ ████████, Atomic Energy Commission, and ████████ ████████, Air Material Command, United States Army, who is the principal army technician at the Nuclear Energy for the Propulsion of Aircraft Research Center at Oak Ridge, Tennessee.

████████ advised that the attached photographs were taken by ████████ in July of 1947. He stated that interview with ████████ revealed that he had been snapping photographs of his family in front of his residence at ████████ ████████ Oak Ridge, Tennessee, late in the afternoon, when he looked into the sky and observed the vapor trail as exhibited by the photograph numbered "1." ████████ stated that he took a snap of this trail, was winding the film to the next number, when he looked into the sky and observed the ball of fire as shown in photograph 2. Upon observing the unusual phenomena, he used his last film in taking photograph #2. ████████ made these photographs available to reporters of the Knoxville News-Sentinel and a story concerning them was run in that paper; however, as shown by the photostatic copy of the newspaper clipping, which is also being submitted herewith to the Bureau, the print was very indistinct; the news story did not contain any factual information; and it was regarded generally by the public at the time as a possible trick.

Later, it was learned by ████████████████████ that ████████ had made several copies of this photograph and had distributed them among his acquaintances at Oak Ridge, Tennessee. Upon ████████ finding that the photographs had received some distribution, he requested ████████ as Head of the ████████████████ to recover as many as possible of the photographs, advise the persons in whose possession they were found to say nothing to anyone concerning them, and to return the said photographs to him for transmission to the United States Air Force Intelligence Service. ████████ advises that he succeeded in rounding up twenty-four copies of these photographs, and that, according to the statements of ████████ no more copies were made or distributed. ████████ further stated that ████████ had appeared extremely concerned over the matter and seemed to be quite emphatic that the matter should be given no more publicity than was absolutely necessary. ████████ also advised that he studied the negatives from which the reproductions were made, and they appeared to be authentic in that trick photography should have been apparent, but from the

RECORDED - 121   62-83894-159

F B I

EX-31   INDEXED - 121   31 JAN 12 1949

FIVE

1

negatives certainly did not appear to be the case. It was ▓▓▓▓▓▓
observation that had the negative been "doped" with some sort of chemical, it
would have removed the emulsion from the face of the film in such a way that
the negative would have been thin at the point which is supposedly a ball of
fire, whereas, in fact, both the vapor trail and the corona of fire are dark 67C
on the negative, indicating that it was an actual exposure. It was the opinion
of ▓▓▓▓▓▓ that the photographs were, without doubt, authentic.

In accordance with Bureau instructions, no active investigation of
this matter was made, but it was deemed advisable to interview▓▓▓▓▓▓▓▓
prior to submitting the photographs to the Bureau.

▓▓▓▓▓▓ predicated his remarks concerning the "flying saucers"
or "mystery missiles" by stating that he knew nothing of an official nature
concerning them, other than the fact that they were believed by air force 67C
intelligence officials to be man-made missiles, rather than some natural
phenomena. It was his further belief that a great deal of information had been
compiled concerning these missiles by air force intelligence, and that research
on the matter was being extensively done at Wright Field, Dayton, Ohio. He also
expressed the opinion that information at the disposal of the United States Army
Air Force Intelligence had, in all probability, been made available to the
Bureau at Washington, D. C.

▓▓▓▓▓▓ then continued with his own ideas as to what might be
the nature of these discs, which ideas he had formulated through review of
those known facts and theoretical conjectures of himself and other scientists
concerning the nature of flying discs and methods of propulsion for such type
of aerial mechanism. According to him, flying discs have long been a theoretical
possibility and, in fact, a possibility which would indicate one of the best
means by which to break through the barriers of the supersonic area. Scientists
have, for many years, been attempting to develop this type of aircraft. Some
experimentation has been done even in the United States, but insofar as is
known in the United States at the present time, there have never been any
practical developments. As a second factor of consideration, ▓▓▓▓▓▓ 67C
stated that insofar as is known to U. S. scientists at this time, there is no
known chemical fuel which would make possible tremendous range of flight such
as is ascribed to the reported "flying saucers." There is only one possible
fuel which could be utilized which is in accord with present theory, and that
is the utilization of atomic-energy.] As further evidence of this possible means
of propulsion, ▓▓▓▓▓▓ called attention to the vapor trail and gaseous
corona described as a ball of fire, which he states might give some evidence
to the fact that a radio-active field is present. He explained that the corona,
or exhaust, has what appears to be layers of intensity which are circular rather
than elongated and have no tendency to trail at the extremities, as would be
the case if a normal type of exhaust from a combustion engine was being utilized
in the propulsion of these aircraft. He continued that the vapor trail left by
the missile appears to be one single line of uniform intensity which is extremely
slow in dissipating. It was pointed out by him that in the case of a normal

- 2 -

2

vapor trail being left by an aircraft moving at extremely high speeds or extremely high altitudes, the vapor trail usually will be from the wing tips and/or the exhaust of the engines, thus presenting several lines. But, in any event, even though only one line were visible, it would be rather quick to dissipate. This indicated to him that the vapor trail represents some atmospheric change along the path of the missile, which would not be the case were it any presently known type of aircraft.

He continued that information furnished by him should be treated with the utmost confidence, in that he was not speaking officially, but as a personal matter of cooperation. He stated that the matter was being given absolutely no dissemination by the air force or other military personnel, and that they had not deemed it advisable to advise him of all information pertaining to the missile. He continued, however, that in his conversation with representatives at Wright Field and in reading reports returned to this country by foreign agents, he had gathered together certain information which might be of assistance in determining whether or not these so-called missiles were authentic, usable and of danger to the United States. First, he pointed out that knowledge of such a possible aircraft is not by any means new, it having been known as early as four years ago that some type of flying disc was being experimented with by the Russians. In addition thereto, he stated that more recent reports have been received from representatives of the Central Intelligence Agency in Southern Europe and Southern Asia to the effect that the Russians were experimenting with some type of radical aircraft or guided missile which could be dispatched for great distances out over the sea, made to turn in flight and return to the base from which it was launched. This fact was extremely worthy of notice as experiments in this country have so far only developed to the point where we are concerned with delivering a missile to the required point of impact, and no consideration has been given to imparting to that missile the ability to return. Secondly, he stated that it is a known fact that the Russians are attempting to develop some type of nuclear energy, that they received a wealth of information concerning nuclear energy at the time of their occupation in Germany, and that they too have at their disposal the limited supply of the necessary fissionable materials. He stated that insofar as any opinion as to whether or not they have the ability and scientific knowledge to create such a nuclear-propelled missile is strictly a matter of conjecture, and that he would hesitate to make any definite statement. He pointed out, however, that the Russians have some very capable scientists in the field of atomic energy and that, in addition thereto, they took into their custody some of the most advanced and capable scientists of the German Nation.

He also stated that a peculiar fact concerning the missiles exists from reports he has received which is worthy of notice, and that is that from all appearances, they usually approach the United States from a northerly direction and have been reported as returning in a northerly direction. None have ever been known to crash, collide or disintegrate over American soil, but it would appear that they come to the United States, cruise around, and go back over the North Pole. He states that insofar as is known to him, there has never

-3-

3

been any piece of one recovered from any source whatever in order that analytical study of its nature could be made. Insofar as was known to him, the only actual material which would be of any value in determining its nature are telephoto photographs which are now in the possession of engineers at Wright Field, Dayton, Ohio. How detailed and how clear these photographs are, he was unable to state. He stated that one report has been received concerning a collision of these missiles with another type of aircraft. This report, according to him, took place a short time prior to the report of numerous discs over the United States, and the report emanated from Czechoslovakia. This report was that a Czecho-slovakian transport had collided with some unidentified missile while in mid-air over the ocean, and that said missile and said transport had been completely disintegrated without recovery of parts or survivors from either. It was the belief of ▓▓▓▓▓▓▓▓▓ that this undescribed missile was perhaps the same type of thing as the flying saucer. Another factor of notice, according to ▓▓▓▓▓▓ ▓▓▓▓ and as is portrayed by the photographs, it would appear that the missiles can be maintained at a certain altitude above the contour of the ground. This could be done by means of some type of radio altimeter or radio control. Natu- rally, the path of the missile is not in exact parallel to the contour, as its purported great speed would create considerable lag in its flight. Another factor which is worthy of note, according to ▓▓▓▓▓▓▓▓▓▓ is that it is normally reported as being seen at tremendously high altitudes and always travel- ing in a straight line. He stated that he himself observed, on one occasion, a single vapor trail coming from some type of aircraft at unbelievably high altitudes, which vapor trail extended from horizon to horizon in a perfectly straight line. He observed the vapor trail while it was in the process of formation and states that it was completely unlike any vapor trail he had ever observed before in all of his experience with the air force. It was his judgment that whatever created the vapor trail was traveling at an unbelievably tremendous speed. This, together with reports that when close to the ground, the missile travels at speeds which make possible visual observation of its actions, would reflect that there is some ability to control the speed of these missiles as well as the altitude.

b7c

▓▓▓▓▓▓▓▓▓▓▓ concluded that this matter, while still purely a matter of guesswork, is nevertheless a source of great concern to the military establish- ment of this country. Great efforts have been expended by the service to determine just what the nature of these missiles might be and, upon so determining, decide whether or not an adequate defense can be established. He also stated that it has given impetus to the research being done by the air force in their own pro- gram of nuclear energy for the propulsion of aircraft to develop guided missiles. He also advised that insofar as was known to him, there was absolutely no con- nection between these missiles and the fact that they were observed close to Oak Ridge, Tennessee. He stated that this was perhaps, and probably, a matter of coincidence and they were seen in this area merely as they were seen in forty- six of the forty-eight states of the United States during the Month of July when so many reports were being received.

b7c

This information is being submitted to the Bureau for whatever value it may be, and no further action in the matter is being contemplated by this office, unless advised to the contrary.

CCM:bk
65-11
Enclosures - 3

-4-

4

TO   DIRECTOR, FBI   DATE: January 31, 1949

FROM   SAC, SAN ANTONIO

SUBJECT: PROTECTION OF VITAL INSTALLATIONS
           BUREAU FILE # 65-58300

CONFIDENTIAL *declassified*
20.. 8/31/77

At recent Weekly Intelligence Conferences of G-2, ONI, OSI, and F.B.I., in the Fourth Army Area, Officers of G-2, Fourth Army have discussed the matter of "Unidentified Aircraft" or "Unidentified Aerial Phenomena" otherwise known as "Flying Discs", "Flying Saucers", and "Balls of Fire". This matter is considered top secret by Intelligence Officers of both the Army and the Air Forces.

It is all known that there have been during the past two years reports from the various parts of the country of the sighting of unidentified aerial objects which have been called in newspaper parlance "flying discs" and "flying saucers". The first such sightings were reported from Sweden, and it was thought that the objects, the nature of which was unknown, might have originated in Russia.

In July 1948 an unidentified aircraft was "seen" by an Eastern Airlines Pilot and Co-Pilot and one or more passengers of the Eastern Airlines Plane over Montgomery, Alabama. This aircraft was reported to be of an unconventional type without wings and resembled generally a "rocket ship" of the type depicted in comic strips. It was reported to have had windows; to have been larger than the Eastern Airlines plane, and to have been traveling at an estimated speed of 2700 miles an hour. It appeared out of a thunderhead ahead of the Eastern Airlines plane and immediately disappeared in another cloud narrowly missing a collision with the Eastern Airlines plane. No sound or air disturbance was noted in connection with this appearance.

During the past two months various sightings of unexplained phenomena have been reported in the vicinity of the A.E.C. Installation at Los Alamos, New Mexico, where these phenomena now appear to be concentrated. During December 1948 on the 5th, 6th, 7th, 8th, 11th, 13, 14th, 20th and 28th sightings of unexplained phenomena were made near Los Alamos by Special Agents of the Office of Special Investigation; Airline Pilots; Military Pilots, Los Alamos Security Inspectors, and private citizens. On January 6, 1949, another similar object was sighted in the same area.

b7c   a Meteorologist of some note, has been generally in charge of the observations near Los Alamos, attempting to learn characteristics of the unexplained phenomena.

Up to this time little concrete information has been obtained.

JEJ:md
S-100-7545
cc: El Paso (2)
    Dallas (2)
    Houston (2)
    Little Rock (2)
    Oklahoma City (2)

RECORDED -

F B I

43 MAR 16 1949

Declassified FBI report regarding the numerous incursions of 'flying discs' near Los Alamos, New Mexico.

There have been day time sightings which are tentatively considered to possibly
resemble the exhaust of some type of jet propelled object. Night-time sightings
have taken the form of lights usually described as brilliant green, similar
to a green traffic signal or green neon light. Some reports indicated that the
light began and ended with a red or orange flash. Other reports have given the
color as red, white, blue-white, and yellowish green. Trailing lights sometimes observed are said to be red. The spectrum analysis of one light indicates
that it may be a copper compound of the type known to be used in rocket
experiments and which completely disintegrates upon explosion, leaving no
debris. It is noted that no debris has ever been known to be located anywhere
resulting from the unexplained phenomena.

Recent observations have indicated that the unidentified phenomena travel at
a rate of speed estimated at a minimum of three miles per second and a maximum
of twelve miles per second, or a mean calculated speed of seven and one-half
miles a second, or 27,000 miles an hour. Their reported course indicates that
they travel on an East - West line with probability that they approach from
the Northern quadrant, which would be the last stage of the great circle route
if they originated in Russia. When observed they seem to be in level flight
at a height of six to ten miles and thus traveling on a tangent to the earth's
surface. They occasionally dip at the end of the path and on two occasions
a definite vertical change in path was indicated. These phenomena have not
been known to have been sighted, however, at any intermediate point between
Russia and Los Alamos, but only at the end of the flight toward the apparent
"target", namely, Los Alamos.

In every case but one the shape of the objects has been reported as round
in a point of light with a definite area to the light's source. One report
gives a diamond shape; another indicates that trailing lights are elongated.
The size is usually compared to one-fourth the diameter of the full moon, and
they have also been compared in size to a basketball with trailing lights the
size of a baseball.

On no occasion has sound been associated directly with the phenomena, but
unexplained-sounds have been reported from Los Alamos. On two occasions
reports have been received of the sighting of multiple units.

Some nine scientific reasons are stated to exist which indicated that the
phenomena observed are not due to meteorites. The only conclusions reached
thus far are that they are either hitherto unobserved natural phenomena or
that they are man made. No scientific experiments are known to exist in this
country which could give rise to such phenomena.

████████████████████████████ are the subject of a letter from the Atlanta office
to the Bureau dated August 10, 1948, entitled, ████████████████████ b7C
INFORMATION CONCERNING."

She has written many letters to Military Authorities concerning her theories
regarding Atomic Energy. She has generally been considered unreliable and
possibly mentally unbalanced. She, however, has submitted to Military
authorities the only theory thus far known that has any credibility at all,
namely, that the lights are manifestations of cosmic rays which are directed
toward a specific point. She further theorizes that such rays may interfere
with the ignition of motors and may account for various unexplained air crashes.

The above is submitted for the confidential information of the Bureau and
offices to which copies of this letter are directed so that these offices may
evaluate any such reports they may have received or may receive in the future.

It is noted that the Fourth Army has the responsibility of protecting vital
installations at Los Alamos, New Mexico, Sandia Base, New Mexico, and Camp
Hood, Texas. Any information developed should be expeditiously transmitted to
G-2, Fourth Army.

It is further noted that G-2 and O.S.I. are actively engaged in investigating
this matter. No investigation is being conducted by this office.

Office Memorandum • UNITED STATES GOVERNMENT

TO : Mr. Ladd   DATE: March 14, 1949

FROM : Mr. Fletcher

SUBJECT: FLYING DISCS

PURPOSE

The approval of the Executives Conference is requested for the attached SAC letter furnishing to the field the type of information desired by the Intelligence Division of the Air Force in connection with the captioned matter.

BACKGROUND

You will recall that by Bureau Bulletin #57, Series 1947, dated October 1, 1947, the field was advised that effective as of that date the Bureau had discontinued its investigative activities in connection with flying discs. The field was advised that all future reports concerning this matter received in the field should be referred to the Air Forces.

Colonel ████████████████████ Air Materiel Command, Nuclear Energy for the Propulsion of Aircraft Research, Oak Ridge, Tennessee, has recently and confidentially advised the Bureau that flying discs are believed by the Air Force to be man-made missiles rather than some natural phenomenon and that as much as four years ago it was learned that some type of flying discs were being experimented upon by the Russians. It was further determined from ████████████████ that most all of the flying discs seen by persons in the United States approached this country from a northerly direction and returned in the same direction, indicating the strong possibility that they are coming from Russia.

The Department of the Air Force has furnished to the Bureau a sufficient number of copies of a memorandum dated February 15, 1949 captioned "Unconventional Aircraft" which can be furnished to our field offices.

STATUS   RECORDED - 76

At the present time this Bureau is conducting no investigation of information received in the field relating to the captioned matter.

RECOMMENDATION

It is recommended that the attached SAC letter and enclosure be forwarded to the field to advise them of the type of questions to be asked of persons who voluntarily submit information relative to "flying discs." Although no active investigation will be conducted by the Bureau, it is believed that the captioned matter is of sufficient importance to the internal security of the country that our field offices should secure as much information as possible from complainants in order to assist the Department of the Air Force.

EHM:EMW
Attachment

FBI document which considers the possibility of UFOs being man-made.

Office Memorandum • UNITED STATES GOVERNMENT

TO : D. M. Ladd   DATE: August 23, 1950

FROM : A. H. Belmont

SUBJECT: SUMMARY OF AERIAL
PHENOMENA IN NEW MEXICO
MISCELLANEOUS - INFORMATION CONCERNING

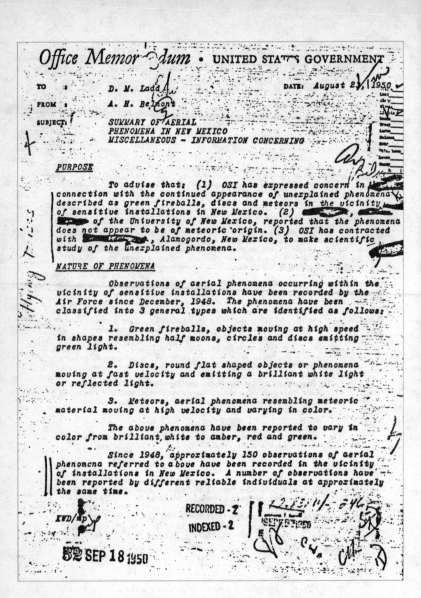

PURPOSE

To advise that: (1) OSI has expressed concern in connection with the continued appearance of unexplained phenomena described as green fireballs, discs and meteors in the vicinity of sensitive installations in New Mexico. (2) ━━━━━, ━━━━━ ━━━ of the University of New Mexico, reported that the phenomena does not appear to be of meteoric origin. (3) OSI has contracted with ━━━ ━━━━━━, Alamogordo, New Mexico, to make scientific study of the unexplained phenomena.

NATURE OF PHENOMENA

Observations of aerial phenomena occurring within the vicinity of sensitive installations have been recorded by the Air Force since December, 1948. The phenomena have been classified into 3 general types which are identified as follows:

1. Green fireballs, objects moving at high speed in shapes resembling half moons, circles and discs emitting green light.

2. Discs, round flat shaped objects or phenomena moving at fast velocity and emitting a brilliant white light or reflected light.

3. Meteors, aerial phenomena resembling meteoric material moving at high velocity and varying in color.

The above phenomena have been reported to vary in color from brilliant white to amber, red and green.

Since 1948, approximately 150 observations of aerial phenomena referred to above have been recorded in the vicinity of installations in New Mexico. A number of observations have been reported by different reliable individuals at approximately the same time.

KWD/mp

RECORDED - 2

INDEXED - 2

52 SEP 18 1950

FBI report revealing the alarm of the CIA's Office of Scientific Intelligence concerning UFO incursions over sensitive military installations.

University of New Mexico, submitted an analysis of the various
observations on May 23, 1950. He concluded, as a result of
his investigation, that approximately half of the phenomena
recorded were of meteoric origin. The other phenomena
commonly referred to as green fireballs or discs he believed
to be U.S. guided missiles being tested in the neighborhood
of the installations. ███████ pointed out that if he were
wrong in interpreting the phenomena as originating with U.S.
guided missiles that a systematic investigation of the observations should be made immediately. ███████ pointed out that
missiles moving with the velocities of the order of those
found for the green fireballs and discs could travel from the
Ural region of the USSR to New Mexico in less than 15 minutes.
He suggested that the observations might be of guided missiles
launched from bases in the Urals.

On the basis of the investigations made by ███████
and the Air Force, it was concluded that the occurrence of the
unexplained phenomena in the vicinity of sensitive installations
was a cause for concern. The Air Force entered into a contract
with ███████████████, Alamogordo, New Mexico, for the
purpose of making scientific studies of the green fireballs and
discs. It was pointed out in the summary furnished by OSI on
July 19, 1950, that the unexplained green fireballs and discs
are still observed in the vicinity of sensitive military and
Government installations.

RESULTS OF AIR FORCE INVESTIGATION

The Air Force together with ███████████████
have established a number of observation posts in the vicinity
of Vaughn, New Mexico, for the purpose of photographing and
determining the speed, height and nature of the unusual
phenomena referred to as green fireballs and discs. On May 24,
1950, personnel of ███████████████ sighted 8 to 10
objects of aerial phenomena. A 24-hour day watch is being
maintained and has been designated Project Twinkle.

CONCLUSIONS

The Albuquerque Office, in a letter dated August 10,
1950, advised that there have been no new developments in connection
with the efforts to ascertain the identity of the strange aerial
phenomena referred to as green fireballs and discs. The Albuquerque
Office advised that Dr. ███████████████ Project Engineer,
had been informed of the Bureau's jurisdiction relative to espionage
and sabotage and arrangements have been made so that the Bureau
will be promptly advised in the event additional information relative
to this project indicates any jurisdiction on the part of the
Bureau.

ACTION

None. The above is for your information.

COPY <u>ONE</u> OF <u>ONE</u>.

SUBJECT: OPERATION MAJESTIC-12 PRELIMINARY BRIEFING FOR
    PRESIDENT-ELECT EISENHOWER.

DOCUMENT PREPARED 18 NOVEMBER, 1952.

BRIEFING OFFICER: ADM. ROSCOE H. HILLENKOETTER (MJ-1)

NOTE: This document has been prepared as a preliminary briefing
only. It should be regarded as introductory to a full operations
briefing intended to follow.

* * * * * *

OPERATION MAJESTIC-12 is a TOP SECRET Research and Development/
Intelligence operation responsible directly and only to the
President of the United States. Operations of the project are
carried out under control of the Majestic-12 (Majic-12) Group
which was established by special classified executive order of
President Truman on 24 September, 1947, upon recommendation by
Dr. Vannevar Bush and Secretary James Forrestal. (See Attachment
"A".) Members of the Majestic-12 Group were designated as follows:

            Adm. Roscoe H. Hillenkoetter
            Dr. Vannevar Bush
            Secy. James V. Forrestal*
            Gen. Nathan F. Twining
            Gen. Hoyt S. Vandenberg
            Dr. Detlev Bronk
            Dr. Jerome Hunsaker
            Mr. Sidney W. Souers
            Mr. Gordon Gray
            Dr. Donald Menzel
            Gen. Robert M. Montague
            Dr. Lloyd V. Berkner

The death of Secretary Forrestal on 22 May, 1949, created
a vacancy which remained unfilled until 01 August, 1950, upon
which date Gen. Walter B. Smith was designated as permanent
replacement.

FBI document which considers the possibility of UFOs being
man-made.

On 24 June, 1947, a civilian pilot flying over the Cascade
Mountains in the State of Washington observed nine flying
disc-shaped aircraft traveling in formation at a high rate
of speed. Although this was not the first known sighting
of such objects, it was the first to gain widespread attention
in the public media. Hundreds of reports of sightings of
similar objects followed. Many of these came from highly
credible military and civilian sources. These reports resulted in independent efforts by several different elements
of the military to ascertain the nature and purpose of these
objects in the interests of national defense. A number of
witnesses were interviewed and there were several unsuccessful
attempts to utilise aircraft in efforts to pursue reported
discs in flight. Public reaction bordered on near hysteria
at times.

In spite of these efforts, little of substance was learned
about the objects until a local rancher reported that one
had crashed in a remote region of New Mexico located approximately seventy-five miles northwest of Roswell Army Air
Base (now Walker Field).

On 07 July, 1947, a secret operation was begun to assure
recovery of the wreckage of this object for scientific study.
During the course of this operation, aerial reconnaissance
discovered that four small human-like beings had apparently
ejected from the craft at some point before it exploded.
These had fallen to earth about two miles east of the wreckage
site. All four were dead and badly decomposed due to action
by predators and exposure to the elements during the approximately one week time period which had elapsed before their
discovery. A special scientific team took charge of removing
these bodies for study. (See Attachment "C".) The wreckage
of the craft was also removed to several different locations.
(See Attachment "B".) Civilian and military witnesses in
the area were debriefed, and news reporters were given the
effective cover story that the object had been a misguided
weather research balloon.

A covert analytical effort organized by Gen. Twining and
Dr. Bush acting on the direct orders of the President, resulted in a preliminary concensus (19 September, 1947) that
the disc was most likely a short range reconnaissance craft.
This conclusion was based for the most part on the craft's
size and the apparent lack of any identifiable provisioning.
(See Attachment "D".) A similar analysis of the four dead
occupants was arranged by Dr. Bronk. It was the tentative
conclusion of this group (30 November, 1947) that although
these creatures are human-like in appearance, the biological
and evolutionary processes responsible for their development
has apparently been quite different from those observed or
postulated in homo-sapiens. Dr. Bronk's team has suggested
the term "Extra-terrestrial Biological Entities", or "EBEs",
be adopted as the standard term of reference for these
creatures until such time as a more definitive designation
can be agreed upon.

Since it is virtually certain that these craft do not originate in any country on earth, considerable speculation has
centered around what their point of origin might be and how
they get here. Mars was and remains a possibility, although
some scientists, most notably Dr. Menzel, consider it more
likely that we are dealing with beings from another solar
system entirely.

Numerous examples of what appear to be a form of writing
were found in the wreckage. Efforts to decipher these have
remained largely unsuccessful. (See Attachment "E".)
Equally unsuccessful have been efforts to determine the
method of propulsion or the nature or method of transmission
of the power source involved. Research along these lines
has been complicated by the complete absence of identifiable
wings, propellers, jets, or other conventional methods of
propulsion and guidance, as well as a total lack of metallic
wiring, vacuum tubes, or similar recognizable electronic
components. (See Attachment "F".) It is assumed that the
propulsion unit was completely destroyed by the explosion
which caused the crash.

A need for as much additional information as possible about
these craft, their performance characteristics and their
purpose led to the undertaking known as U.S. Air Force Project
SIGN in December, 1947. In order to preserve security, liason
between SIGN and Majestic-12 was limited to two individuals
within the Intelligence Division of Air Materiel Command whose
role was to pass along certain types of information through
channels. SIGN evolved into Project GRUDGE in December, 1948.
The operation is currently being conducted under the code name
BLUE BOOK, with liason maintained through the Air Force officer
who is head of the project.

On 06 December, 1950, a second object, probably of similar
origin, impacted the earth at high speed in the El Indio -
Guerrero area of the Texas - Mexican boder after following
a long trajectory through the atmosphere. By the time a
search team arrived, what remained of the object had been almost
totally incinerated. Such material as could be recovered was
transported to the A.E.C. facility at Sandia, New Mexico, for
study.

Implications for the National Security are of continuing importance in that the motives and ultimate intentions of these
visitors remain completely unknown. In addition, a significant
upsurge in the surveillance activity of these craft beginning
in May and continuing through the autumn of this year has caused
considerable concern that new developments may be imminent.
It is for these reasons, as well as the obvious international
and technological considerations and the ultimate need to
avoid a public panic at all costs, that the Majestic-12 Group
remains of the unanimous opinion that imposition of the
strictest security precautions should continue without interruption into the new administration. At the same time, contingency plan MJ-1949-04P/78 (Top Secret - Eyes Only) should
be held in continued readiness should the need to make a
public announcement present itself. (See Attachment "G".)

COPY ONE OF ONE.

        ENUMERATION OF ATTACHMENTS:

    •ATTACHMENT "A".........Special Classified Executive
                            Order #092447. (TS/EO)

    •ATTACHMENT "B".........Operation Majestic-12 Status
                            Report #1, Part A. 30 NOV '47.
                            (TS-MAJIC/EO)

    •ATTACHMENT "C".........Operation Majestic-12 Status
                            Report #1, Part B. 30 NOV '47.
                            (TS-MAJIC/EO)

    •ATTACHMENT "D".........Operation Majestic-12 Preliminary
                            Analytical Report. 19 SEP '47.
                            (TS-MAJIC/EO)

    •ATTACHMENT "E".........Operation Majestic-12 Blue Team
                            Report #5. 30 JUN '52.
                            (TS-MAJIC/EO)

    •ATTACHMENT "F".........Operation Majestic-12 Status
                            Report #2. 31 JAN '48.
                            (TS-MAJIC/EO)

    •ATTACHMENT "G".........Operation Majestic-12 Contingency
                            Plan MJ-1949-04P/78: 31 JAN '49.
                            (TS-MAJIC/EO)

    •ATTACHMENT "H".........Operation Majestic-12, Maps and
                            Photographs Folio (Extractions).
                            (TS-MAJIC/EO)

TOP SECRET / MAJIC

September 24, 1947.

MEMORANDUM FOR THE SECRETARY OF DEFENSE

Dear Secretary Forrestal:

As per our recent conversation on this matter, you are hereby authorized to proceed with all due speed and caution upon your undertaking. Hereafter this matter shall be referred to only as Operation Majestic Twelve.

It continues to be my feeling that any future considerations relative to the ultimate disposition of this matter should rest solely with the Office of the President following appropriate discussions with yourself, Dr. Bush and the Director of Central Intelligence.

[signature: Harry Truman]

6

July 14, 1954

MEMORANDUM FOR GENERAL TWINING

SUBJECT: NSC/MJ-12 Special Studies Project

The President has decided that the MJ-12 SSP briefing should take place <u>during</u> the already scheduled White House meeting of July 16, rather than following it as previously intended. More precise arrangements will be explained to you upon arrival. Please alter your plans accordingly.

Your concurrence in the above change of arrangements is assumed.

ROBERT CUTLER
Special Assistant
to the President

7

THE PRESIDENT'S APPOINTMENTS
FRIDAY, JULY 16, 1954.

8.50 — The President will receive the Governor of
the Farm Credit Administration and the
Members of the Federal Farm Credit Board

9.00 — Cabinet Meeting

11.00 — The President will sign S. 3291, An Act
"Authorizing the President to present
a gold medal to Irving Berlin"

12.15 — The President will receive a group of
Congressmen, who wish to pay their respects and pledge their continuing support
of the President's program.

1.00 — (LUNCH)

8

REPORT OF AIR FORCE RESEARCH REGARDING
THE "ROSWELL INCIDENT"

EXECUTIVE SUMMARY

The "Roswell Incident" refers to an event that supposedly happened in July, 1947, wherein the Army Air Forces (AAF) allegedly recovered remains of a crashed "flying disc" near Roswell, New Mexico. In February, 1994, the General Accounting Office (GAO), acting on the request of a New Mexico Congressman, initiated an audit to attempt to locate records of such an incident and to determine if records regarding it were properly handled. Although the GAO effort was to look at a number of government agencies, the apparent focus was on the Air Force. SAF/AAZ , as the Central Point of Contact for the GAO in this matter, initiated a systematic search of current Air Force offices as well as numerous archives and records centers that might help explain this matter. Research revealed that the "Roswell Incident" was not even considered a UFO event until the 1978-1980 time frame. Prior to that, the incident was dismissed because the AAF originally identified the debris recovered as being that of a weather balloon. Subsequently, various authors wrote a number of books claiming that, not only was debris from an alien spacecraft recovered, but also the bodies of the craft's alien occupants. These claims continue to evolve today and the Air Force is now routinely accused of engaging in a "cover-up" of this supposed event.

The research located no records at existing Air Force offices that indicated any "cover-up" by the USAF or any indication of such a recovery. Consequently, efforts were intensified by Air Force researchers at numerous locations where records for the period in question were stored. The records reviewed did not reveal any increase in operations, security, or any other activity in July, 1947, that indicated any such unusual event may have occurred. Records were located and thoroughly explored concerning a then-TOP SECRET balloon project, designed to attempt to monitor Soviet nuclear tests, known as Project Mogul. Additionally, several surviving project personnel were located and interviewed, as was the only surviving person who recovered debris from the original Roswell site in 1947, and the former officer who initially identified the wreckage as a balloon. Comparison of all information developed or obtained indicated that the material recovered near Roswell was consistent with a balloon device and most likely from one of the Mogul balloons that had not been previously recovered. Air Force research efforts did not disclose any records of the recovery of any "alien" bodies or extraterrestrial materials.

INTRODUCTION

Air Force involvement in the alleged UFO-related incident popularly known as the "Roswell Incident" began as the result of a January 14, 1994, Washington Post article (Atch 1) which announced Congressman Steven Schiff's intent to initiate a General Accounting Office (GAO) effort to resolve this controversial matter. Having previously been involved in numerous Freedom of Information Act (FOIA) and Congressional

1

The USAF report concluding that the incident at Roswell was in fact the result of the top secret Project Mogul; that the likely source of the wreckage recovered was one of the balloon trains.

requests on "unusual aircraft," to include Unidentified Flying Objects (UFOs), The Director, Security and Special Program Oversight, Office of the Secretary of the Air Force, (SAF/AAZ) believed the Air Force would become involved in any GAO effort involving this subject.

Thus, in late January, 1994, SAF/AAZ directed its research/declassification team, SAF/AAZD, to attempt to locate any official records relative to this matter. These initial research efforts focused on records at the Air Force Historical Research Agency (AFHRA), Maxwell AFB, AL, the Air Force Safety Agency (AFSA) at Kirtland AFB, NM and the National Archives and Records Administration (NARA).

On February 15, 1994, the GAO officially notified Secretary of Defense William J. Perry that, it was initiating an audit of the Department of Defense (DoD) policies and procedures for acquiring, classifying, retaining, and disposing of official government documents dealing with weather balloon, aircraft, and similar crash incidents (Atch 2). This notification was subsequently passed to the Department of Defense Inspector General who in turn officially notified the Secretaries of the Services and other affected parties of the audit in a February 23, 1994, memo (Atch 3). This memorandum indicated that the "GAO is anxious to respond to Representative Schiff's request and to dispel any concerns that the DoD is being unresponsive." These were the first official US Government documents that indicated that the purpose of the GAO was to review "crash incidents involving weather balloons and unknown aircraft, such as UFOs and foreign aircraft, and (2) the facts involving the reported crash of an UFO in 1949 (sic, 1947) at Roswell, New Mexico ... (and an) alleged DoD cover-up."

An entrance meeting of potentially concerned parties was held in the offices of the DoD Inspector General on February 28, 1994. During this meeting it was learned that, while the audit officially would be reviewing the records of a number of DoD (and possibly other Executive Branch entities), the bulk of the effort would be focused on Air Force records and systems. The audit was officially given the GAO code 701034, and entitled "Records Management Procedures Dealing With Weather Balloon, Unknown Aircraft, and Similar Crash Incidents." Although this official title appeared rather broad, there was no misunderstanding that the real purpose was to attempt to locate records and/or information on the "Roswell Incident." This incident, explained later in more detail, generally dealt with the claim that in July of 1947, the US Army Air Forces (USAAF) recovered a flying saucer and /or its alien occupants which supposedly crashed near Roswell, New Mexico. When the USAAF ultimately became the United States Air Force (USAF) in September, 1947, the USAF inherited equipment, personnel, records, policies, and procedures from the AAF. In this particular case, the Air Force also inherited the allegation that it had "covered up" the "Roswell Incident" and has continued to do so for the next 47 years.

Within the Air Force, the Office of the Administrative Assistant to the Secretary of the Air Force (SAF/AA) is responsible both for information management procedures (SAF/AAI) and security policy and oversight (SAF/AAZ). Because of this organization, SAF/AA was

2

the logical entity to assist the GAO in its audit and SAF/AAZ was officially named as the Central Point of Contact for this endeavor (Atch 4). Subsequently, the then-Administrative Assistant, Mr. Robert J. McCormick, issued a tasking memorandum dated March 1, 1994 (Atch 5), to a number of current Air Staff and Secretariat offices that might possibly have records related to such an incident if, indeed, something had actually occurred. This search for records was purposely limited to Air Force records and systems since:

(a) The Air Force had no authority to compel other agencies to review their records;
(b) The Air Force would have no way to monitor the completeness of their efforts if they did; and
(c) the overall effort was the task and responsibility of the GAO—not the Air Force.

During the in-briefing process with GAO, it was learned that this audit was, indeed, generated at the specific request of Congressman Steven Schiff of New Mexico. Earlier, Congressman Schiff had written to the Department of Defense Legislative Liaison Office for information on the "Roswell Incident" and had been advised that it was part of the former UFO "Project Bluebook" that had previously been turned over to NARA by the Air Force. Congressman Schiff subsequently learned from NARA that, although they did, indeed, have the "Bluebook" materials, the "Roswell Incident" was not part of that report. Congressman Schiff, apparently perceiving that he had been "stonewalled" by the DoD, then generated the request for the aforementioned audit.

It is within this context that the following research and assistance efforts were conducted in support of the GAO. This report is intended to stand as the final official Air Force response regarding this matter.

THE "ROSWELL INCIDENT"—WHAT WAS ORIGINALLY REPORTED IN 1947

The modern preoccupation with what ultimately came to be called Unidentified Flying Objects (UFOs) actually began in June, 1947. Although some pro-UFO researchers argue that sightings of UFOs go back to Biblical times, most researchers will not dispute that anything in UFO history can compare with the phenomenon that began in 1947. What was later characterized as "the UFO Wave of 1947" began with 16 alleged sightings that occurred between May 17 and July 12, 1947, (although some researchers claim there were as many as 800 sightings during that period). Interestingly, the "Roswell Incident" was not considered one of these 1947 events until the 1978-1980 time frame. There is no dispute, however, that something happened near Roswell in July, 1947, since it was reported in a number of contemporary newspaper articles; the most famous of which were the July 8 and July 9 editions of the Roswell Daily Record. The July 8 edition reported "RAAF Captures Flying Saucer On Ranch In Roswell Region," while the next day's edition reported, "Ramey Empties Roswell Saucer" and "Harassed Rancher Who Located 'Saucer' Sorry He Told About It."

The first story reported that the Intelligence Officer of the 509th Bomb Group, stationed at Roswell AAF, Major Jesse A. Marcel, had recovered a "flying disc" from the range lands of an unidentified rancher in the vicinity of Roswell and that the disc had been "flown to higher headquarters." That same story also reported that a Roswell couple claimed to have seen a large unidentified object fly by their home on July 2, 1947.

The July 9 edition of the paper noted that Brigadier General Roger Ramey, Commander of the Eighth Air Force at Forth Worth, Texas, stated that upon examination the debris recovered by Marcel was determined to be a weather balloon. The wreckage was described as a ."..bundle of tinfoil, broken wood beams, and rubber remnants of a balloon...." The additional story of the "harassed rancher" identified him as W.W. Brazel of Lincoln County, New Mexico. He claimed that he and his son, Vernon, found the material on June 14, 1947, when they "came upon a large area of bright wreckage made up of rubber strips, tinfoil, a rather tough paper, and sticks." He picked up some of the debris on July 4 and ."..the next day he first heard about the flying discs and wondered if what he had found might have been the remnants of one of these." Brazel subsequently went to Roswell on July 7 and contacted the Sheriff, who apparently notified Major Marcel. Major Marcel and "a man in plain clothes" then accompanied Brazel home to pick up the rest of the pieces. The article further related that Brazel thought that the material:

> ."..might have been as large as a table top. The balloon which held it up, if that is how it worked, must have been about 12 feet long, he felt, measuring the distance by the size of the room in which he sat. The rubber was smoky gray in color and scattered over an area about 200 yards in diameter. When the debris was gathered up the tinfoil, paper, tape, and sticks made a bundle about three feet long and 7 or 8 inches thick, while the rubber made a bundle about 18 or 20 inches long and about 8 inches thick. In all, he estimated, the entire lot would have weighed maybe five pounds. There was no sign of any metal in the area which might have been used for an engine and no sign of any propellers of any kind. Although at least one paper fin had been glued onto some of the tinfoil. There were no words to be found anywhere on the instrument although there were letters on some of the parts. Considerable scotch tape and some tape with flowers printed upon it had been used in the construction. No string or wire were to be found but there were some eyelets in the paper to indicate that some sort of attachment may have been used. Brazel said that he had previously found two weather balloons on the ranch, but that what he found this time did not in any way resemble either of these."

EVOLUTION OF THE EVENT FROM 1947 TO THE PRESENT

General Ramey's press conference and rancher Brazel's statement effectively ended this as a UFO-related matter until 1978, although some UFO researchers argue that there were several obtuse references to it in 1950's era literature. Roswell, for example, is not referred to in the official USAF investigation of UFOs reported in Project Bluebook or its predecessors, Project Sign and Project Grudge, which ran from 1948-1969 (which Congressman Schiff subsequently learned when he made his original inquiry).

In 1978, an article appeared in a tabloid newspaper, the National Inquirer, which reported the former intelligence officer, Marcel, claimed that he had recovered UFO debris near Roswell in 1947. Also in 1978, a UFO researcher, Stanton Friedman, met with Marcel and began investigating the claims that the material Marcel handled was from a crashed UFO. Similarly, two authors, William L. Moore and Charles Berlitz, also engaged in research which led them to publish a book, The Roswell Incident, in 1980. In this book they reported they interviewed a number of persons who claimed to have been present at Roswell in 1947 and professed to be either first or second hand witnesses to strange events that supposedly occurred. Since 1978-1980, other UFO researchers, most notably Donald Schmitt and Kevin Randle, claim to have located and interviewed even more persons with supposed knowledge of unusual happenings at Roswell. These included both civilian and former military persons.

Additionally, the Robert Stack-hosted television show "Unsolved Mysteries" devoted a large portion of one show to a "re-creation" of the supposed Roswell events. Numerous other television shows have done likewise, particularly during the last several years and a made-for-TV movie on the subject is due to be released this summer. The overall thrust of these articles, books and shows is that the "Roswell Incident" was actually the crash of a craft from another world, the US Government recovered it, and has been "covering up" this fact from the American public since 1947, using a combination of disinformation, ridicule, and threats of bodily harm, to do so. Generally, the US Air Force bears the brunt of these accusations.

From the rather benign description of the "event" and the recovery of some material as described in the original newspaper accounts, the "Roswell Incident" has since grown to mythical (if not mystical) proportions in the eyes and minds of some researchers, portions of the media and at least part of the American public. There are also now several major variations of the "Roswell story." For example, it was originally reported that there was only recovery of debris from one site. This has since grown from a minimal amount of debris recovered from a small area to airplane loads of debris from multiple huge "debris fields." Likewise, the relatively simple description of sticks, paper, tape and tinfoil has since grown to exotic metals with hieroglyphics and fiber optic-like materials. Most versions now claim that there were two crash sites where debris was recovered; and at the second site, alleged bodies of extraterrestrial aliens were supposedly retrieved. The number of these "alien bodies" recovered also varied. These claims are further complicated by the fact that UFO researchers are not in agreement among themselves as to exactly where these recovery sites were located or even the dates of the alleged crash(es).

5

Consistently, however, the AAF was accused of securing these sites, recovering all the material therefrom, keeping locals away, and returning the recovered wreckage (and bodies) to Roswell under extremely tight security for further processing and later exploitation.

Once back at Roswell AAF, it is generally alleged that special measures were taken to notify higher headquarters and arrangements made to have recovered materials shipped to other locations for analysis. These locations include Ft. Worth, Texas, the home of the Eighth Air Force Headquarters; possibly Sandia Base (now Kirtland AFB), New Mexico; possibly Andrews AAF, Maryland, and always to Wright Field, now known as Wright-Patterson AFB, Ohio. The latter location was the home of "T-2" which later became known as the Air Technical Intelligence Center (ATIC) and the Air Materiel Command (AMC), and would, in fact, be a logical location to study unknown materials from whatever origin. Most of the Roswell stories that contain the recovery of alien bodies also show them being shipped to Wright Field. Once the material and bodies were dispersed for further analysis and/or exploitation, the government in general, and the Army Air Forces in particular, then engaged in covering up all information relating to the alleged crash and recovery, including the use of security oaths to military persons and the use of coercion (including alleged death threats) to others. This, as theorized by some UFO researchers, has allowed the government to keep the fact that there is intelligent extraterrestrial life from the American public for 47 years. It also supposedly allowed the US Government to exploit recovered extraterrestrial materials by reverse engineering them, ultimately providing such things as fiber optic and stealth technology. The "death threats," oaths, and other forms of coercion alleged to have been meted out by the Army Air Forces personnel to keep people from talking have apparently not been very effective, as several hundred people are claimed to have come forward (without harm) with some knowledge of the "Roswell Incident" during interviews with non-government researchers and the media.

Adding some measure of credibility to the claims that have arisen since 1978 is the apparent depth of research of some of the authors and the extent of their efforts. Their claims are lessened somewhat, however, by the fact that almost all their information came from verbal reports many years after the alleged incident occurred. Many of the persons interviewed were, in fact, stationed at, or lived near Roswell during the time in question, and a number of them claim military service. Most, however, related their stories in their older years, well after the fact. In other cases, the information provided is second or third-hand, having been passed through a friend or relative after the principal had died. What is uniquely lacking in the entire exploration and exploitation of the "Roswell Incident" is official positive documentary or physical evidence of any kind that supports the claims of those who allege that something unusual happened. Conversely, there has never been any previous documentary evidence produced by those who would debunk the incident to show that something did not happen; although logic dictates that bureaucracies do not spend time documenting non-events.

SEARCH STRATEGY AND METHODOLOGY

6

To insure senior Air Force leadership that there were no hidden or overlooked files that might relate to the "Roswell Incident;" and to provide the GAO with the best and most complete information available, SAF/AAZ constructed a strategy based on direct tasking from the Office of the Secretary, to elicit information from those functional offices and organizations where such information might logically be contained. This included directing searches at current offices where special or unusual projects might be carried out, as well as historical organizations, archives, and records centers over which the Air Force exerted some degree of control. Researchers did not, however, go to the US Army to review historical records in areas such as missile launches from White Sands, or to the Department of Energy to determine if its forerunner, the Atomic Energy Commission, had any records of nuclear-related incidents that might have occurred at or near Roswell in 1947. To do so would have encroached on GAO's charter in this matter. What Air Force researchers did do, however, was to search for records still under Air Force control pertaining to these subject areas.

In order to determine parameters for the most productive search of records, a review was first conducted of the major works regarding the "Roswell Incident" available in the popular literature. These works included: The Roswell Incident, (1980) by William Moore and Charles Berlitz; "Crashed Saucers: Evidence in Search of Proof," (1985) by Moore; The UFO Crash at Roswell, (1991) by Kevin Randle and Donald Schmitt; The Truth About the UFO Crash at Roswell, (1994) also by Randle and Schmitt; The Roswell Report: A Historical Perspective, (1991), George M. Eberhart, Editor; "The Roswell Events," (1993) compiled by Fred Whiting; Crash at Corona (1992) by Stanton T. Friedman and Don Berliner, as well as numerous other articles written by a combination of the above and other researchers. Collectively, the above represent the "pro" UFO writers who allege that the government is engaged in a conspiracy. There are no specific books written entirely on the theme that nothing happened at Roswell. However, Curtis Peebles in Watch the Skies! (1994) discussed the development of the UFO story and growth of subsequent claims as a phenomenon. There has also been serious research as well as a number of detailed articles written by so-called "debunkers" of Roswell and other incidents, most notably Philip J. Klass who writes The Skeptical Inquirer newsletter, and Robert Todd, a private researcher. The concerns and claims of all the above authors and others were considered in conducting the USAF records search.

It was also decided, particularly after a review of the above popular literature, that no specific attempt would be made to try to refute, point by point, the numerous claims made in the various publications. Many of these claims appear to be hearsay, undocumented, taken out of context, self-serving, or otherwise dubious. Additionally, many of the above authors are not even in agreement over various claims. Most notable of the confusing and now ever-changing claims is the controversy over the date(s) of the alleged incident, the exact location(s) of the purported debris and the extent of the wreckage. Such discrepancies in claims made the search much more difficult by greatly expanding the volume of records that had to be searched.

An example of trying to deal with questionable claims is illustrated by the following example: One of the popular books mentioned that was reviewed claimed that the writers had submitted the names and serial numbers of "over two dozen" personnel stationed at Roswell in July, 1947, to the Veterans Administration and the Defense Department to confirm their military service. They then listed eleven of these persons by name and asked the question: "Why does neither the Defense Department nor the Veteran's Administration have records of any of these men when we can document that each served at Roswell Army Air Field." That claim sounded serious so SAF/AAZD was tasked to check these eleven names in the Personnel Records Center in St. Louis. Using only the names (since the authors did not list the serial numbers) the researcher quickly found records readily identifiable with eight of these persons. The other three had such common names that there could have been multiple possibilities. Interestingly, one of the listed "missing" persons had a casualty report in his records reflecting that he died in 1951, while the writers claimed to have interviewed him (or a person of the exact same name) in 1990.

While the historical document search was in progress, it was decided to attempt to locate and interview several persons identified as still living who could possibly answer questions generated by the research. This had never been officially done before, although most of the persons contacted reported that they had also been contacted in the past by some of the listed authors or other private researchers. In order to counter possible future arguments that the persons interviewed were still "covering up" material because of prior security oaths, the interviewees were provided with authorization from either the Secretary of the Air Force or the Senior Security Official of the Air Force that would officially allow discussion of classified information, if applicable, or free them from any prior restriction in discussing the matter, if such existed. Again, the focus was on interviewing persons that could address specific issues raised by research and no consideration was given to try and locate every alleged witness claimed to have been contacted by the various authors. For example, one of the interviewees thought vital to obtain an official signed, sworn statement from was Sheridan Cavitt, Lt Col, USAF (Retired) who is the last living member of the three persons universally acknowledged to have recovered material from the Foster Ranch. Others were also interviewed as information developed (discussed in detail later). Additionally, in some cases survivors of deceased persons were also contacted in an attempt to locate various records thought to have been in the custody of the deceased.

Even though Air Force research originally started in January, 1994, the first official Air Force-wide tasking was directed by the March 1, 1994, memorandum from SAF/AA, (Atch 5) and was addressed to those current Air Staff elements that would be the likely repository for any records, particularly if there was anything of an extraordinary nature involved. This meant that the search was not limited to unclassified materials, but also would include records of the highest classification and compartmentation.

The specific Air Staff/Secretariat offices queried included the following:
(a) SAF/AAI, Directorate of Information Management
(b) SAF/AQL, Directorate of Electronics and Special Programs

8

(c) AF/SE, Air Force Safety
(d) AF/HO, Air Force Historian
(e) AF/IN, Air Force Intelligence (including Air Force Intelligence Agency—AFIA, and the National Air Intelligence Center, NAIC)
(f) AF/XOW, Directorate of Weather
(g) (added later) The Air Force Office of Special Investigations (AFOSI)

In addition to the above Air Staff and Secretariat offices, SAF/AAZ also reviewed appropriate classified records for any tie-in to this matter. With regards to highly classified records, it should be noted that any programs that employ enhanced security measures or controls are known as a Special Access Programs (SAPs). The authority for such programs comes from Executive Order 12356 and flows from the Department of Defense to the Services via DoD Directive 5205.7. These programs are implemented in the Air Force by Policy Directive 16-7, and Air Force Instruction 16-701. These directives contain detailed requirements for controlling and reporting, in a very strict manner, all SAPs. This includes a report from the Secretary of the Air Force to the Secretary of Defense (and ultimately to Congress) on all SAPs submitted for approval, and a certification that there are no "SAP-like" programs being operated. These reporting requirements are stipulated in public law.

It followed then, that if the Air Force had recovered some type of extraterrestrial spacecraft and/or bodies and was exploiting this for scientific and technology purposes, then such a program would be operated as a SAP. SAF/AAZ, the Central Office for all Air Force SAPs, has knowledge of, and security oversight over, all SAPs. SAF/AAZ categorically stated that no such Special Access Program(s) exists that pertain to extraterrestrial spacecraft/aliens.

Likewise, the Secretary of the Air Force and the Chief of Staff, who head the Special Program Oversight Committee which oversees all sensitive programs in the Air Force, had no knowledge of the existence of any such program involving, or relating to the events at Roswell or the alleged technology that supposedly resulted therefrom. Besides the obvious irregularity and illegality of keeping such information from the most senior Air Force officials, it would also be illogical, since these officials are responsible for obtaining funding for operations, research, development, and security. Without funding such a program, operation, or organization could not exist. Even to keep such a fact "covered-up" in some sort of passive "caretaker status" would involve money. More importantly, it would involve people and create paperwork.

The aforementioned March 1, 1994, SAF/AA tasking generated negative responses (Atch 6-12) from all recipients; i.e. all offices reported that they had no information that would explain the incident. Consequently, these negative responses led to an increase in the already on-going historical research at records centers and archives.

The extensive archival and records center search was systematically carried out at by the SAF/AAZD Declassification Review Team. This team is composed entirely of Air Force

Reserve personnel who have extensive training and experience in large scale review of records. (Previous efforts include the Southeast Asia Declassification Review, declassification of POW/MIA records, and the review of the Gulf War Air Power Survey records). The team members all had the requisite security clearances for classified information and had the authority of the Secretary of the Air Force to declassify any classified record they found that might be related to Roswell. SAF/AAZD conducted reviews at a number of locations, including: the National Archives in Washington, DC; the National Personnel Records Center, St. Louis, MO; the National Archives, Suitland MD; the National Records Center, Suitland, MD; Naval Research Laboratory, Washington, DC; Federal Records Center, Ft Worth, TX; the INSCOM Archives, Ft. Meade, MD; National Air and Space Museum, Washington, DC; Air Force Historical Research Agency, Maxwell AFB, AL; Center for Air Force History, Bolling AFB, DC; Phillips Laboratory, Hanscom AFB, MA and Kirtland AFB, NM; Rome Laboratory, Griffiss AFB, NY; and the Library of Congress, Washington, DC.

A listing of the specific record areas searched is appended as Atch 13. The areas included all those subject areas logically believed to possibly contain any reference to activities at Roswell AAF during the period of time in question. It is anticipated that detractors from this effort will complain that "they did not search record group x , box y, or reel z, etc.; that's where the real records are!" Such complaints are unavoidable and there is no possible way that the millions of records under Air Force control could be searched page by page. The team endeavored to make logical searches in those places where records would likely be found. They were assisted in this task by archivists, historians, and records management specialists, including experienced persons who have continually worked in Army and Air Force records systems since 1943. The team also searched some record areas that were recommended by serious private researchers such as Robert Todd, who had independently obtained almost encyclopedic knowledge of the complexities of Air Force records systems, particularly as related to this subject area.

Not surprisingly, the research team found the usual number of problems in many of the records centers (particularly St. Louis) with misfiling, lost or misplaced documents, mismarking of documents, or the breaking up of record groups over the years and refiling in different systems. This included, for example, a small amount of missing "decimal files" from the 509th Bomb Group at Roswell that covered the years 1945-1949, that were marked on the index as "destroyed." The researchers noted that there was no pattern to any anomalies found and that most discrepancies were minor and consistent with what they had found in the past on similar projects.

WHAT THE ROSWELL INCIDENT WAS NOT

Before discussing specific positive results that these efforts revealed, it is first appropriate to discuss those things, as indicated by information available to the Air Force, that the "Roswell Incident" was not:

An Airplane Crash

Of all the things that are documented and tracked within the Air Force, among the most detailed and scrupulous are airplane crashes. In fact, records of air crashes go back to the first years of military flight. Safety records and reports are available for all crashes that involved serious damage, injury, death, or a combination of these factors. These records also include incidents involving experimental or classified aircraft. USAF records showed that between June 24, 1947, and July 28, 1947, there were five crashes in New Mexico alone, involving A-26C, P-51N, C-82A, P-80A and PQ-14B aircraft; however, none of these were on the date(s) in question nor in the area(s) in question.

One of the additional areas specifically set forth by GAO in its efforts was to deal with how the Air Force (and others) specifically documented ."..weather balloon:..and other crash incidents." In this area, the search efforts revealed that there are no air safety records pertaining to weather balloon crashes (all weather balloons "crash" sooner or later); however, there are provisions for generating reports of "crashes" as ground safety incidents in the unlikely chance that a balloon injures someone or causes damage. However, such records are only maintained for five years.

A Missile Crash

A crashed or errant missile, usually described as a captured German V-2 or one of its variants, is sometimes set forth as a possible explanation for the debris recovered near Roswell. Since much of this testing done at nearby White Sands was secret at the time, it would be logical to assume that the government would handle any missile mishap under tight security, particularly if the mishap occurred on private land. From the records reviewed by the Air Force, however, there was nothing located to suggest that this was the case. Although the bulk of remaining testing records are under the control of the US Army, the subject has also been very well documented over the years within Air Force records. There would be no reason to keep such information classified today. The USAF found no indicators or even hints that a missile was involved in this matter.

A Nuclear Accident

One of the areas considered was that whatever happened near Roswell may have involved nuclear weapons. This was a logical area of concern since the 509th Bomb Group was the only military unit in the world at the time that had access to nuclear weapons. Again, reviews of available records gave no indication that this was the case. A number of records still classified TOP SECRET and SECRET-RESTRICTED DATA having to do with nuclear weapons were located in the Federal Records Center in St. Louis, MO . These records, which pertained to the 509th, had nothing to do with any activities that could have been misinterpreted as the "Roswell Incident." Also, any records of a nuclear-related incident would have been inherited by the Department of Energy (DOE), and, had one occurred, it is likely DOE would have publicly reported it as part of its recent declassification and public release efforts. There were no ancillary records in Air Force files to indicate the potential existence of such records within DOE channels, however.

An Extraterrestrial Craft

11

The Air Force research found absolutely no indication that what happened near Roswell in 1947, involved any type of extraterrestrial spacecraft. This, of course, is the crux of this entire matter. "Pro-UFO" persons who obtain a copy of this report, at this point, most probably begin the "cover-up is still on" claims. Nevertheless, the research indicated absolutely no evidence of any kind that a spaceship crashed near Roswell or that any alien occupants were recovered therefrom, in some secret military operation or otherwise. This does not mean, however, that the early Air Force was not concerned about UFOs. However, in the early days, "UFO" meant Unidentified Flying Object, which literally translated as some object in the air that was not readily identifiable. It did not mean, as the term has evolved in today's language, to equate to alien spaceships. Records from the period reviewed by Air Force researchers as well as those cited by the authors mentioned before, do indicate that the USAF was seriously concerned about the inability to adequately identify unknown flying objects reported in American airspace. All the records, however, indicated that the focus of concern was not on aliens, hostile or otherwise, but on the Soviet Union. Many documents from that period speak to the possibility of developmental secret Soviet aircraft overflying US airspace. This, of course, was of major concern to the fledgling USAF, whose job it was to protect these same skies.

The research revealed only one official AAF document that indicated that there was any activity of any type that pertained to UFOs and Roswell in July, 1947. This was a small section of the July Historical Report for the 509th Bomb Group and Roswell AAF that stated: "The Office of Public Information was quite busy during the month answering inquiries on the 'flying disc,' which was reported to be in possession of the 509th Bomb Group. The object turned out to be a radar tracking balloon" (included with Atch 11). Additionally, this history showed that the 509th Commander, Colonel Blanchard, went on leave on July 8, 1947, which would be a somewhat unusual maneuver for a person involved in the supposed first ever recovery of extraterrestrial materials. (Detractors claim Blanchard did this as a ploy to elude the press and go to the scene to direct the recovery operations). The history and the morning reports also showed that the subsequent activities at Roswell during the month were mostly mundane and not indicative of any unusual high level activity, expenditure of manpower, resources or security.

Likewise, the researchers found no indication of heightened activity anywhere else in the military hierarchy in the July, 1947, message traffic or orders (to include classified traffic). There were no indications and warnings, notice of alerts, or a higher tempo of operational activity reported that would be logically generated if an alien craft, whose intentions were unknown, entered US territory. To believe that such operational and high-level security activity could be conducted solely by relying on unsecured telecommunications or personal contact without creating any records of such activity certainly stretches the imagination of those who have served in the military who know that paperwork of some kind is necessary to accomplish even emergency, highly classified, or sensitive tasks.

An example of activity sometimes cited by pro-UFO writers to illustrate the point that something unusual was going on was the travel of Lt. General Nathan Twining, Commander of the Air Materiel Command, to New Mexico in July, 1947. Actually,

12

records were located indicating that Twining went to the Bomb Commanders' Course on July 8, along with a number of other general officers, and requested orders to do so a month before, on June 5, 1947 (Atch 14).

Similarly, it has also been alleged that General Hoyt Vandenberg, Deputy Chief of Staff at the time, had been involved directing activity regarding events at Roswell. Activity reports (Atch 15), located in General Vandenberg's personal papers stored in the Library of Congress, did indicate that on July 7, he was busy with a "flying disc" incident; however this particular incident involved Ellington Field, Texas and the Spokane (Washington) Depot. After much discussion and information gathering on this incident, it was learned to be a hoax. There is no similar mention of his personal interest or involvement in Roswell events except in the newspapers.

The above are but two small examples that indicate that if some event happened that was one of the "watershed happenings" in human history, the US military certainly reacted in an unconcerned and cavalier manner. In an actual case, the military would have had to order thousands of soldiers and airman, not only at Roswell but throughout the US, to act nonchalantly, pretend to conduct and report business as usual, and generate absolutely no paperwork of a suspicious nature, while simultaneously anticipating that twenty years or more into the future people would have available a comprehensive Freedom of Information Act that would give them great leeway to review and explore government documents. The records indicate that none of this happened (or if it did, it was controlled by a security system so efficient and tight that no one, US or otherwise, has been able to duplicate it since. If such a system had been in effect at the time, it would have also been used to protect our atomic secrets from the Soviets, which history has showed obviously was not the case). The records reviewed confirmed that no such sophisticated and efficient security system existed.

WHAT THE "ROSWELL INCIDENT" WAS

As previously discussed, what was originally reported to have been recovered was a balloon of some sort, usually described as a "weather balloon," although the majority of the wreckage that was ultimately displayed by General Ramey and Major Marcel in the famous photos (Atch 16) in Ft. Worth, was that of a radar target normally suspended from balloons. This radar target, discussed in more detail later, was certainly consistent with the description of July 9 newspaper article which discussed "tinfoil, paper, tape, and sticks." Additionally, the description of the "flying disc" was consistent with a document routinely used by most pro-UFO writers to indicate a conspiracy in progress—the telegram from the Dallas FBI office of July 8, 1947. This document quoted in part states: ."..The disc is hexagonal in shape and was suspended from a balloon by a cable, which balloon was approximately twenty feet in diameter. ...the object found resembles a high altitude weather balloon with a radar reflector. ...disc and balloon being transported..."

Similarly, while conducting the popular literature review, one of the documents reviewed was a paper entitled "The Roswell Events" edited by Fred Whiting, and sponsored by the

13

Fund for UFO Research (FUFOR). Although it was not the original intention to comment on what commercial authors interpreted or claimed that other persons supposedly said, this particular document was different because it contained actual copies of apparently authentic sworn affidavits received from a number of persons who claimed to have some knowledge of the Roswell event. Although many of the persons who provided these affidavits to the FUFOR researchers also expressed opinions that they thought there was something extraterrestrial about this incident, a number of them actually described materials that sounded suspiciously like wreckage from balloons. These included the following:

Jesse A. Marcel, MD (son of the late Major Jesse Marcel; 11 years old at the time of the incident). Affidavit dated May 6, 1991. " ... There were three categories of debris: a thick, foil like metallic gray substance; a brittle, brownish-black plastic-like material, like Bakelite; and there were fragments of what appeared to be I-beams. On the inner surface of the I-beam, there appeared to be a type of writing. This writing was a purple-violet hue, and it had an embossed appearance. The figures were composed of curved, geometric shapes. It had no resemblance to Russian, Japanese or any other foreign language. It resembled hieroglyphics, but it had no animal-like characters...."

Loretta Proctor (former neighbor of rancher W.W. Brazel). Affidavit dated May 5, 1991. ."..Brazel came to my ranch and showed my husband and me a piece of material he said came from a large pile of debris on the property he managed. The piece he brought was brown in color, similar to plastic...'Mac' said the other material on the property looked like aluminum foil. It was very flexible and wouldn't crush or burn. There was also something he described as tape which had printing on it. The color of the printing was a kind of purple..."

Bessie Brazel Schreiber (daughter of W.W. Brazel; 14 years old at the time of the incident). Affidavit dated September 22, 1993. ."..The debris looked like pieces of a large balloon which had burst. The pieces were small, the largest I remember measuring about the same as the diameter of a basketball. Most of it was a kind of double-sided material, foil-like on one side and rubber-like on the other. Both sides were grayish silver in color, the foil more silvery than the rubber. Sticks, like kite sticks, were attached to some of the pieces with a whitish tape. The tape was about two or three inches wide and had flower-like designs on it. The 'flowers' were faint, a variety of pastel colors, and reminded me of Japanese paintings in which the flowers are not all connected. I do not recall any other types of material or markings, nor do I remember seeing gouges in the ground or any other signs that anything may have hit the ground hard. The foil-rubber material could not be torn like ordinary aluminum foil can be torn..."

Sally Strickland Tadolini (neighbor of WW Brazel; nine years old in 1947). Affidavit dated September 27, 1993. ."..What Bill showed us was a piece of what I still think as fabric. It was something like aluminum foil, something like satin, something like well-tanned leather in its toughness, yet was not precisely like any one of those materials. ...It

14

was about the thickness of very fine kidskin glove leather and a dull metallic grayish silver, one side slightly darker than the other. I do not remember it having any design or embossing on it..."

Robert R. Porter (B-29 flight Engineer stationed at Roswell in 1947). Affidavit dated June 7, 1991. ."..On this occasion, I was a member of the crew which flew parts of what we were told was a flying saucer to Fort Worth. The people on board included...and Maj Jesse Marcel. Capt. William E. Anderson said it was from a flying saucer. After we arrived, the material was transferred to a B-25. I was told they were going to Wright Field in Dayton, Ohio. I was involved in loading the B-29 with the material, which was wrapped in packages with wrapping paper. One of the pieces was triangle-shaped, about 2 1/2 feet across the bottom. The rest were in small packages, about the size of a shoe box. The brown paper was held with tape. The material was extremely lightweight. When I picked it up, it was just like picking up an empty package. We loaded the triangle shaped package and three shoe box-sized packages into the plane. All of the packages could have fit into the trunk of a car. ...When we came back from lunch, they told us they had transferred the material to a B-25. They told us the material was a weather balloon, but I'm certain it wasn't a weather balloon..."

In addition to those persons above still living who claim to have seen or examined the original material found on the Brazel Ranch, there is one additional person who was universally acknowledged to have been involved in its recovery, Sheridan Cavitt, Lt Col, USAF, (Ret) . Cavitt is credited in all claims of having accompanied Major Marcel to the ranch to recover the debris, sometimes along with his Counter Intelligence Corps (CIC) subordinate, William Rickett, who, like Marcel, is deceased. Although there does not appear to be much dispute that Cavitt was involved in the material recovery, other claims about him prevail in the popular literature. He is sometimes portrayed as a closed-mouth (or sometimes even sinister) conspirator who was one of the early individuals who kept the "secret of Roswell" from getting out. Other things about him have been alleged, including the claim that he wrote a report of the incident at the time that has never surfaced.

Since Lt Col Cavitt, who had first-hand knowledge, was still alive, a decision was made to interview him and get a signed sworn statement from him about his version of the events. Prior to the interview, the Secretary of the Air Force provided him with a written authorization and waiver to discuss classified information with the interviewer and release him from any security oath he may have taken. Subsequently, Cavitt was interviewed on May 24, 1994, at his home. Cavitt provided a signed, sworn statement (Atch 17) of his recollections in this matter. He also consented to having the interview tape-recorded. A transcript of that recording is at Atch 18. In this interview, Cavitt related that he had been contacted on numerous occasions by UFO researchers and had willingly talked with many of them; however, he felt that he had oftentimes been misrepresented or had his comments taken out of context so that their true meaning was changed. He stated unequivocally, however, that the material he recovered consisted of a reflective sort of material like aluminum foil, and some thin, bamboo-like sticks. He thought at the time, and continued to do so today, that what he found was a weather balloon and has told other private researchers that. He also remembered finding a small "black box" type of instrument, which he thought at the time was probably a radiosonde. Lt Col Cavitt also reviewed the famous Ramey/Marcel photographs (Atch 16) of the wreckage taken to Ft. Worth (often claimed by UFO researchers to have been switched and the remnants of a balloon substituted for it) and he identified the materials depicted in those photos as consistent with the materials that he recovered from the ranch. Lt Col Cavitt also stated that he had never taken any oath or signed any agreement not to talk about this incident and had never been threatened by anyone in the government because of it. He did not even know the "incident" was claimed to be anything unusual until he was interviewed in the early 1980's.

Similarly, Irving Newton, Major, USAF, (Ret) was located and interviewed. Newton was a weather officer assigned to Fort Worth, who was on duty when the Roswell debris was sent there in July, 1947. He was told that he was to report to General Ramey's office to view the material. In a signed, sworn statement (Atch 30) Newton related that .".I walked into the General's office where this supposed flying saucer was lying all over the floor. As soon as I saw it, I giggled and asked if that was the flying saucer...I told them that this was a balloon and a RAWIN target..." Newton also stated that .".while I was examining the debris, Major Marcel was picking up pieces of the target sticks and trying to convince me that some notations on the sticks were alien writings. there were figures on the sticks, lavender or pink in color, appeared to be weather faded markings, with no rhyme or reason (sic). He did not convince me that these were alien writings." Newton concluded his statement by relating that .".During the ensuing years I have been interviewed by many authors, I have been quoted and misquoted. The facts remain as indicated above. I was not influenced during the original interview, nor today, to provide anything but what I know to be true, that is, the material I saw in General Ramey's office was the remains of a balloon and a RAWIN target."

Balloon Research
The original tasking from GAO noted that the search for information included "weather balloons." Comments about balloons and safety reports have already been made, however the SAF/AAZ research efforts also focused on reviewing historical records involving balloons, since, among other reasons, that was what was officially claimed by the AAF to have been found and recovered in 1947. ⁻

As early as February 28, 1994, the AAZD research team found references to balloon tests taking place at Alamogordo AAF (now Holloman AFB) and White Sands during June and July 1947, testing "constant level balloons" and a New York University (NYU)/Watson Labs effort that used "...meteorological devices ... suspected for detecting shock waves generated by Soviet nuclear explosions"−a possible indication of a cover story associated with the NYU balloon project. Subsequently, a 1946 HQ AMC memorandum was surfaced, describing the constant altitude balloon project and specified that the scientific data be classified TOP SECRET Priority 1A. Its name was Project Mogul (Atch 19).

Project Mogul was a then-sensitive, classified project, whose purpose was to determine the state of Soviet nuclear weapons research. This was the early Cold War period and there was serious concern within the US government about the Soviets developing a weaponized atomic device. Because the Soviet Union's borders were closed, the US Government sought to develop a long range nuclear explosion detection capability. Long range, balloon-borne, low frequency acoustic detection was posed to General Spaatz in 1945 by Dr. Maurice Ewing of Columbia University as a potential solution (atmospheric ducting of low frequency pressure waves had been studied as early as 1900).

As part of the research into this matter, AAZD personnel located and obtained the original study papers and reports of the New York University project. Their efforts also revealed that some of the individuals involved in Project Mogul were still living. These persons included the NYU constant altitude balloon Director of Research, Dr. Athelstan F. Spilhaus; the Project Engineer, Professor Charles B. Moore; and the military Project Officer, Colonel Albert C. Trakowski .

All of these persons were subsequently interviewed and signed sworn statements about their activities. A copy of theses statements are appended at Atch 20-22. Additionally, transcripts of the interview with Moore and Trakowski are also included (equipment malfunctioned during the interview of Spilhaus) (Atch 23-24). These interviews confirmed that Project Mogul was a compartmented, sensitive, effort. The NYU group was responsible for developing constant level balloons and telemetering equipment that would remain at specified altitudes (within the acoustic duct) while a group from Columbia was to develop acoustic sensors. Doctor Spilhaus, Professor Moore, and certain others of the group were aware of the actual purpose of the project, but they did not know of the project nickname at the time. They handled casual inquiries and/or scientific inquiries/papers in terms of "unclassified meteorological or balloon research." Newly hired employees were not made aware that there was anything special or classified about their work; they were told only that their work dealt with meteorological equipment.

An advance ground team, led by Albert P. Crary, preceded the NYU group to Alamogordo AAF, New Mexico, setting up ground sensors and obtaining facilities for the NYU group. Upon their arrival, Professor Moore and his team experimented with various configurations of neoprene balloons; development of balloon "trains" (see illustration, Atch 25); automatic ballast systems; and use of Naval sonobuoys (as the Watson Lab acoustical sensors had not yet arrived). They also launched what they called "service flights." These "service flights" were not logged nor fully accounted for in the published Technical Reports generated as a result of the contract between NYU and Watson Labs. According to Professor Moore, the "service flights" were composed of balloons, radar reflectors and payloads specifically designed to test acoustic sensors (both early sonobuoys and the later Watson Labs devices). The "payload equipment" was expendable and some carried no "REWARD" or "RETURN TO..." tags because there was to be no association between these flights and the logged constant altitude flights which were fully acknowledged. The NYU balloon flights were listed sequentially in their reports (i.e.,

17

A,B, 1,5,6,7,8,10 ...) yet gaps existed for Flights 2-4 and Flight 9. The interview with Professor Moore indicated that these gaps were the unlogged "service flights."

Professor Moore, the on-scene Project Engineer, gave detailed information concerning his team's efforts. He recalled that radar targets were used for tracking balloons because they did not have all the necessary equipment when they first arrived in New Mexico. Some of the early developmental radar targets were manufactured by a toy or novelty company. These targets were made up of aluminum "foil" or foil-backed paper, balsa wood beams that were coated in an "Elmer's-type" glue to enhance their durability, acetate and/or cloth reinforcing tape, single strand and braided nylon twine, brass eyelets and swivels to form a multi-faced reflector somewhat similar in construction to a box kite (see photographs, Atch 26). Some of these targets were also assembled with purplish-pink tape with symbols on it (see drawing by Moore with Atch 21).

According to the log summary (Atch 27) of the NYU group, Flight A through Flight 7 (November 20, 1946-July 2, 1947) were made with neoprene meteorological balloons (as opposed to the later flights made with polyethylene balloons). Professor Moore stated that the neoprene balloons were susceptible to degradation in the sunlight, turning from a milky white to a dark brown. He described finding remains of balloon trains with reflectors and payloads that had landed in the desert: the ruptured and shredded neoprene would "almost look like dark gray or black flakes or ashes after exposure to the sun for only a few days. The plasticizers and antioxidants in the neoprene would emit a peculiar acrid odor and the balloon material and radar target material would be scattered after returning to earth depending on the surface winds." Upon review of the local newspaper photographs from General Ramey's press conference in 1947 and descriptions in popular books by individuals who supposedly handled the debris recovered on the ranch, Professor Moore opined that the material was most likely the shredded remains of a multi-neoprene balloon train with multiple radar reflectors. The material and a "black box," described by Cavitt, was, in Moore's scientific opinion, most probably from Flight 4, a "service flight" that included a cylindrical metal sonobuoy and portions of a weather instrument housed in a box, which was unlike typical weather radiosondes which were made of cardboard. Additionally, a copy of a professional journal maintained at the time by A.P. Crary, provided to the Air Force by his widow, showed that Flight 4 was launched on June 4, 1947, but was not recovered by the NYU group. It is very probable that this TOP SECRET project balloon train (Flight 4), made up of unclassified components; came to rest some miles northwest of Roswell, NM, became shredded in the surface winds and was ultimately found by the rancher, Brazel, ten days later. This possibility was supported by the observations of Lt Col Cavitt (Atch 17-18), the only living eyewitness to the actual debris field and the material found. Lt Col Cavitt described a small area of debris which appeared, "to resemble bamboo type square sticks one quarter to one half inch square, that were very light, as well as some sort of metallic reflecting material that was also very light ... I remember recognizing this material as being consistent with a weather balloon."

Concerning the initial announcement, "RAAF Captures Flying Disc," research failed to locate any documented evidence as to why that statement was made. However, on July

10, 1947, following the Ramey press conference, the Alamogordo News published an article with photographs demonstrating multiple balloons and targets at the same location as the NYU group operated from at Alamogordo AAF. Professor Moore expressed surprise at seeing this since his, was the only balloon test group in the area. He stated, "It appears that there was some type of umbrella cover story to protect our work with Mogul." Although the Air Force did not find documented evidence that Gen. Ramey was directed to espouse a weather balloon in his press conference, he may have done so because he was either aware of Project Mogul and was trying to deflect interest from it, or he readily perceived the material to be a weather balloon based on the identification from his weather officer, Irving Newton. In either case, the materials recovered by the AAF in July, 1947, were not readily recognizable as anything special (only the purpose was special) and the recovered debris itself was unclassified. Additionally, the press dropped its interest in the matter as quickly as they had jumped on it. Hence, there would be no particular reason to further document what quickly became a "non-event."

The interview with Colonel Trakowski (Atch 23-24) also proved valuable information. Trakowski provided specific details on Project Mogul and described how the security for the program was set up, as he was formerly the TOP SECRET Control Officer for the program. He further related that many of the original radar targets that were produced around the end of World War II were fabricated by toy or novelty companies using a purplish-pink tape with flower and heart symbols on it. Trakowski also recounted a conversation that he had with his friend, and superior military officer in his chain of command, Colonel Marcellus Duffy, in July, 1947. Duffy, formerly had Trakowski's position on Mogul, but had subsequently been transferred to Wright Field. He stated: ."..Colonel Duffy called me on the telephone from Wright Field and gave me a story about a fellow that had come in from New Mexico, woke him up in the middle of the night or some such thing with a handful of debris, and wanted him, Colonel Duffy, to identify it. ...He just said 'it sure looks like some of the stuff you've been launching at Alamogordo' and he described it, and I said 'yes, I think it is.' Certainly Colonel Duffy knew enough about radar targets, radiosondes, balloon-borne weather devices. He was intimately familiar with all that apparatus."

Attempts were made to locate Colonel Duffy but it was ascertained that he had died. His widow explained that, although he had amassed a large amount of personal papers relating to his Air Force activities, she had recently disposed of these items. Likewise, it was learned that A.P. Crary was also deceased; however his surviving spouse had a number of his papers from his balloon testing days, including his professional journal from the period in question. She provided the Air Force researchers with this material. It is discussed in more detail within Atch 32. Overall, it helps fill in gaps of the Mogul story.

During the period the Air Force conducted this research, it was discovered that several others had also discovered the possibility that the "Roswell Incident" may have been generated by the recovery of a Project Mogul balloon device. These persons included Professor Charles B. Moore, Robert Todd, and coincidentally, Karl Pflock, a researcher who is married to a staffer who works for Congressman Schiff. Some of these persons

19

provided suggestions as to where documentation might be located in various archives, histories and libraries. A review of Freedom of Information Act (FOIA) requests revealed that Robert Todd, particularly, had become aware of Project Mogul several years ago and had doggedly obtained from the Air Force, through the FOIA, a large amount of material pertaining to it; long before the AAZD researchers independently seized on the same possibility.

Most interestingly, as this report was being written, Pflock published his own report of this matter under the auspices of FUFOR, entitled "Roswell in Perspective" (1994). Pflock concluded from his research that the Brazel Ranch debris originally reported as a "flying disc" was probably debris from a Mogul balloon; however, there was a simultaneous incident that occurred not far away, that caused an alien craft to crash and that the AAF subsequently recovered three alien bodies therefrom. Air Force research did not locate any information to corroborate that this incredible coincidence occurred, however.

In order to provide a more detailed discussion of the specifics of Project Mogul and how it appeared to be directly responsible for the "Roswell Incident," a SAF/AAZD researcher prepared a more detailed discussion on the balloon project which is appended to this report as Atch 32.

Other Research
In the attempt to develop additional information that could help explain this matter, a number of other steps were taken. First, assistance was requested from various museums and other archives (Atch 28) to obtain information and/or examples of the actual balloons and radar targets used in connection with Project Mogul and to correlate them with the various descriptions of wreckage and materials recovered. The blueprints for the "Pilot Balloon Target ML307C/AP Assembly" (generically, the radar target assembly) were located at the Army Signal Corps Museum at Fort Monmouth and obtained. A copy is appended as Atch 29. This blueprint provides the specification for the foil material, tape, wood, eyelets, and string used and the assembly instructions thereto. An actual device was also obtained for study with the assistance of Professor Moore. (The example actually procured was a 1953-manufactured model "C" as compared to the Model B which was in use in 1947. Professor Moore related the differences were minor). An examination of this device revealed it to be simply made of aluminum-colored foil-like material over a stronger paper-like material, attached to balsa wood sticks, affixed with tape, glue, and twine. When opened, the device appears as depicted in Atch 31 (contemporary photo) and Atch 25 (1947 photo, in a "balloon train"). When folded, the device is in a series of triangles, the largest being four feet by two feet ten inches. The smallest triangle section measures two feet by two feet ten inches. (Compare with descriptions provided by Lt Col Cavitt and others, as well as photos of wreckage).

Additionally, the researchers obtained from the Archives of the University of Texas-Arlington (UTA), a set of original (i.e. first generation) prints of the photographs taken at the time by the Fort Worth Star-Telegram, that depicted Ramey and Marcel with the

20

wreckage. A close review of these photos (and a set of first generation negatives also subsequently obtained from UTA) revealed several intesting observations. First, although in some of the literature cited above, Marcel allegedly stated that he had his photo taken with the "real" UFO wreckage and then it was subsequently removed and the weather balloon wreckage substituted for it, a comparison shows that the same wreckage appeared in the photos of Marcel and Ramey. The photos also depicted that this material was lying on what appeared to be some sort of wrapping paper (consistent with affidavit excerpt of crew chief Porter, above). It was also noted that in the two photos of Ramey he had a piece of paper in his hand. In one, it was folded over so nothing could be seen. In the second, however, there appears to be text printed on the paper. In an attempt to read this text to determine if it could shed any further light on locating documents relating to this matter, the photo was sent to a national level organization for digitizing and subsequent photo interpretation and analysis. This organization was also asked to scrutinize the digitized photos for any indication of the flowered tape (or "hieroglyphics, depending on the point of view) that were reputed to be visible to some of the persons who observed the wreckage prior to it getting to Fort Worth. This organization reported on July 20, 1994, that even after digitizing, the photos were of insufficient quality to visualize either of the details sought for analysis. This organization was able to obtain measurements from the "sticks" visible in the debris after it was ascertained by an interview of the original photographer what kind of camera he used. The results of this process are provided in Atch 33, along with a reference diagram and the photo from which the measurements were made. All these measurements are compatible with the wooden materials used in the radar target previously described.

CONCLUSION

The Air Force research did not locate or develop any information that the "Roswell Incident" was a UFO event. All available official materials, although they do not directly address Roswell *per se*, indicate that the most likely source of the wreckage recovered from the Brazel Ranch was from one of the Project Mogul balloon trains. Although that project was TOP SECRET at the time, there was also no specific indication found to indicate an official pre-planned cover story was in place to explain an event such as that which ultimately happened. It appears that the identification of the wreckage as being part of a weather balloon device, as reported in the newspapers at the time, was based on the fact that there was no physical difference in the radar targets and the neoprene balloons (other than the numbers and configuration) between Mogul balloons and normal weather balloons. Additionally, it seems that there was over-reaction by Colonel Blanchard and Major Marcel, in originally reporting that a "flying disc" had been recovered when, at that time, nobody for sure knew what that term even meant since the it had only been in use for a couple of weeks.

Likewise, there was no indication in official records from the period that there was heightened military operational or security activity which should have been generated if this was, in fact, the first recovery of materials and/or persons from another world. The post-War US Military (or today's for that matter) did not have the capability to rapidly identify, recover, coordinate, cover-up, and quickly minimize public scrutiny of such an event. The claim that they did so without leaving even a little bit of a suspicious paper trail for 47 years is incredible.

It should also be noted here that there was little mentioned in this report about the recovery of the so-called "alien bodies." This is for several reasons: First, the recovered wreckage was from a Project Mogul balloon. There were no "alien" passengers therein. Secondly, the pro-UFO groups who espouse the alien bodies theories cannot even agree among themselves as to what, how many, and where, such bodies were supposedly recovered. Additionally, some of these claims have been shown to be hoaxes, even by other UFO researchers. Thirdly, when such claims are made, they are often attributed to people using pseudonyms or who otherwise do not want to be publicly identified, presumably so that some sort of retribution cannot be taken against them (notwithstanding that nobody has been shown to have died, disappeared or otherwise suffered at the hands of the government during the last 47 years). Fourth, many of the persons making the biggest claims of "alien bodies" make their living from the "Roswell Incident." While having a commercial interest in something does not automatically make it suspect, it does raise interesting questions related to authenticity. Such persons should be encouraged to present their evidence (not speculation) directly to the government and provide all pertinent details and evidence to support their claims if honest fact-finding is what is wanted. Lastly, persons who have come forward and provided their names and made claims, may have, in good faith but in the "fog of time," misinterpreted past events. The review of Air Force records did not locate even one piece of evidence to indicate that the Air Force has had any part in an "alien" body recovery operation or continuing cover-up.

During the course of this effort, the Air Force has kept in close touch with the GAO and responded to their various queries and requests for assistance. This report was generated as an official response to the GAO, and to document the considerable effort expended by the Air Force on their behalf. It is anticipated that that they will request a copy of this report to help formulate the formal report of their efforts. It is recommended that this document serve as the final Air Force report related to the Roswell matter, for the GAO, or any other inquiries.

RICHARD L. WEAVER, COL, USAF
DIRECTOR, SECURITY AND SPECIAL
PROGRAM OVERSIGHT

Attachments
1. Washington Post Article, "GAO Turns to Alien Turf in New Probe,"
January 14, 1994
2. GAO Memo, February 15, 1994
3. DoD/IG Memo, February 23, 1994
4. SAF/FM Memo, February 24, 1994, w/Indorsement

INDEX

ACKNOWLEDGEMENTS

The author would like to acknowledge permission to quote from *Above Top Secret* by Timothy Good (Sidwick & Jackson) and *Phenomenon* edited by John Spencer and Hilary Evans (Futura). Also useful in research and recommended to the reader is *Project Blue Book* edited by Brad Steiger (Ballantine).

Thanks are also due to Peter Moore and Alan Hayling at Channel Four, who commissioned the documentary *Incident at Roswell* which was shown as part of the Channel Four Science Fiction Weekend in August 1995. The documentary was broadcast as part of Channel Four's highly acclaimed *Secret History* series, and despite its inclusion in a science fiction extravaganza maintained the high standards of journalism and film-making that have become the hallmark of *Secret History* – achieving a high rating and a greater number of viewers than an episode of *The X Files* shown at the same time.

The film was in part made possible by the contribution of one of Britain's most talented documentary producers, John Purdie of Union Pictures, who has been responsible for producing some of the most distinguished documentary programmes of the last two decades, including the award-winning BBC series *Sailor*. John lent his considerable reputation to a project that could have all too easily invited ridicule from his colleagues – that it instead achieved the opposite is a vindication of his skill and judgement. John established a comprehensive wealth of research and a collection of credible witnesses for the film which resulted in a compelling documentary – complemented by the inclusion of the fascinating and controversial 'Alien Autopsy' footage, which received massive publicity in the weeks prior to transmission. Our collaboration on the film was the beginning of a fascinating journey and, more importantly, a new friendship. The production company is one of the UK's most successful independent television and film organisations. The executive producer who worked on the project, Franc Roddam, made an invaluable contribution, and by having his name in the credits gave me an added *frisson*, having been a teenage fan of the Who (for whom Franc directed the unsurpassable rock 'n' roll movie *Quadrophenia*).

Thanks also to Cherry, Helen and Kitty at Union for friendship, tea and sympathy, smiles and assistance in logistics; and to Gala at Channel Four, I hope we can produce something similar in the future.

In America, Marc Barasch was instrumental in getting the project underway, and was a dedicated source of knowledge and research and provided a wealth of detail and a body of evidence that helped to underwrite what became a serious documentary on a subject vulnerable to scepticism. Many thanks to him for his company and conversation on the succession of endless drives along the long and straight highways of New Mexico on search of witnesses and locations.

David Reynolds at Bloomsbury had the courage and conviction to commission a book which many others had already turned down, and I am grateful to him and his supportive staff at Bloomsbury for their patience, and to Richard Dawes for his assistance in editing. Thanks also to Christabel and Peter Kent for tickets, dinner and friendship, Christopher Olgiati for oceanic conversations about the many mysteries of Roswell, and John Haslet for his tireless support and use of his fax machine.

Last but not least, thanks to my wife, Marion, for tolerating the intrusion of aliens and flying saucers after the Mafia and hit-men that were the subjects of my previous books. Also thanks to my two sons, Alexander and Edward, who graciously forsook valuable time on the computer, which could have been used for a bewildering variety of space-based computer games instead of a book about UFOs and Roswell. I trust that one day they will find it was a worthwhile sacrifice!

The book is dedicated to them.

Tim Shawcross, 31 March 1997

ABOUT THE AUTHOR

Tim Shawcross has worked in television for twenty years as a series editor, director and producer. He has worked on Granada's *World in Action*, the BBC's *Panorama*, Thames Television's *This Week* and Channel Four's *Secret History*. His numerous documentaries include *Mountbatten, The War Against the Mafia* and *Chernobyl: The Inside Story*. He is the author of *Men of Honour* and *The War Against the Mafia*.

Tim Shawcross directed Channel Four's *Secret History: Incident at Roswell*. With fellow film-makers John Purdie and Marc Barasch, he conducted the most exhaustive research into Roswell ever undertaken by independent investigators, interviewing numerous witnesses in Roswell, Fort Worth, Washington and elsewhere. As a follow-up to the film, Shawcross has uncovered additional new research from a variety of sources, and has boldly gone where no man has gone before in order to produce the most comprehensive and revealing book about the Roswell Incident and the reality of 'flying saucers'.